The author was able to make use of exceptionally detailed and thorough sources in his research. In part because of the international attention focused on Danzig, party records were created at the national level that illuminate even the petty details of local squabbles. The German, British, and Polish foreign offices, with the help of their local representatives, generated records that closely follow events in the Free City of Danzig and relate them to larger questions of European diplomacy. The League of Nations created masses of material on Danzig, and the international position of the Free City attracted journalists and scholarly observers.

The story of the Free City of Danzig is fascinating in itself. However, its ultimate value lies in the odd and varied angles from which it allows the historian to view the total structure of Hitler's world.

HERBERT S. LEVINE has published articles in various scholarly journals; this is his first book.

HITLER'S FREE CITY

HITLER'S FREE CITY

A History of the Nazi Party in Danzig, 1925–39

Herbert S. Levine

The University of Chicago Press Chicago and London

HERBERT S. LEVINE is assistant professor of history. He has published articles in various scholarly journals; this is his first book. [1973]

The University of Chicago Press, Chicago 60637
The University of Chicago Press, Ltd., London
 Published 1973
Printed in the United States of America
International Standard Book Number: 0-226-47565-4
Library of Congress Catalog Card Number: 73-75780

To the victims

Contents

Preface

The mythological world of my childhood was densely populated by Nazi demons. The naïve questions I asked about them and the horrors they perpetrated have never received definitive answers and may never receive them, but the reader should regard this book as a small effort in that direction. It is a book about national socialism, National Socialists, and their followers and sympathizers. Only secondarily does it deal with matters of resistance and diplomacy or even with the unhappy city of Danzig itself. These matters provide the setting, but the Nazi party provides the story.

The work began as a Yale doctoral dissertation. I owe a great debt to Yale, not least for the financial support that made possible a lengthy stay in Europe in 1968. An even greater debt is owed to Professor Hans W. Gatzke, who saw the dissertation through to its completion, and to Professors Henry A. Turner and Piotr S. Wandycz, who enriched it with their suggestions. At a later stage, the manuscript was read by Professor Dietrich Orlow, of Boston University, and by Professor Anna M. Cienciala, of the University of Kansas, whose constructive criticism did much to form the finished work. The American Philosophical Society was generous enough to supply a grant-in-aid, which made possible a second research trip, in 1970.

Nothing at all could have been accomplished without the assistance of the staffs of the archives and libraries at which I worked. Particular thanks are due to Mr. Robert Wolfe, of the National Archives in Washington, to Mr. Heinz Wewer, formerly of the Berlin Document Center, and to Dr. Sven Welander, of the United Nations Library in Geneva.

The moral and financial support given by my parents, George and Fannie Levine, and by my parents-in-law, Michael and

Margaret Baker, is acknowledged as sincerely as is possible in this setting, and the same and more may be said of my debt to Martha Levine, without whose creative encouragement very little would have been done.

Abbreviations

See "Note on Sources," p. 163, for further information on abbreviations used in the notes and an explanation of reference technique.

AA:	Auswärtiges Amt (German Foreign Office)
ASDN:	Archives de la Société des Nations (League of Nations Archives)
BA:	Bundesarchiv (West German Federal Archives)
BDC:	Berlin Document Center of the United States State Department
DGFP:	*Documents on German Foreign Policy*
DGKD:	Deutsches Generalkonsulat Danzig (German Consulate-General in Danzig)
FO:	(British) Foreign Office
HA:	Hauptarchiv der NSDAP (Central Archives of the NSDAP)
KGRP:	Komisarz Generalny Rzeczypospolitej Polskiej w Gdańsku (Commissariat-General of the Republic of Poland in Danzig)
LNOJ:	*League of Nations Official Journal*
Moderow MS:	W. Moderow, "Die Freie Stadt Danzig," manuscript in United Nations Library, Geneva
NA:	National Archives of the United States

Abbreviations

PA: Politisches Archiv des Auswärtigen Amts (Political Archives of the West German Foreign Office)

PRO: Public Record Office, London

WAP: Wojewódzkie Archiwum Państwowe w Gdańsku (Polish Provincial State Archives in Danzig)

Hitler's Free City

Introduction

In May 1939 an uncomfortable question was raised by a voice on the French political Right. Marcel Déat asked his countrymen if they ought to prepare themselves "to die for Danzig." He answered his rhetorical question in the negative.[1] The slogan "Why die for Danzig?" became a rallying point for those in Britain and France opposed to fighting a war against Hitler for the sake of Polish pretensions involving a little-known Baltic seaport. It is widely recognized today that Déat was raising a false issue. The war against nazism was not a war for Danzig, not even a war for Poland. It was a struggle made necessary by the growth of an aggressive evil in the heart of Europe.[2] But events in the tiny free city did have an importance of their own, quite apart from their exploitation by contemporary propagandists of various persuasions.

The Free City of Danzig, a permanent ward of the League of Nations sandwiched between Poland and Germany, held a unique place in European history between the two world wars. The city also held a singular place in the history of national socialism. Although the NSDAP (*Nationalsozialistische Deutsche Arbeiterpartei;* Nazi party) came to power in Danzig soon after its victory in the Reich, the Nazis did not manage to drive all opposition underground until 1937. They were forced to govern and to hold elections under the eyes of the high commissioner of the League of Nations and to consider the international effects of their domestic policies. In Danzig, Nazi techniques of government and persuasion were subjected to a much harsher, and more public, test than they were in Germany.[3] Danzig was not a typical German town. In it, rather ordinary Germans, and rather ordinary Nazis, were exposed to extraordinary pressures.

Those factors that made Danzig atypical, today make its history an exceptionally suitable focus for a study of national socialism. Every Gau (region) of the NSDAP created records at both the local and national levels. The Gau Danzig archives, so far as is known, no longer exist in a significant form. But in part because of the international sensitivity of the area, party records were created at the national level that illuminate even petty details of local squabbles. Most significant here are the party personnel records to be found in the Berlin Document Center of the United States State Department.

Other classes of records were created that either do not exist or exist in a much less significant form for cities within Germany. No other Gau of the NSDAP was subjected to so varied a scrutiny. Within the German government, Danzig was the special responsibility of the German Foreign Office, which was represented in the free city by a consul-general. The German Foreign Office documents closely follow internal Danzig developments, relate them to the larger context of German foreign policy, and illuminate the conflicts that determined that policy. The records of the Polish Commissariat-General in Danzig add more observations on local affairs, now set in the context of German-Polish relations. The League of Nations, the international authority responsible for the free city, created masses of relevant published and unpublished material. The British Foreign Office was intimately associated with Danzig through Britain's role in the League, and it recorded every clue Danzig gave to Hitler's plans for revision of the European status quo. And finally, the international position of the free city attracted journalists and scholarly observers, as well as propagandists.

These sources make possible a multifaceted approach to the enigma of national socialism. Unfortunately, the very complexity of the Danzig situation, which created such a variety of source material, also created a great potential for misunderstanding my purpose. Danzig played an important role in international affairs, but the present work does not purport to be a history of that role. Several aspects of European and German history in the interwar period are discussed as they are illuminated by the Danzig materials: Anglo-German and Polish-German relations, the situation of the League, and the destruction of the Jewish community. Particular attention is paid to the relationship between national socialism and the German opposition, since the latter had possibilities for development in Danzig that did not exist in the Reich after the Nazi seizure of power. But all these matters remain peripheral to the central concern of the work. The special problems that Danzig presented to the Nazi movement are seen here as stimuli that set in motion certain processes of political evaluation and decision-making, both in Danzig and in the Reich.[4]

It must also be emphasized that I had no intention of producing a local history of Danzig, or even a complete history of the Danzig NSDAP. I deal with local matters only insofar as they shed light on larger issues. Indeed the sources ordinarily used to produce local histories are largely unavailable for Danzig. The community itself was destroyed in 1945, and most of the principal actors are now dead or, in one case, uncommunicative. Interviews and correspondence could therefore be utilized to only a limited extent. Local newspapers were used, but most local government records proved inaccessible. Further gaps in the local record were created by the loss of the Gau files, and by the fact that none of the major participants was tried at Nuremberg or anywhere else in Western Europe. Denazification materials exist only for minor figures. I was able to visit and work in Danzig, now the Polish city of Gdansk, but restored buildings and scattered rubble proved to be mute witnesses, of limited use to the work at hand.

From the evidence that does exist, which is presented in the course of the narrative, it appears that the sociological and psychological makeup of the Danzig NSDAP was not significantly different from that of the Reich party. Political differences normally had discernible political explanations. Extensive research into the local history of the Third Reich has begun and is continuing, but it is doubtful that Danzig has a great role to play here.[5] The examination of events in Danzig that follows may contribute to a greater understanding of the Third Reich as it appeared on the local level, but this aspect of the inquiry remains limited by the lack of complete local documentation. The great advantage of a study of Danzig lies in the odd and varied angles from which it allows the historian to view the total structure of Hitler's world.

1 Danzig before the Nazi Takeover

More than a quarter century has passed since 1945, but the horror and pathos of recent history still obsess the traveler who ventures into those lands formerly known as West and East Prussia, the ancient meeting place and battleground of German and Slav. A timbered German hall, the largest building in its village, sports a white eagle on a red-enameled plaque—Polish municipal offices are housed here now. The unfinished Reichsautobahn east from Elbing to Königsberg is a two-lane country road to nowhere, cut short before an impassable Soviet border. Cows graze on the shoulders and children play on the cracked pavement, Polish children whose fathers may have fled from Vilna or crept from the ruins of Bialystok or Warsaw. The Germans have left other monuments—the barracks and railroad siding of the concentration camp at Stutthof. A stone pyramid has been built here by the Poles over a great mound of sand mixed with human bones. But the land remains the same. The marshes and forests where the East Prussian Junkers once hunted stag and boar are unchanged, as are the pleasant farms and gentle hills of West Prussia. The sluggish waters of the Vistula still find their way to the sea.

The Vistula rises near the town of Cieszyn, in the mountains that form the present border between Poland and Czechoslovakia. It takes a bend to the east and flows through the city of Cracow. Turning north, it bisects Warsaw and then curves north and west to the Baltic. It is largely empty of traffic today. The river trade has been done in by silt, railroads, and war, but the Vistula was once one of the great highways of Europe, the commercial link between Poland and the west, the life of Danzig.

Danzig before the Nazi Takeover

Danzig before 1918

A chronicle records that Saint Adelbert of Prague took ship at a settlement called Gydannicz, near the mouth of the Vistula, in the year 997. This Gydannicz later appears as a Slavic fishing village surrounding the castle of a family of Pommerellian princes. Increased international trade was brought to the area in the thirteenth century by German merchants from the cities of the Hanseatic League. In the fourteenth and fifteenth centuries, under the lordship of the Teutonic Knights, the original Slavic population was absorbed into a German trading center of growing wealth and power, which came to be called Danzig. In 1454 Danzig, exasperated over the restraints imposed by its lords, cooperated with the Polish king to destroy the state established by the knights.[1]

Merchant Danzig became a virtually independent city, a leading member of the Hanseatic League, bound to Poland by a union under the Polish crown but distinct from the Polish state. Polish grain, amber, furs, and lumber were floated down the Vistula on barges to be transshipped at Danzig's wharves near the Crane Gate. In the sixteenth century Danzig was the most important port on the Baltic and a major population center. The close economic ties between Danzig and Poland in this period are self-evident, and their existence has never been denied. But the nature of the political relationship was hotly disputed after the First World War. German scholars and publicists insisted that the sole political tie binding Danzig and Poland between 1454 and the Prussian annexation in 1793 was the union under the Polish crown, which remained largely formal and ineffective. On the other hand, Polish historians have treated Danzig as a semiautonomous dependency of Poland. The intricacies of this debate need not detain us here.[2]

The weakening and impoverishment of Poland and the disruption of Baltic trade by the Swedish wars of the seventeenth century caused Danzig to drift gradually into insignificance. As a result of the Second Partition of Poland in 1793, Danzig became part of Prussia. After a ruinous interlude from 1807 to 1814 as a "free city" under Napoleonic patronage, the town was returned to Prussia. The French occupation destroyed what was left of Danzig's trade, and the city's population declined.[3] The citizens learned not to cherish their "freedom" too highly; it was a manifest anachronism in the transformed east-central Europe of the nineteenth century.

Under Prussian rule Danzig experienced slow growth and moderate prosperity. As the capital of the province of West Prussia the city attracted civil servants, and the garrisoning of Prussian troops aided its economy. A further source of income was the development of the nearby town of Zoppot as a seaside resort with a well-known casino. In 1854 a royal (later imperial) navy yard was established, and a shipbuilding industry grew up around it and the privately owned Schichau Works. A modern commercial harbor was finished by 1903, but the city ranked only fifth among German ports in total freight turnover.[4] Thanks partly to the slow pace of its economic development, Danzig never lost its distinctive architectural characteristics. The core of the city was built around sixteenth-century dwellings and public buildings of a unique style more reminiscent of Holland and Belgium than of northern Germany. Structures that were added in the nineteenth century followed the pattern established by the imported architects of the Dutch Renaissance. In the center of Danzig, dominated by the city hall and the towering Marienkirche, a Hanseatic merchant would not have felt out of place.[5]

But things had been changing behind the ancient patrician housefronts. Prussian-German officials and military men dominated the life of the city, overshadowing the old merchant families. Trade gave way to administration as the town's chief interest. At the beginning of the twentieth century Danzig was both more and less provincial than it had been 350 years before. Hanseatic Danzig had traded with the entire world, but its political interests and emotional loyalties had been bound up in the purely local patriotism of a city-state. Prussian Danzig, even as it lost all international significance, became fully involved in the national development of the German people, sharing in the formative events of 1848, 1871, and 1914. When Germany met defeat in 1918, Danzigers reacted no differently than other Germans.[6] They did not at first realize that the defeat of Germany was to mean their political separation from their fellow countrymen.

The Free City

The Free City of Danzig was created by the Paris Peace Conference at the end of the First World War as a compromise among conflicting interpretations of Wilson's Thirteenth Point:

> An independent Polish State should be erected which should include the territories inhabited by indisputably Polish populations, which should be assured a free and secure access to the sea, and whose political and economic independence and territorial integrity should be guaranteed by international covenant.

The commission that considered the Polish question at the Peace Conference concluded that "a free and secure access to the sea" could only be assured to Poland by allowing her to annex Danzig, along with most of the German provinces of Posen and West Prussia. Wilson's stipulation that the territories taken from Germany be "indisputably Polish" in population would have to be ignored. The commission's report was presented to the Supreme Council of the Peace Conference on 19 March 1919 by Jules Cambon of France.[7]

David Lloyd George, the British prime minister, immediately objected that the report did not take into account the principle of national self-determination. Danzig was unquestionably German. Could any German government be expected to sign a treaty that so flagrantly violated the Fourteen Points? Lloyd George was supported by Wilson.[8] The American president was doubtless glad to vindicate the principle of national self-determination in a relatively small issue. He had already abandoned it in favor of political expediency in more important matters, such as Italy's northern frontier. Poland would be offended at not getting Danzig, but Poland's offense was nothing compared with Italy's. The refusal to give Danzig to Poland was a cheap reaffirmation of a hopelessly compromised principle.

The task of designing a precise solution to the Danzig dispute was given to James W. Headlam-Morley, of the British delegation, and to Sidney Mezes, of the American delegation.[9] Danzig was to be autonomous, Poland was to receive full guarantees regarding access to the sea, and the Danzigers were to be assured that they would be allowed to govern themselves free of Polish interference. It was ultimately decided by the Supreme Council that Danzig, Zoppot, and the surrounding rural districts should become an independent international entity under the supervision of the League of Nations. A German counteroffer envisioned the granting of limited rights to Poland in a Danzig that would remain, with the rest of West Prussia, an integral part of the Reich.[10] But the German proposal was rejected, and Danzig became a free city under articles 100 through 108 of the Treaty of Versailles.

The solution satisfied none of those most directly concerned. To the Poles the creation of the free city seemed to destroy much of the value of the cession of West Prussia by Germany, which gave Poland a seacoast but no harbor worthy of the name. All economic concessions granted to Poland in the free city might well prove worthless if the local government were in truth to be independent and therefore German in nationality and sympathy. The Poles did not deny that Danzig's population was German. As Premier Ignace Paderewski dejectedly foresaw, an independent Danzig would remain under the control of the Reich and would some day return to the Reich.[11] But the Germans and Danzigers were no happier.

To the Germans the creation of the free city was part of a hypocritical dictated peace that ignored the principle of national self-determination whenever it might lead to advantages for Germany. They did not acknowledge the role the principle had played in keeping Danzig from Poland. The Germans claimed Danzig for the Reich on ethnic grounds. At the same time, they argued for a retention of West Prussia, with its largely Polish population, by declaring a "Polish corridor" to be economically and politically insupportable. Determined as they were to retain every scrap of territory possible, the Germans were unable to consider the conditions of the peace settlement objectively, to determine whether the loss of Danzig and the corridor substantially weakened the Reich.[12] The Danzigers, the Germans most immediately affected, were in even less of a position objectively to weigh the possible economic advantages of an arrangement that could lead to a monopoly of Polish trade by the free city.[13] From the first news of the possibility of separation from the Reich through the final signing of the Treaty of Versailles, the population of Danzig busied itself with petitions and mass demonstrations, and serious incidents between Germans and Poles took place. But all protests against the decisions of Paris were fruitless.

Although the creation of the free city harkened back to the Hanseatic precedent, that precedent had lost all meaning to the Danzigers and could not serve as a model for an independent "national" life. But once the treaty was signed, the responsible authorities in Danzig, headed by Mayor Heinrich Sahm, eagerly took up the business of organizing an independent administration and cooperated with the League of Nations high commissioner in arranging elections to a constituent assembly.[14] The commendable zeal of Danzig's politicians and bureaucrats was not due to a revival of local patriotism. The Danzigers were desperately anxious to avoid any excuse for Polish intervention. Bad as their new status seemed, it was better than the direct seizure of the city by Poland, which could only be avoided by loyal cooperation with the League. This fact governed the generally good relationship between Danzig and the League until 1933. The special relationship between Danzig and Poland was defined by a bilateral convention signed in Paris in November 1920, which was followed by the formal proclamation of the free city. Its constitution was submitted to the council of the League for approval. Most of the constitution was put into immediate operation, and the final amended draft was accepted by the council on 11 May 1922.[15] The status of the free city had now been determined in detail. In general, Danzigers had little reason to complain about the manner in which the Treaty of Versailles had been applied. Thanks to British diplomatic pressure, vague points had been interpreted in favor of the Danzigers. In particular, Poland had failed to gain control of Danzig's harbor and waterways. Control had instead been given to the harbor board, composed equally of Poles and Danzigers with a neutral president. Poland was furthermore never able to obtain a permanent mandate as military protector of the free city and could only hope to intervene legally with military force if authorized to do so, in a specific instance, by the League.

The League fulfilled three separate functions in relation to the free city. It was the guarantor of Danzig's constitution, the arbiter between Danzig and Poland, and the military protector of Danzig.[16] In practice, the League's activities were limited to the first two categories, since Danzig did not require military protection until long after the League had ceased to function effectively. League interests in Danzig were represented by a resident high commissioner, who served as the channel of communication between Geneva and the free city. He informed the League of the situation in Danzig and acted as a court of first instance in all disputes between Danzig and Poland. Appeals from his decisions could be made by either party to the League council. Prior to 1933, most of the high commissioners' time was taken up by Polish-Danzig quarrels. Only after the Nazi takeover was it necessary for the high commissioners to call on the council in its role as guarantor of the constitution. It was at this time that a report on the draft constitution, written by Viscount Ishii of Japan in 1920 and accepted by the council, assumed vital importance. Ishii had concluded that Danzig's public life would have to be conducted in accordance with the constitution, and that the constitution could not be changed without the approval of the League.[17]

Relations between Danzig and Poland were made difficult by a basic disagreement over the nature of the free city. At every turn the Poles tried to deny the sovereign character of Danzig. The Danzig government, on the other hand, insisted on the unrestricted sovereignty of the free city, which it also termed a "free state." Although one high commissioner did agree that "Danzig is a State in the International sense of the word and is entitled to the use of expressions denoting that fact," this opinion was not generally accepted outside Germany and the free city itself.[18] Danzig's special relationship with Poland imposed such limitations on its sovereignty that it would be best to regard it as a "statelike" creation of international treaties, in a category of its own.[19]

Poland controlled the formal conduct of Danzig's foreign affairs, owned the railways, operated its own harbor post office, and won the right to maintain a small munitions depot. Danzig was part of the Polish customs area, and most of its customs revenue went to Poland, according to a formula based on the Danzig-Polish population ratio. The free city could not construct fortifications or maintain an army. The administration of the harbor and waterways was in the hands of the binational harbor board.[20] But despite these rather peculiar arrangements, the everyday life of the city was surprisingly normal. Quarrels over the details of Danzig's status did not usually disturb the smooth functioning of the railroads, the postal administration, or the harbor. The administrators and technical experts, Danzigers and Poles alike, tended to leave the political wrangling to their chiefs, while they got on with their more prosaic tasks.[21]

Poland was represented in Danzig by a commissioner-general, although the Danzig government guarded its sovereign status by referring to him only as the "Polish Diplomatic Representative." To avoid awkward moments, the commissioner-general was addressed in Danzig as "Minister."[22] This official was responsible for Polish relations with the Danzig authorities, the harbor board, and the high commissioner. He provided consular services to Polish nationals, Danzigers, and others in the free city and was also the coordinator of the political and cultural activities of the Polish minority. Political coordination was no easy task, since the Poles in Danzig reflected the factional divisions in Poland itself. Some control was maintained through the distribution of considerable amounts of Polish state money by the commissioner-general.[23]

The Polish minority in Danzig fell into two categories: citizens of Poland and citizens of Danzig. The former were normally recent immigrants, the latter Poles who had lived in the city at least since the war. Although the number of Danzig citizens who considered themselves Polish declined between 1920 and 1930, if we may take the declining vote for Polish candidates as a guide, the number of Polish citizens in the free city increased.

Since Danzig was obliged to allow any Polish citizen to take up residence, and since Polish merchants and farm laborers often resided in Danzig on a temporary basis, the precise number of Poles in Danzig at any given date is difficult to determine. It appears that the number of Polish citizens resident in Danzig increased from five thousand in 1923 to seventeen thousand in 1934. By 1934 about 6 percent of the total population of four hundred thousand spoke Polish.[24] The population picture was complicated by the presence in Danzig of perhaps three thousand Jews with Polish citizenship; some spoke Polish as their native language, and some did not. The commissioners-general defended the economic and political interests of all Polish citizens,[25] but the Polish Jews in Danzig remained a distinct national group. A smaller section of the Jewish community, those Jews who had been in Danzig since before 1914, tended to identify with the German segment of the population.[26]

Politically, Danzig was a miniature version of Germany. Its constitution was modeled on those of the Weimar Republic and the German city-state of Lübeck. The representative body was the Volkstag (Popular Assembly), elected by universal suffrage under proportional representation. The Volkstag chose the senate, an executive body with a president who was the head of the government. There was no head of state. For reasons of economy the Volkstag was reduced from 120 to 72 members when the constitution was amended in 1930. The number of senators was now fixed at 10, 6 of whom were to be unsalaried. At the same time the senators were made individually and collectively subject to parliamentary recall, and provision was made for the self-dissolution of the Volkstag.[27]

Just as the Polish political organizations in Danzig mirrored political differences in Poland, so political parties in Germany had their counterparts in the free city. The Danzig versions of the German National People's party (*Deutschnationale Volkspartei;* DNVP) and the Communist party of Germany (*Kommunistische Partei Deutschlands;* KPD) were actually local branches of their parent Reich organizations. This was also true of the National Socialists. The local Center party and the Social Democratic party (*Sozialdemokratische Partei Deutschlands;*

SPD) were formally independent entities, but they were no less influenced by their Reich counterparts. Only with Danzig's liberals were the connections to the Reich less clear. Four competing liberal groups were able to elect candidates in the late twenties. They were divided by economic issues of purely local significance.

The free city continued to cultivate close ties with Germany. Many of Danzig's officials came from the Reich, served a tour of duty, and then returned, continuing the prewar pattern. Heinrich Sahm, first senate president, arrived as mayor in 1919 from another Prussian post, served as president from 1920 to 1930, and then became mayor of Berlin. Danzig law followed German law in granting citizenship automatically with an official appointment. Special arrangements completed in 1921 allowed officials to transfer from the German or Prussian to the Danzig civil service and back without any loss in seniority or other privileges.[28] In this way Danzig was able to maintain an administration similar in most respects to that of any German town.

Danzig's foreign relations were formally conducted through the Polish government, but this proved no obstacle to a close working relationship between Berlin and the free city. Contact was maintained through visits by Danzig officials to the German foreign ministry, and through the German consul-general in Danzig. All major aspects of Danzig's foreign and domestic policy were concerted with Berlin and were often supported by open or hidden German subsidies. The Volkstag frequently adopted legislation identical with that passed in the Reichstag. The common goal was the reunification of Danzig and the corridor with the Reich. Danzigers were even willing to sacrifice their own economic interests in the service of German foreign policy. As a contemporary Italian observer accurately concluded, the free city's policies were "determined entirely by Germany's expectations of Treaty revision." [29] The obvious dependence of Danzig on Reich direction after the Nazi assumption of power continued a practice as old as the free city itself.

Before the Nazi takeover, Danzig was governed by a series of coalitions. The Catholic Center party participated in all governments. Its cooperation was always essential, but political initiative was left to its coalition partners. From 1920 to 1923 the government was led by the conservative and nationalistic DNVP. After an interval of Social Democratic rule from June to December 1923, control returned to the DNVP. The SPD formed its second, and last, government in 1927. At this time President Sahm resigned his membership in the DNVP and remained in office.[30] The SPD was inclined to compromise with Poland and thus to reject the intransigent German nationalism of the DNVP as unrealistic. Tensions eased, business was relatively good, and the high commissioner did not have to hand down a single decision in 1928 and 1929.[31]

The elections of November 1930 went against the Social Democrats, as had the September Reichstag elections in Germany. In both cases the worsening economic situation shifted the vote to the extremist parties—the Nazis and the Communists. A minority government was formed in the Reich under a Centrist, Heinrich Brüning, who governed by means of the emergency powers of the Reich president, Paul von Hindenburg. In Danzig, a minority government of Centrists, German Nationalists, and liberals took power under the presidency of Ernst Ziehm of the DNVP. This minority senate also ruled largely by decree, empowered to do so by an enabling act passed with the help of the NSDAP.

The effects of the economic crisis were particularly severe in Danzig, since it became involved in a trade war with Poland. Poland discriminated against Danzig in favor of the new Polish port of Gdynia. Gdynia had formerly been a tiny fishing village on the coast just beyond the border of the free city. It attracted the attention of Polish planners after the Polish-Soviet war of 1920. Danzig's harbor workers, moved by both anti-Polish feelings and socialist sympathy with the Soviets, had refused to unload munitions destined for Poland's hard-pressed armies.[32] For reasons of military security alone, it appeared that Poland needed a port in its own territory. Beginning in 1924, Poland constructed a large artificial harbor at Gdynia with the aid of Dutch engineers and French capital. During the next fifteen years, Gdynia grew into a city of over one hundred thousand people.

The growth of Gdynia seemed particularly threatening to Danzigers after the slump in the Polish export-import trade that accompanied the depression. They carried the matter to the League of Nations in 1931 and 1932. On the one hand, the Danzigers claimed, the Poles insisted on the continued separation of the free city from the Reich on the grounds that only the status quo could guarantee Poland's economic and political security. On the other hand, Danzig was being cheated of the economic benefits that ought to have accompanied this arrangement. If the free city had been created to assure Poland's access to the sea, and if this access were now safely afforded by Gdynia, then Danzig ought to return to the Reich.[33]

By early 1933 Gdynia had surpassed Danzig in total freight turnover.[34] To the Danzigers the new harbor was clear proof that the Poles, motivated by fanatical hatred of everything German and disappointed in their attempts to control Danzig politically, were determined to strangle it economically. To the Poles, Gdynia was the answer to Danzig's continued political, economic, and cultural dependence on Germany, as well as to the "treachery" of 1920. The Poles refused to countenance treaty revision as a matter of principle. At the same time, they reserved the right to buttress their security by supplemental arrangements such as the building of Gdynia. The Danzigers were caught between Polish intransigence and their own national pride, with a still disarmed Germany offering no hope for a revision of their status by force. Embittered and impoverished, Danzig defended an unwanted independence "for the sake of her national character." [35] This was the situation the Nazis inherited when they became rulers of the free city on 20 June 1933.

2 The Early History of the NSDAP in Danzig, 1925–30

The victorious National Socialist movement well understood the propagandistic value of its own past. The Munich Putsch of 9 November 1923, in reality little more than a minor street clash, became the heroic "bloody parade" at a wave of Joseph Goebbels's magic wand. Another wave, and a gang of beer hall brawlers was transformed into the selfless brotherhood of "old fighters." But not even the Nazi talent for rewriting history could do anything with the early days of the movement in the Free City of Danzig. One account wisely limited discussion of the period from 1925 to 1930 to a single sentence.[1] This reticence was justified. The Nazis in Danzig before 1930 produced no triumph, or even defeat, of which the party could later be proud. The Danzig NSDAP seemed so insignificant to contemporaries that it was rarely mentioned in non-Nazi sources. But enough documents have survived to enable us to piece together the story.[2] It is worth the effort of a brief retelling because it provides a basis for judging party achievements after 1930, and because it affords an insight into certain traits of Nazi political character that never disappeared, even though they may have been obscured by the brilliance of later victories.

The First Nazis

On 9 November 1923, the day of the Beer Hall Putsch in Munich, there was only one National Socialist in the free city. Hans Albert Hohnfeldt, a minor official in the Tax Office, was a native Danziger, fond of boasting that his ancestors had held citizens' rights since 1597. Now twenty-six years old, he had been in the army during the world war, and by his own account had fought against revolution in the Naval Brigade II *Ehrhardt* and the

Free Corps *Schlageter*.[3] Returning home from the Reich after the revolutionary period, he found Danzig separated from Germany and threatened by Polish control. His experience with the swastika-wearing Ehrhardt Brigade had presumably already introduced him to the *völkisch* or racial nationalist ideology common among the disillusioned war veterans and free corps men.[4]

The term *völkisch* is most literally translated as "populist." *Völkisch* politicians believed themselves to be appealing to the broad masses of little men, who had been taken in by Jewish exploitive capitalism, and by Jewish Marxism as well. They were violent in language, irrational in argument, and failures in politics. Before the First World War, *völkisch* movements, distinguished by crude anti-Semitism and some form of socialistic program, had never succeeded in electing more than thirteen deputies to the Reichstag at one time. In the confusion after the war, in the widespread climate of despair created by the German inflation, the opportunities for *völkisch* agitation seemed greater than before. But despite the acceptance of *völkisch* ideas in certain reactionary and neoromantic literary circles, the aura of failure still clung to *völkisch* political movements.[5] Only gradually was the NSDAP to prove an exception.

Hohnfeldt found his way to the *völkisch* groups in his old home town, now an endangered outpost of German race and culture. These organizations had dropped their personal and ideological differences for campaign purposes and had formed the German Social party (*Deutsch-Soziale Partei;* DSP), allied with the party of the same name in the Reich. Hohnfeldt joined in 1922 and soon became party chairman. He joined the Nazi party in the following year.[6] Since the Nazis had no organization in Danzig in 1923, he was active only in the DSP. The membership of the DSP increased from about one hundred to about one thousand during 1923. In the November Volkstag elections the DSP gained ten thousand votes and seven seats, and Hohnfeldt entered the Volkstag the following January.

He soon left the DSP, presumably because of personal disagreements with the other leaders, although he continued as a member of the parliamentary group in the Volkstag. Hohnfeldt was a vain and quarrelsome man, incapable of providing real leadership. His political activities were motivated less by ideological conviction than by a desire to dominate other individuals. The groups with which he involved himself accordingly remained as small as his meager talent for domination. He was the littlest of little Hitlers. His initial entry into the NSDAP had no practical effect. After the dissolution of the party following Hitler's arrest and imprisonment in Landsberg, Hohnfeldt was left on his own, as a disruptive member of the tiny *völkisch* movement in Danzig.[7]

When the party was refounded by Hitler in early 1925, Hohnfeldt sensed a new opportunity. Even before he was readmitted to the NSDAP, he began working on its behalf. On 21 October an infant Danzig Ortsgruppe (local group) of the NSDAP held its first meeting. By the end of November 1925, there were about 130 Nazis in Danzig, and the Ortsgruppe was divided into three Bezirksgruppen (wards): Danzig-town, Langfuhr, and Zoppot. Langfuhr was a lower-middle-class residential community separating the cities of Danzig and Zoppot; there were no rural Bezirksgruppen. Hohnfeldt was left a free hand in organizational matters. Party headquarters (the Reichsleitung of the NSDAP) confined its role to collecting fees, registering members, and supplying application forms and party emblems. The party emblems were sent in flat envelopes so that they would look like letters rather than packages, since the Ortsgruppe could not afford the duty. The membership increase soon slowed. After reaching a peak of 140, the figures began a slight decline. Hohnfeldt made enemies, who tended to return to the DSP. A full-fledged Gau Danzig was nevertheless formed on 11 March 1926, with the Bezirksgruppen becoming Ortsgruppen. Gauleiter Hohnfeldt could boast only about 125 followers.[8]

The Gau Danzig was overorganized. The Danzig-town Ortsgruppe, with 76 members the largest in the Gau, was divided into eight Bezirksgruppen of its own. For the 125 Nazis in Danzig there were 27 officers and deputies at the Ortsgruppe and Gau levels. If the officers of the Bezirksgruppen are included, at least one-third of the membership must have been composed of officeholders. The Gauleitung consisted of Hohnfeldt as Gauleiter, Wilhelm von Wnuck as secretary, and Karl Waiblinger as treasurer. Wnuck will appear many times in the following narrative, but Waiblinger soon dropped out of sight. The officers of Gau and Ortsgruppen were almost all minor white-collar employees and artisans.[9] With the partial exception of Wnuck and Hohnfeldt, none of these early officers had any real importance or influence after 1930. They seem to have been men of limited talent, left in charge only so long as the Gau Danzig remained a backwater in a comparatively weak NSDAP.

Hohnfeldt did his best to give an air of militancy to the movement. A youth group affiliated itself with the Gau, and the first Danzig SA (*Sturmabteilung;* "storm troopers") was formed on 28 March 1926 with forty-five members. Even before the formation of the SA, the commander of the irregular citizens' militia (*Einwohnerwehr*), the closest thing to an army in the demilitarized free city, was disturbed by a "distorted" report that Hohnfeldt had instructed Nazi members of the militia not to equate their duty to defend law and order with a duty to protect the present governmental system.[10]

The Gauleiter was less worried about the Danzig authorities than about his fellow "revolutionaries," the Communists. At this time the NSDAP was proceeding nationally according to an "urban plan," which called for expansion into workers' districts.[11] The formation of a Danzig SA was connected with Hohnfeldt's attempt to move into Schidlitz-Emaus, a workers' quarter and hitherto "Marxist territory." The first meeting in the area, an "anti-May Day" rally, unfortunately attracted two hundred members of the Red Front and closed to the derisive singing of the Internationale. Despite all, a new Ortsgruppe Schidlitz-Emaus, with thirty members, was founded on 20 May. By the end of July 1926, Gau membership totaled three hundred. An SS (*Schutzstaffel;* "protection squad") of twenty men was formed. The rest of the SA (of which the SS was an elite section) had about seventy-five members, most of whom could not afford uniforms. Almost one-third of the Gau belonged to the SA and SS. The policy of militancy paid some small dividends in increased membership, but neither the SA nor the Communists behaved in the determined fashion of later years, and no serious violence developed.[12]

Party offices changed hands frequently, especially at the lower levels. Wilhelm von Wnuck, however, remained Gau secretary and Ortsgruppenleiter (local group leader) of Langfuhr. There was no interference from Munich headquarters, which accepted all changes without comment. Only once did the Reichsleitung intervene. The financial situation of the Gau was poor. The Reich treasurer of the NSDAP, Franz Xaver Schwarz, was unwilling to make any special arrangement to help the Gau beyond accepting the parity of German mark and Danzig gulden for party fees, which he felt was a considerable concession (1 gulden = .80 mark). Hohnfeldt decided to help himself. In December 1926, he founded the "National Socialist German Workers' Aid Society," chaired by Wnuck, and set up as an independent organization for "'tactical reasons." It was to collect contributions for the needy of German "race" and to provide an additional source of funds for the Gau. Munich rejected the project on the grounds that it would lead to a splintering of effort and would overburden party members. For the first time the Reichsleitung intervened in Hohnfeldt's activities, over a question of finances. Under Franz Xaver Schwarz, the financial affairs of the party were more centrally controlled than its political activity.[13]

The Reichsleitung showed mild interest in Danzig with the approach of the Volkstag elections of November 1927. A new policy adopted by the party at the national level stressed the importance of electoral victories as evidence of political vitality. This was the first opportunity for the NSDAP to test itself in the free city. Hohnfeldt entered the campaign with subordinates considered by him both capable and loyal. Wnuck was now deputy Gauleiter, and Walter Maass was named deputy for the SA. Wnuck worked as a bookkeeper for the International Shipbuilding and Engineering Company, Ltd., a firm that operated the former imperial navy yard (Danziger Werft) with the aid of foreign capital. Maass, like Hohnfeldt, was a civil servant, working in the Danzig Customs Office. The Reichsleitung did its best to strengthen the prestige of this company of clerks, offering speakers from the Reich for the election campaign.[14] Even so, the Danzig NSDAP proved unequal to the test of its first election.

The campaign of 1927 came at a poor time for the *völkisch* forces. The population had by now somewhat recovered from the shock of separation from the Reich. Business was better than at any time before 1920, and the port of Gdynia was still a potential threat rather than a serious competitor. The intense German patriotism of some Danzigers could find adequate expression in the anti-Polish stand taken by the DNVP, and the workers, enjoying relatively full employment, had no reason to be dissatisfied with the leadership of the SPD. There was also the Communist alternative, for those workers who clung to the concept of class warfare or who wished to register a vote against the "system." The Center continued its hold on the Catholic vote. The *völkisch* politicians could only appeal to the perennially dissatisfied and to the radically anti-Semitic, a small number in these quiet times. But the *völkisch* parties were in any case more interested in fighting each other than in appealing to the broad electorate.

Once again Hohnfeldt found himself at, or projected himself into, the center of contention. In April the NSDAP and the DSP began negotiations with a view to producing the normal single list of *völkisch* candidates. Hohnfeldt broke off talks when the DSP demanded his resignation as Gauleiter as a condition of its cooperation. The NSDAP shrank to a tiny group of Hohnfeldt's personal supporters. The party polled only fourteen hundred votes in November, after a campaign that the Reichsleitung could not bring itself to support with funds from an already stretched treasury. Hohnfeldt was the only Nazi to enter the new Volkstag. The DSP did little better, with only two thousand votes.

Hohnfeldt was now rejected by his followers. In June 1928 he resigned as Gauleiter in favor of Walter Maass. As usual, the Reichsleitung showed no interest in intervening. The NSDAP was consolidating internally, and a number of other incompetent or inflexible local leaders lost their positions at about the same time.[15] As for Maass, he had no leadership ambitions. He would accept only the post of deputy Gauleiter, even without a chief. The party continued to exist through 1928 and 1929 and even attracted some old members and gained a few new ones, but it failed to draw any attention outside the narrow *völkisch* group.[16] Neither the NSDAP nor the DSP attempted to remedy this situation by associating themselves with respectable, "nonpartisan" patriotic demonstrations, such as those on the tenth anniversary of the signing of the hated Treaty of Versailles (28 June 1929).[17] An energetic Nazi leadership, had it existed in Danzig, would certainly have taken some advantage of this major public occasion.

In late 1929 a great growth in Reich party membership began, accompanied by successes in several local elections. The Danzig backwater, although not a vital matter, was something of a political liability. The publicity to be gained from a strong NSDAP in an internationally sensitive area like the free city may have attracted the Reichsleitung, although no direct evidence exists. Whatever its precise reasons, the Reichsleitung made its first attempt to clean up the Danzig situation. Hohnfeldt had proven an incapable leader, and Maass lacked the ambition to lead. Finally, in late 1929, Gauleiter Erich Koch of East Prussia was given full authority in Danzig as provisional Gau administrator.[18] The change marks a new period in the development of the NSDAP in Danzig. For the first time, the Gau was drawn into the broad stream of Nazi politics with its ever-changing fronts, and the purely provincial quarrels of the Gau became part of the larger struggles within the national movement.

The SA Rebellion

Erich Koch was a brutal man with a talent for making enemies. Even so, he could have provided a central focus for the Danzig NSDAP, an external authority to judge between factions, not bound to any of them. Success in this task was denied him by a new arrival in Danzig, Bruno Fricke, who had recently returned to Europe from Nazi activities in South America. Fricke came to Danzig as a result of Koch's attempt to bring the organizational level of the Gau up to Reich standards. Danzig lacked a salaried business manager, even though such officials had been usual in other Gaue since 1926.[19] Fricke took up the new post of Gau business manager in Danzig in February or March 1930.[20] He also became the leader of the local SA. He introduced a militant spirit into the SA, which increased from less than one hundred to one hundred and fifty men under his leadership, while the SS remained at its old level of twenty members.[21]

Fricke seems to have inspired remarkable loyalty among his followers, and his influence was partly responsible for the growth of party membership from about four hundred in 1929 to eight hundred in June 1930.[22] Fricke's SA took to the streets, and Nazi agitation in the free city increased. So did the receptivity of the public, as the first effects of the depression were felt.[23] It was in June that the attention of the Polish commissioner-general was first drawn to Nazi meetings at which the international status of Danzig was denounced, although he was still far more concerned with the use of the free city as a convention center by various Reich organizations.[24] Koch resented the competition of the new SA leader, and a conflict was inevitable. Although the causes of the conflict were essentially local, its outline and outcome were determined by the political situation within the NSDAP as a whole.

In his capacity as leader of the Danzig SA, Fricke was a subordinate and an ally of the "Supreme SA Leader—East," Captain Walter Stennes. Stennes was a former police officer who had already challenged Koch's authority in East Prussia. In 1931 Stennes was to rebel openly against the Reichsleitung, only to be expelled from the party.[25] Fricke followed Stennes in viewing the SA as the only viable force in the NSDAP, and in attempting to control the political activity of the party through its "military" arm. Party leaders opposed to Stennes, notably Gregor Strasser, the member of the Reichsleitung most concerned with organizational affairs, tried at this time to enforce a strict separation between the SA and the PL (*Politische Leitung;* the "political leadership"), to prevent the former from taking over the latter.[26] The conflict in the Reich was repeated on a smaller scale in Danzig.

In the face of the threat from Fricke, the older leaders of the

Gau, including Maass and Hohnfeldt, united behind Koch. Maass had already been replaced as deputy Gauleiter by Wilhelm von Wnuck, who had been a stable force in Gau politics.[27] Old quarrels were made up. Koch, on his own authority, suspended Fricke from his post as business manager and gave that position to Arthur Greiser, a much decorated former flying officer from the province of Poznan who had been active in the DSP and the nationalist veterans' organization, the Stahlhelm.[28] On 30 July 1930 Koch felt strong enough to demand of the Reichsleitung that Fricke be expelled from the party for usurping the prerogatives of the political leadership and for carrying out this "deliberate sabotage" at the direction of Stennes.[29] The Gau was divided into two camps: the "political" group headed by Koch, Wnuck, Greiser, Maass, and Hohnfeldt, and the SA led by Bruno Fricke. Fricke was supported by Stennes, and the political faction could count on Gregor Strasser and the Reichsleitung. Fricke eventually gained the support of a majority of the Ortsgruppenleiter and more active members in Danzig. The argument was not decided, however, on its local merits, but on the broader basis of Nazi politics.

The Reichsleitung cooperated with Koch and suspended Fricke despite objections from Stennes. Fricke faced party court (USCHLA) proceedings blatantly rigged against him. But on 21 August Koch made the mistake of calling a general Danzig membership meeting, intended to mark the defeat of the SA. Angry SA men invaded the meeting. Danzig SS commander Erich Peters lost control of his men, who joined with the SA. Koch was powerless, and the old political leaders of the Gau felt constrained to resign their posts. In exchange, Fricke generously requested the SA to allow the vanquished to leave the field unharmed.[30] As it happened, several days afterward the Berlin SA revolted against Gauleiter Joseph Goebbels, and Hitler seemed for a time to give in to SA demands for greater independence and influence within the party.[31] The Danzig SA revolt appeared as a local expression of a national plot by the SA against the political leadership, and both sides did not hesitate to call for support on the national level. Koch returned to the fight with the backing of the Reichsleitung, which finally expelled Fricke from the party on 1 September, declared the Gau Danzig to be dissolved, and placed the individual party members under the direct authority of Munich. Koch was commissioned to reorganize the Danzig NSDAP.[32]

Bloodshed was avoided, if only because the SA had an overwhelming preponderance of force on its side. Direct action by the political leadership was impossible. Skirmishes did occur. For example, Koch's ally, SS leader Erich Peters, did a bit of eavesdropping on an SA meeting, only to be discovered. The SA reported that Peters fled, with several storm troopers at his heels. Taking refuge in the ladies' toilet of a tavern, he leveled a pistol at the approaching SA men and cried out, with more of a sense of drama than of place: "I stand here in the name of Adolf Hitler. Whoever comes closer will be shot." The police then arrived to rescue Peters, who escaped from the affray with no damage save to his reputation.[33]

In September, the SA and the Ortsgruppenleiter supporting Fricke went so far as to choose a new Gauleitung. The records of the rebellion incidentally show that the NSDAP had attracted a number of new members of a rather higher social class than had previously been represented. Several physicians and attorneys were among Fricke's supporters. The rebels never failed to protest their loyalty to Hitler, but their support of Fricke after his expulsion from the party was hardly compatible with the famous Nazi "leadership principle." [34] Hitler had already reacted vigorously in another case, when Ortsgruppenleiter had attempted to dismiss their Gauleiter by majority vote.[35] The confidence of the rebels was based, not only on the strength of their local position, but also on a misreading of the national situation within the NSDAP. They were proceeding on the belief that Stennes had already won his victory, that Fricke's expulsion was only an expression of Gregor Strasser's desperate attempts to cling to power, and that Hitler would shortly reinstate Fricke and denounce Koch. But time was pressing. An election to the Volkstag was to take place in November.

Since the elections were run on the same principle of proportional representation and straight-ticket voting used in the Reich, each party had to submit a list of candidates, which would be published in the official Danzig law gazette. The first three names on each list would appear on the ballot. The proportion of the total vote a party received determined the number of its mandates, which were given to the candidates according to their order on the list. In the coming elections the Nazis in Danzig expected to profit from the worsening economic situation and the example of Nazi success in Germany. This expectation increased after the Reichstag elections of 14 September gave the NSDAP 107 seats. The list of Volkstag candidates to be presented became a matter of crucial importance, since the men whose names led the list would be assured of the prestige and salary that went with membership in the Volkstag. Election to the Volkstag was the only form of patronage available to the NSDAP. Fricke's supporters feared that the already defeated political faction would attempt to reverse the situation by controlling the list of nominations.

Everything possible was done by the SA faction to prevent a reversal of their victory. They took over the party office, which Koch had closed. They arranged election parades and speeches, in which Fricke participated. They bombarded Hitler's offices in Munich with complaints that Koch and his candidate for business manager, Arthur Greiser, were planning to rig the party nominations. In carrying out their internal party squabble, they indirectly generated a certain amount of public interest in the affairs of the NSDAP.[36] But election victory was not the only goal of the National Socialist movement. The situation at the end of September 1930 was most disturbing to the Reichsleitung and could not help but disturb Hitler. There had been a gross failure in the Nazi chain of command.

For all their apparent success, the leaders of the Fricke group, including Fricke himself, were aware that their victory would eventually prove meaningless unless it were confirmed by Hitler. It had more than once been demonstrated that no faction could openly challenge Hitler's leadership and remain within the party. The legitimacy of lesser leaders depended absolutely on the approval of the Führer.[37] In late September, Hitler finally moved to clarify the situation. He commissioned Hermann Göring to arrange a settlement. Göring arrived in Danzig on

3 October and stayed only briefly to make a public speech and to hold discussions with party leaders. He was impressed by Fricke's local strength, and his first reaction was to give the victory to the SA, although without arranging for Fricke's own readmittance to the party. A Fricke man was installed as provisional head of the SS, the dissolution of the Gau was revoked, and a provisional Gauleitung was appointed, with Greiser as Gauleiter and a Fricke supporter as deputy.[38]

Greiser had been associated with Koch and the old political leadership of the Gau, but it was understood that he would remain as Gauleiter only until a new man could arrive from the Reich. The control of the Fricke group over SA and SS was confirmed, and Greiser was saddled with a Fricke man as deputy Gauleiter. Greiser himself was bitterly disappointed at Göring's decisions and wrote to him that he could not "quite accept the fact that our principle of command and of the authority of leadership had to be sacrificed to the demand of a majority." [39] Greiser had received a lesson in Nazi politics that he was never to forget. Throughout his long party career, which lasted until 1945, he was never to misjudge for long the potentialities of his own position, or to take risks on the assumption that his demonstrated loyalty to Nazi "principles" would protect him.

After Göring left Danzig, the Reichsleitung and the new provisional Danzig Gauleitung went to work on the problem of a list of candidates for the Volkstag election. The result of their labors was a compromise list, rather weighted in the direction of the Fricke group in the first part (those candidates with a real chance of election). Fricke himself was not included, and his expulsion from the party was allowed to stand. Hans Albert Hohnfeldt, who still symbolized the old leadership, was also left off the list. Most of those who appeared in the leading positions, including Greiser, were men who were willing to work with the national leadership, whatever their previous factional affiliation.[40] But the party in Danzig remained badly split. The political faction was especially convinced that it had been treated unfairly. The SA, overestimating the extent of its triumph, was unreliable and capable of alienating the public through excessive zeal. It seemed hardly likely that the two groups could work together for an election success. The most sensible members of both factions agreed on the need for a new departure. Everything now depended on the expected "comrade from the Reich," on the man who would come with a strong hand and clear authority. Hitler sent Albert Forster.

3

Growth and Victory, 1930–33

Not quite three years after the SA rebellion in Danzig ran its ambiguous course, the NSDAP received an absolute majority of the votes in an election for a new Volkstag. The success of the NSDAP in attaining power in the free city seems particularly impressive when compared with the disastrous mediocrity of its later efforts at government. The factors making for Nazi success may be divided into two categories: the internal and the external. The internal factors included the changes in personnel and organization that transformed the Gau Danzig after October 1930. The external factors included the basic ingredients of public life in the free city—the economic, ethnological, and international aspects of the Danzig situation—over which the party could exercise little control, and the changing political constellation, which was amenable to Nazi influence. In the management of their internal affairs, and in their ability to exploit external circumstances, the Nazis were superior to their opponents. But it required the final, crushing circumstance of the Nazi takeover of power in Germany to assure local victory in Danzig. The task of the Gau Danzig of the NSDAP was not so much an independent assumption of the government of the free city as it was preparation for the day when Danzig would have to follow the lead of a Nazi Reich.

Albert Forster

Albert Forster, the man who was to lead the NSDAP to power in Danzig, was twenty-one years old when he joined the party in September 1923. He was the youngest son of the administrator of the state prison in Fürth, a small city in Franconia (northern Bavaria). Forster had been too young to share in the "front experience" of the world war or to be much influenced by the revolutionary events of 1918 and 1919. He came to political awareness at the very moment he encountered the NSDAP, bringing nothing into the party but an eagerness to learn and to be of help. This inclination survived the dissolution of the party after the Munich Putsch, and Forster was back in the ranks by March 1925. He soon became Ortsgruppenleiter of Fürth. Meanwhile he had lost his position as a bank teller, and he remained unemployed until 1928. Nazi accounts later attributed Forster's unfortunate employment record to his penchant for anti-Semitic agitation, and this may well have been true. Fürth's Jewish community was relatively large, and sensible employers would have shunned a man with Forster's reputation for Nazi fanaticism.

That same fanaticism, along with his strong personal attachment to Hitler and his ability as a speaker, gave Forster a modest fame in Bavarian Nazi circles. His career in the party was advanced by his patron and Gauleiter, Julius Streicher of Nuremberg. Forster made himself especially useful in promoting the sale of Streicher's pornographic, anti-Semitic publication, *Der Stürmer*. His Nazi activities did not cease when he again found employment, in 1928. He was hired by the German National Commercial Employees' Association as a clerk, was given training in Hamburg for a more advanced position, and was assigned in 1930 to the association's local organization in the small industrial city of Harburg. Streicher did not forget him, and his name was placed third on the list of NSDAP Reichstag candidates from Franconia. After the great Nazi election victory of 14 September 1930, Forster became a member of the 107-man Nazi delegation; at age twenty-eight he was the youngest member of the Reichstag.[1]

After Hermann Göring returned from Danzig in October 1930, he suggested to Hitler that Forster be appointed to reorganize the troubled Gau.[2] Göring's reasons are not known. Forster may have seemed a good choice because he had not been involved on either side of the Stennes controversy. He also enjoyed the salary and the free railway pass that went with being a Reichstag deputy, and so his new assignment cost the party nothing. He had had some experience as an Ortsgruppenleiter, but he was not currently occupying a party post for which a replacement would have to be found. In any case, Forster was given no time to pursue his new career as a legislator. On 15 October Hitler gave him a grant of plenary power in Danzig, although formal appointment as Gauleiter came somewhat later.[3] Forster's train pulled into Danzig's cavernous central station on 24 October, a day that Nazi propaganda retrospectively labeled "the turning point" in the history of the local party.[4]

Faced with the complicated problem of running the Gau on the eve of an election, Forster discovered that the old political faction retained a certain amount of vitality. Even more important, the older leaders made plain their willingness to follow Forster as Gauleiter, if he could produce a new settlement at the expense of the obstreperous SA men.[5] Forster's obvious political interests, as a new man on the scene, led him partially to reverse the results of Göring's brief visit. Greiser became deputy Gauleiter, displacing the Fricke supporter who had been appointed by Göring. Only the Gau treasurer, Paul Wittenberg, continued to represent the Fricke faction in the new Gauleitung. The SA itself presented a particularly difficult problem. Forster assured himself of control over the organization by arranging for the appointment of a new local commander, Max Linsmayer, a youthful friend from Fürth.[6]

The crisis situation created by the approaching election was used by Forster to consolidate his position while uniting the party. He pushed party members into an election campaign marked by a series of massive public rallies unlike any they had ever seen. Joseph Goebbels even came to speak on election eve. The "wave of meetings" (*Versammlungswelle*), which crested with the appearance of the most prominent speaker available, was a technique that had been employed by the Nazis with great success before the September Reichstag elections.[7] Now it was used in Danzig for the first time. Forster made good use of the resources he found on hand. Greiser had already held one rally in mid-October and had begun arrangements for later meetings.[8]

He remained in charge of organization. The enthusiasm of the militant SA was not dampened but was effectively channeled into the campaign.

All efforts were justified by the results of the voting on 16 November. The Nazis capitalized on Danzig's unfortunate economic situation, and on the example of the recent Reichstag elections, to attract 16.1 percent of the total vote (compared with 18.3 percent in the Reich) and to increase their representation in the new, smaller Volkstag from 1 seat in 120 to 12 seats in 72. Even the League high commissioner was forced to take note of the Nazi achievement. The new Nazi Volkstag deputies represented the SA faction and the old leadership more or less equally, and the quarrel was permanently buried in the exuberance of victory.[9]

With the election over, Forster turned to peripheral aspects of Gau organization. The Hitler Youth and its female counterpart, the League of German Girls, were soon represented in Danzig.[10] More important was the foundation of a Gau newspaper to compete with the papers published under the auspices of the more established political parties. An "unofficial" Nazi weekly played a part in the election campaign. On 5 February 1931 it was replaced by an official weekly Gau newspaper, the *Vorposten* ("Outpost"), which listed Forster as publisher and Greiser as the first editor in chief. The *Vorposten* was soon printing five thousand copies every week.[11] The paper, which became a daily in 1933, survived until the end of the Second World War.

In the Reich, the agricultural depression had driven surprising numbers of rural voters into the arms of the NSDAP in 1928, even though party propaganda had largely ignored agricultural problems. A series of decisions in late 1928 and early 1929 had resulted in the abandonment of the party's efforts to win German workers and in a new emphasis on attracting patriotic middle-class and rural voters. This "rural-nationalist" strategy was not applied in Danzig until after Forster's arrival.[12] In October 1930, there were only three small, isolated Ortsgruppen in the rural areas of the free city, and most of the rural population had never been reached by Nazi organizing efforts. Forster had had considerable experience as a rural speaker in Bavaria, where his reception had been poor, and in Schleswig-Holstein, where the reaction had been much more favorable.[13] The rural areas of the free city, which contained 30 percent of the population, resembled Schleswig-Holstein in that they were north German, primarily Protestant, specialized in dairy production, and suffered from severe economic difficulties. After the immediate rush of the election campaign was over, Forster personally addressed himself to spreading national socialism in the villages. His earlier experience bore fruit in detailed guidelines for his subordinates.[14]

Unlike the other political parties, the Nazis did not go into semihibernation after the elections but actually stepped up their activity.[15] In the year from October 1930 to October 1931, the NSDAP held 44 mass meetings and 2,100 smaller public meetings, trained six speakers in special courses, and spent 10,967 gulden on blanketing town and country alike with propaganda of all kinds. In the same period, the Gauleitung claimed, the membership of the SA increased from 150 to 1,500, the SS jumped from 20 to 200, and the total membership of the Gau grew from under 1,000 to over 5,000.[16] The cramped and uninspiring headquarters at Hundegasse 52 proved inadequate, and the Gauleitung and SA moved to a larger and more impressive set of rooms at Jopengasse 11, in the heart of the business and shopping district.[17] The move to new quarters symbolized the creation of a new party.

Official party statistics chart the growth of the Gau as follows: [18]

June 1930:	800 members
December 1930:	1,310
June 1931:	3,897
December 1931:	5,623
June 1932:	8,879
December 1932:	9,519

The great increase in party and SA membership completely overwhelmed the old leaders, few of whom rose to positions of importance in the "new" party. Those who did maintain themselves until the takeover of power in 1933 disappeared from the Danzig scene after 1935. The major exception was Arthur Greiser. The Gau was first divided into Kreise in 1932. (The Kreis was an administrative unit intermediate between Ortsgruppe and Gau.) Of the twenty-nine Gau officials and nine Kreisleiter who held office in 1936, only three officials and one Kreisleiter had been in any way prominent in the party before Forster's arrival. Most of the remainder had joined the NSDAP in 1931 and 1932.[19] It appears that Forster was following a very deliberate personnel policy.

The growth of the Gau under Forster secured his own power in the party. The new members associated Danzig with Forster as they associated the NSDAP as a whole with Hitler. For many years it was impossible for any of Forster's subordinates to challenge his leadership. Something similar had happened in the small but rapidly expanding NSDAP in 1921 and 1922. The growth of the party had been presided over by Hitler in his capacity as propaganda chief and principal speaker. The new members had come to identify the NSDAP with Hitler, whose propaganda activities had attracted them to the party and who was the most dynamic of the members of the party directorate. The greater the increase in membership, the more the influence of the party's actual founders had been undermined, until it was possible for Hitler to seize dictatorial power over the young movement.[20]

The NSDAP and Public Life in Danzig, 1931–32

The NSDAP made little impression on the public life of the free city prior to the elections in the Reich and in Danzig in the fall of 1930. This situation changed radically in 1931 and 1932, both because of the increased effectiveness of Nazi propaganda under the new leadership and because changes in the quality of public life created a climate more receptive to the appeal of national socialism.

It has become something of a truism to see in the growth of Nazi influence in the Reich the result of the fears engendered in the German population, and particularly in the middle classes, by the great depression that followed the failure of the American stock market.[21] A close look at the situation in Danzig will not endanger this interpretation. But it should be pointed out that the economy of the free city had never been particularly healthy. It was dependent on the unstable Polish economy and vulnerable to discriminatory Polish economic policies, which were themselves the natural result of Danzig's own efforts to retain its German character at whatever economic cost.[22] Unemployment was a chronic problem, even in relatively prosperous times. From 1926 to 1929 unemployed workers amounted to almost twenty thousand during the slow winter months and between twelve and fifteen thousand during the summer. If dependents of the unemployed are included, between 10 and 17 percent of the population was on the dole at any given time during this period.[23] The improvement noticeable in 1928 and 1929 was slight. Considerable economic distress may thus be taken as a constant factor in the life of the free city, even before 1930. Constant too was anti-Polish German nationalism. And yet, the NSDAP failed to make its mark. The sharpening of both economic distress and national feeling after 1930 certainly aided the Nazis, but success would have remained beyond the reach of the party had it not been for the reorganization and revitalization carried out by Albert Forster and backed by the example of growing Nazi influence in the Reich.

The effects of the world depression made themselves felt in Danzig in 1930. In December of that year unemployment already stood at twenty-five thousand. Two years later, the number had risen to thirty-nine thousand. Only Reich subsidies enabled the government to continue assistance payments.[24] The total export-import trade of Poland dropped sharply between 1931 and 1932. The share routed through Danzig dropped in favor of the Polish port of Gdynia, and so the depression was felt far more in Danzig than in Gdynia, which lay just beyond the border of the free city. President Ernst Ziehm's German National–Center coalition senate, which took office in January 1931, proved much less willing to compromise with the Poles than had the previous senate, which had been led by the Social Democrats. The League high commissioner had not been called upon to settle any

Polish-Danzig disputes in 1928 and 1929. In 1930 he rendered only two decisions, neither of which was appealed. Between October 1931 and November 1932 he handed down no less than eight decisions. Most of them involved vital economic matters, and every one of them was appealed before the League council by one or both parties. The question of Gdynia, in particular, occupied the attention of the council and the disputants.[25]

Economic crisis aside, the political atmosphere of Danzig in this period was dominated by fear of Polonization. Anti-Polish sentiments were expressed by the leaders of all parties, other than the Communists. The Catholic Center party showed no sympathy for its Polish coreligionists, and Catholic politicians and clergy fought against all attempts at penetration of the church organization by Poles.[26] The DNVP, as the leading government party, adopted a vociferously anti-Polish attitude. Even the SPD, attacked by its enemies as being lax in the defense of Danzig's German culture, did not hesitate to raise the Polish bogey when politically appropriate. A typical attack on Ziehm in the Social Democratic *Volksstimme* labeled him "the hope of the Poles." [27]

Try as the Danzig government might, the free city's ethnic and economic difficulties were dependent on forces almost totally beyond its control. Some small amelioration of the economic catastrophe might have been gained by a program of thoroughgoing compromise with Poland, but the success of such a policy depended on the reasonableness of Polish demands and on the good sense of the Danzig electorate. Unfortunately, so sensitive were the Danzigers on the national issue that no serious Polish demand appeared reasonable. The voters turned to those parties that promised a fight against the Polish enemy. Given the weakness of the free city, this fight could not possibly succeed. On the contrary, it invited effective Polish economic retaliation. The political anger created by economic fears was diverted by nationalism away from the only course that stood even a small chance of success. The anger of the electorate, denied an outlet in successful political action, became hysterical. The Nazis made themselves the beneficiaries.

The NSDAP, as a party outside the government, benefited

from the unsolvable nature of Danzig's problems. The difficulties of the threatened agricultural and urban middle classes received special attention. Serious solutions were not proposed. Instead, Nazi propaganda concentrated on the undeniable facts of distress and on the identification of enemies. The universal Jewish foe was expanded to include the Poles, who were normally referred to as "Polacks." [28] Since many of the Polish citizens resident in Danzig as merchants and commercial agents were in fact Jewish, the identification of Jew and Pole in the public mind was easily accomplished. The Nazi campaign against the international status quo established by the Treaty of Versailles also fitted the Danzig situation. The masthead of the weekly *Vorposten* attacked the very existence of the free city: "Back to the Reich. Against the Tyranny of Treaties." [29] Nor did the Nazis confine themselves to words. Assaults on Poles and Polish citizens of Jewish origin by members of the NSDAP occurred with increasing frequency from October 1930.[30]

The increase in political street violence in Germany during 1931 and 1932 had its parallel in Danzig. The SA clashed repeatedly with the Communists and with the Social Democratic Arschufo (*Arbeiterschutzformationen;* Workers' Defense Formations). Shots were only rarely exchanged, but knives and improvised weapons were used. Remarkably enough, there was only one fatality. Sixteen-year-old Horst Hoffmann died after he and his SA companions fought with the Arschufo in the village of Kahlbude on 15 November 1931. He was immediately declared a martyr by the NSDAP.[31]

In Danzig, as in Germany, the NSDAP fed off the radicalization of the public atmosphere and contributed to it. The endless succession of meetings, SA marches, inflammatory handbills, and violent articles in the *Vorposten* frightened and attracted the electorate. The elections to the county assemblies (Kreistage) on 17 May 1931 brought large gains for the NSDAP. The campaign had been marked by violence in the rural districts.[32] National socialism penetrated into the civil service, and Nazi sympathies were noted in the officer corps of the police as early as March 1931, despite the bad feeling caused by police action against SA breaches of the peace.[33]

The growing impact of national socialism on Danzig's public life was demonstrated on 9 April 1932 when Hitler landed briefly at the airport in Danzig-Langfuhr on his way to a rally in East Prussia. The Führer was greeted, not only by the massed ranks of the SA, but also by thousands of cheering Danzigers and, most ominously, by a high-ranking Danzig police official at the head of a uniformed company of his men.[34] The NSDAP, with its successes in the Reich and its vigorous methods at the local level, had made itself the most visible force on the Danzig political scene. But street violence and propaganda did not in themselves lead to power. They were tools to be exploited by the party in its relations with the government. The ambiguous relationship between the senate and the NSDAP set for the Nazi leaders their most difficult and delicate political tasks.

The NSDAP and the Government

After the elections of 16 November 1930, the seats in the Volkstag were divided among the parties as indicated in table 1. Some of

TABLE 1

Division of Volkstag Seats by Party, 1927 and 1930

Party	Year	
	1927	1930
Center	18	11
DNVP	25	10
Deutsche Volksgemeinschaft	—	3
KPD (Communists)	8	7
Liberal parties	17	7
NSDAP	1	12
Polish parties	3	2
Railway and harbor workers' list	—	1
SPD	42	19
Other parties	6	—
Total	120	72

Source: Adapted from *Taschenbuch*, p. 157.

the entries in table 1 require a word of explanation. The railway and harbor workers' list was presented by the professional associations representing these workers, who felt that their German national character was threatened by their employment by the Polish state and the binational harbor board. The *Deutsche Volksgemeinschaft* (Community of the German People) was headed by a former member of the DNVP, Julius Hoppenrath, and specialized in extreme anti-Polish nationalism.[35] Hoppenrath became senator for finance in the new government. There were no less than four parties in Danzig that considered themselves "liberal." In the new Volkstag the liberal deputies sat together with the deputies of the railway and harbor workers and the *Deutsche Volksgemeinschaft* in a parliamentary group known as the "Block of National Unity" (*Block der nationalen Sammlung*) and commonly called the "Bourgeois Block." The block numbered eleven deputies. There were two Polish parties, divided both on the basis of personality and on their attitude toward the government in Warsaw. The Polish parties had a great deal of difficulty attracting electoral support, since most of the Poles resident in Danzig were citizens of Poland and were therefore ineligible to vote.

Given the distribution of mandates, there were two possibilities for majority governments: a "left" senate of SPD, Center, and the Bourgeois Block, and a "right" senate of Center, Block, DNVP, and NSDAP. The Center, which had participated in the senate continuously since the founding of the free city, occupied the key position. Party chairman Monsignor Anton Sawatzki decided to move to the right. He was motivated by the tension between Brüning and the SPD in the Reich, and by a belief that the SPD had proved incapable of solving Danzig's economic and financial problems. Sawatzki accordingly asked Ernst Ziehm of the DNVP to open negotiations with the Nazis.[36]

There were two precedents for Nazi membership in right-wing coalitions, in Thuringia in 1929 and in Brunswick in 1930. Many Nazi supporters in Danzig, in and out of the party, expected that the gains at the polls would be followed by participation in the senate.[37] Hitler himself had just offered Brüning a coalition in return for three cabinet positions and had been disappointed by Brüning's refusal. Even while the Danzig elections were being held, talks were continuing in the Reich between the Nazis and other groups on the possibility of coalition.[38] Forster was nevertheless told by Hitler, reportedly on Göring's advice, that the NSDAP would not participate in the new senate.[39] There is no evidence on the Führer's motives. It was instead decided to support a right-wing minority government, if one could be formed.

In early December, Göring returned to Danzig for talks with political leaders.[40] Ernst Ziehm was told that the NSDAP could not enter the senate before it was represented in the Reich government, but that the party was willing to support any coalition directed "against the Marxists." Ziehm, for the DNVP, and would-be fellow senators from the Center and the Bourgeois Block, demanded a written guarantee from the Nazi Volkstag deputies that they would in all cases vote with the new, minority government and would not introduce any proposal in the Volkstag without the senate's prior consent. After much hesitation, Göring persuaded the local Nazis to agree. Agreement was made easier because both sides acknowledged the need for an enabling law to permit government by decree. The Volkstag would be largely eliminated from the legislative process, and the Nazis would not have to vote for unpopular austerity measures. Ziehm felt he had driven a good bargain, since the NSDAP would be forced to bear "a share in the responsibility of government, without sharing in the advantages." [41]

This view was short-sighted. Thanks to Nazi propaganda techniques, the party had no need for the public exposure that went with government participation, while the coalition parties were exposed most unpleasantly in this period of economic hardship and austerity programs. The Nazis also proved able to dispense with some of the rewards of political patronage, although these were welcome enough when the proper time came. The new minority senate would inevitably be dependent on the NSDAP, despite the written guarantee. In fact, the Nazis would enjoy the advantages of government, without its responsibilities.

Forster may have been disappointed at first, but he soon recognized that the NSDAP would benefit from the arrangement. His first task was to assure his constituents of the wisdom of non-participation. The Nazi rank and file was told that the new senate would be dependent on the NSDAP, and that the evil of another "Marxist" government would be avoided. Party members were assured that the Nazis would enter the senate as soon as they could be certain of a dominant position, and when there was at least one National Socialist in the Reich cabinet, who could prevent an anti-Nazi German government from cutting off the flow of financial support to Danzig.[42] Forster may have believed himself that the present arrangement was temporary at most, since even Hitler was predicting that the Nazis would control the Reich government by February 1931.[43]

After Ziehm took office as senate president on 9 January 1931, the Nazis supplemented their continuing "wave of meetings" with performances in the Volkstag. Arthur Greiser, as leader of the Nazi parliamentary group, gained special repute for his vituperative attacks on Poles and Social Democrats. The coalition parties seemed to welcome Greiser's parliamentary offensive against the common Polish and Marxist enemies, and the DNVP was particularly anxious to cooperate. In March the government parties went so far as to join with the NSDAP to elect Wilhelm von Wnuck the new president of the Volkstag, replacing Social Democrat Julius Gehl. The SPD did not bother to contest the election.[44] A pattern was soon established. The "bourgeois" parties cooperated with the NSDAP in their eagerness to weaken the SPD, but the Social Democrats stood on their dignity and refused to fight to maintain their few remaining positions of power.

The Nazis did not limit their attacks to the SPD. The Center was accused of collaboration with the "Reds," and the liberal parties were supposed to be friendly to the Jews and the Poles.[45] But the *Vorposten* tended to support government actions and emphasized the influence the Nazis had over the senate.[46] The DNVP was not at first attacked. In return, Ziehm took on the task of defending the NSDAP against complaints by the Polish commissioner-general and the League high commissioner. Nazi street violence and boycott campaigns against Poles and Jews provoked both these officials. Polish protests had the clear intent of proving the senate incapable of maintaining order in the free city and justifying a Polish intervention with the permission of the League of Nations. In defending the NSDAP, the senate was defending its own ability to keep order.[47] In any case, the Nazis were only doing what the government parties would have wished to do, had they not been burdened with the responsibility of avoiding League or Polish intervention.

Relations between NSDAP and DNVP were not seriously disturbed until March 1932, when the DNVP was subjected to violent abuse in the *Vorposten*. This was the natural result of the Reich presidential campaign, which saw Hitler opposing both Hindenburg and the DNVP candidate, Theodor Düsterberg. The attacks abated in April, when the DNVP agreed to support Hitler in the runoff election. The great increases won by the Nazis in the Reich and Prussian elections may have encouraged the party to show less restraint in Danzig. By June, the *Vorposten* and Nazi speakers were once again attacking the DNVP, along with all other parties. Gerhard Weise, DNVP leader in Zoppot, was selected for special abuse.[48]

The DNVP did not reply in kind. Ziehm may have been influenced by the attempts of Reich Chancellor Franz von Papen, supported by the DNVP, to come to an agreement with Hitler.[49] Ziehm's dependence on the parliamentary support of the NSDAP left him little choice. When the antics of the SA and the propaganda of the *Vorposten* caused difficulties with Poland, the government continued to make the Nazis' excuses for them. The senate refused to allow the contention of the Polish commissioner-general that the NSDAP was a subversive organization and should be banned. Since League High Commissioner Manfredi Gravina accepted the senate's position and considered the banning of the NSDAP unconstitutional, the commissioner-general's protests led nowhere.[50]

The senate's permissive attitude is well illustrated by an incident involving Arthur Greiser. Greiser, who had been appointed a Danzig delegate to the harbor board, published an article in the *Vorposten* in June, in which he claimed that the board served only Polish interests and demanded that it be abolished. The *Vorposten* continued the campaign through July.[51] On 2

August 1932 the professional association of Polish harbor board employees adopted a resolution denouncing the Nazi attacks and warning that Greiser would bear full responsibility for any "incidents" that might occur. Greiser appeared several days later in the office of a harbor board engineer active in the Polish employees' association and told him that he considered the resolution a threat. The Nazi then displayed a revolver, playfully tossed it about, and claimed he was ready for any attack. The incident was interpreted by Commissioner-General Kazimierz Papée and the Polish press as a menacing of the Polish engineer. The senate, in its reply to Papée's protest, dismissed the affair as a friendly joke.[52]

Chancellor von Papen failed to "tame" the NSDAP in the summer of 1932. The Reichstag, elected in July, was dissolved again in September, with elections set for 6 November. In August Forster visited Hitler at the latter's retreat on the Obersalzberg. Forster was accompanied by SA leader Max Linsmayer and by the Gau's adviser on agriculture, Dr. Hermann Rauschning. The Gauleiter told Hitler that the senate was refusing to cooperate with the NSDAP. The enabling law, which was the basis of Ziehm's decree-issuing power, was due to expire in September. Forster requested Hitler's permission to take advantage of the crisis to press for new elections in Danzig. Hitler hesitated, explaining that he feared a ban of the NSDAP in the Reich, in which case he might consider transferring party headquarters to Danzig. He asked Forster and Rauschning if Danzig would extradite a "political criminal" to the Reich. Perhaps it would be best to cultivate good relations with the senate. Rauschning thought the idea impractical, and it was not brought up again. Hitler allowed Forster to renounce the agreement to support the senate, and this was done with great fanfare on 4 September.[53]

Forster's initiative was not, in fact, due to any sudden worsening of relations with the senate. He was worried by the mood of his party, which might best be described as depressed. The Reichstag elections of 31 July had failed to bring a promised majority. The membership, and especially the militant elements of the SA, became uneasy. Hitler's celebrated "legal" method of taking power seemed to be leading nowhere. This mood affected the SA men in Danzig even more than those in the Reich. The Danzig SA was isolated, cooperation with the militia (*Einwohnerwehr*) was poor, and the way to power appeared blocked.[54] Forster's renunciation of support for the senate was intended to break this depression.

The party immediately launched a vigorous propaganda campaign against the senate and moved to dissolve the Volkstag. This motion was actually brought forward jointly with the KPD, to assure it the necessary number of signatures.[55] This is one index of Forster's desperate mood. The motion was defeated only by the combined votes of the government parties and the SPD, all equally fearful of new elections. Although, as the *Vorposten* admitted, the motion stood no chance of passage, it was effective propaganda. It encouraged the membership by giving the party an appearance of militancy, and it forced the senate to cooperate publicly with the SPD. At last, the opposition of the NSDAP to all parties of the hated "system" was plain for every voter to see.[56]

Both the Nazis in Danzig and those in the Reich had ample reason for despondency at the end of 1932. In the November Reichstag elections the Nazis lost ground for the first time, and by a full two million votes. In the Thuringian elections in December the loss was even greater, amounting to 40 percent of the vote polled in that state in July. Party debts mounted, and the SA took to the streets, not to fight, but to beg with tin cans. General Kurt von Schleicher, appointed chancellor in December, tempted Gregor Strasser with the post of vice-chancellor. Strasser refused to accept without party approval, but he was suspected by Hitler of treachery. His resultant resignation shook the party.[57]

In January 1933 the situation began to improve, as complicated negotiations opened between Hitler, former Chancellor von Papen, and Alfred Hugenberg of the DNVP. The Nazis in Danzig played no part. On 30 January 1933 it was announced that a "national" government had been appointed in the Reich. Hitler was chancellor, Papen was vice-chancellor, and the cabinet included German Nationalists and Nazis. In Danzig, political observers confidently expected a similar reformation of the senate.

Hermann Rauschning and the Nazi Victory

On 8 January 1932 the *Vorposten* carried an article on the agricultural situation in the free city by the "Gau technical adviser on agriculture," Dr. Hermann Rauschning. Prior to this time, Rauschning's name had been unknown to the Nazi reading public. Since he was to play a vital role in Danzig's affairs during 1933 and 1934, a few words on his background and outlook are appropriate.

Rauschning, the son of an army officer, was born in 1877 in the West Prussian town of Torun (Thorn). He spent his younger years in Prussian cadet schools and then turned to the study of the history of music, in which he earned a doctorate in 1911. After having been badly wounded during the First World War, he obtained employment in 1920 in the library of the German community of Poznan. Here he became involved in political activity on behalf of the German minority in the former Prussian provinces of Posen and West Prussia, now restored to Poland as Poznan and Pomorze. As a result of this activity, he was forced to leave Poland in 1927. Rauschning took advantage of this turn of fate to fulfill a long-held ambition to become a farmer, and he purchased a small property in Danzig territory. In 1929 he acquired a larger farm, Warnau, in the Kreis Grosses Werder.[58] Farming drew him into politics once again.

Rauschning was to break with national socialism in 1934. After 1936, exile took him to Switzerland, France, Britain, and the United States. As one of the relatively few conservative German emigrés, he devoted himself to warning his fellow conservatives in the west of the dangers of Hitler's movement. In the course of his literary attacks on Hitler, he explained why he had been attracted to national socialism. His discoverable activities between 1931 and 1934 tend to bear out these later apologiae.[59] Rauschning was above all a German patriot. His first book, *Die Entdeutschung Westpreussens und Posens,* was intended to help the German cause by depicting statistically the results of Poland's anti-German policies in her new western territories.[60] Rauschning was a conservative as well as a nationalist, and a monarchist at heart. Although initially a member of the DNVP, he found the party unsatisfactory and identified himself with that small group of writers and politicians known now as "Germany's new conservatives." [61] Rauschning himself adopted Hugo von Hofmannsthal's term and referred to a "conservative revolution." He considered himself a follower of Edgar J. Jung, who criticized democracy as "the rule of inferiors" and saw the conservative revolution as a revival of Christian values on which would be built a new, organic, elitist order.[62] This was the type of society Rauschning hoped could be constructed with the help of national socialism, "a movement that might still be intellectually shaped." [63]

Practically speaking, Rauschning "came into politics from the agrarian side." [64] The farms of the Danzig area were known for their high quality of stock and dairy products, but even before 1914 the average indebtedness of Danzig farms was higher than anywhere else in Prussia.[65] The dislocations caused by the creation of the free city, which forced Danzig farmers to compete with cheaper Polish products, depressed the area's agriculture beyond recovery, despite Reich efforts to find a remedy.[66]

The farmers saw a possible solution in the anti-Polish stand taken by the NSDAP.[67] The Ziehm senate failed to solve the farm problem and soon exhausted its support in the rural areas. In the summer of 1931, Rauschning broke with the DNVP over agricultural policy. Personal disagreements between Rauschning and Ziehm also played a part. The two men so disliked each other that they could not even cooperate in 1935, when both belonged to the anti-Nazi opposition.[68] Rauschning joined the NSDAP in 1931, as the rural credit crisis reached its peak. The summer crisis was particularly severe in his own Grosses Werder. He was elected by his neighbors to head the Kreis branch of the Agricultural League (*Landbund*) on a program of liberalized trade regulations and increased exports.[69] Since Rauschning had also become Gau technical adviser on agriculture, his election to the Agricultural League post was a major victory for the NSDAP in its continuing campaign to capture the rural districts.

Rauschning was carrying out locally a plan organized by the chief Nazi agricultural specialist, Walther Darré. Darré worked through the Gau agricultural advisers in order to take over the major organization of German farmers, the Agricultural League.

Hitler favored the plan with his personal blessing, and it prospered. The national organization of the league was captured by early 1932. In February of that year Rauschning was elected Agricultural League chairman in the free city.[70] The NSDAP made itself the political champion of Danzig's farmers.

Despite Rauschning's successful drive to take over the Agricultural League, he remained unknown outside agricultural and party circles until the spring of 1933.[71] His sudden rise to prominence in April and May and his election as senate president had little to do with the details of his earlier political activities and a great deal to do with the course of Albert Forster's negotiations with the senate after Hitler's assumption of power in the Reich.

The change in government in the Reich on 30 January 1933 came at an embarrassing moment for the senate. President Ziehm and Senator Hinz of the DNVP (who held the portfolios of agriculture and the interior) had initiated a deportation action against Gauleiter Forster, and the courts were considering government libel suits against him as publisher of the *Vorposten*. These actions were now quietly dropped. This did not alter the distaste felt by leading Nazis for Ziehm and Hinz. The latter was disliked by the SA and by the party as a whole as senator for the interior, and by Rauschning and the Agricultural League in his capacity as senator for agriculture. The German consul-general, Baron Edmund von Thermann, nonetheless expected that "within a short time a coalition similar to the Berlin model will be created, as regularly tends to happen." [72] His expectations were reinforced by the published statements of local Nazis, who spoke of cooperation with the DNVP on the Reich pattern. But the NSDAP did not at the same time refrain from accusing Ziehm of collusion with Poland, or from ridiculing him for his de facto dependence on the SPD since the Nazis had ceased to support the government. Talks did begin on allowing the NSDAP into the government, but they quickly broke down over Nazi insistence that the presidency and the Department of the Interior had to go to National Socialists.[73]

Danzig's international position made the political situation even more difficult. Carried away by the events of 30 January, the local Nazis proclaimed the early return of the free city to the Reich and demanded an immediate end to the Polish-Danzig customs union. It was widely assumed that they were only announcing the actual intentions of the new Reich chancellor. The senate chose this tense period to announce that the harbor police, a special detachment responsible to the harbor board, would henceforth be responsible only to Danzig police authorities. The Poles responded in early March by suddenly increasing their garrison on the Westerplatte, the small neck of land in Danzig's harbor allotted to them as a munitions depot. They did this without seeking the required permission of the high commissioner. The Westerplatte affair was taken up by a special session of the League council, and the Poles were forced to withdraw their reinforcements. The senate agreed to restore harbor board control over the harbor police.[74] Many Danzigers felt that a full-scale Polish intervention, which would have used the excuse of Nazi activities, had been very narrowly avoided. President Ziehm declared that the public activities of the NSDAP constituted a menace to Danzig's security, and he ordered them stopped. He acted only after an interview with Hitler, and he believed he had received the chancellor's prior agreement to the step.[75]

Since the Danzig Nazis refused to enter the senate unless they were given the leading posts, negotiations made no headway. Ziehm decided that he could not continue to rule unless a new enabling law were passed by the Volkstag; the old law had expired the previous September. But at this point Ziehm was deserted by the Bourgeois Block, some of whose members had been negotiating with the Nazis on their own. The German Foreign Office, aware of Danzig's international position and anxious to avoid the tensions of an election, now mediated between the NSDAP and the DNVP with the idea of taking the Nazis into the senate while allowing Ziehm to remain as president until July, by which time, it was hoped, the international situation would have cooled down. This tack proved unsuccessful.

Ziehm decided to resolve the impasse by calling for elections, and the Volkstag dissolved itself on 13 April, with voting set for

28 May. The negotiations had been doomed to failure from the start, since Forster had chosen Rauschning as Nazi representative, and since Rauschning was absolutely opposed to any coalition under Ziehm's presidency, no matter how temporary. In choosing Rausching, Forster had, quite possibly with deliberation, made compromise impossible.

No direct decision by Hitler was involved here. Danzig politicians were municipal politicians, suited by their experience and cast of mind to the running of a modestly important city hall. An accident of history now required them to make national policies on an international stage. The hothouse atmosphere in the free city made it difficult for public figures to overcome their personal animosities. Thus it happened that Ziehm did not imitate the leader of the German DNVP, Alfred Hugenberg. For better or worse, the senate president refused to help the Nazis into power.[76]

On 7 April Rauschning was introduced by the *Vorposten* as the "future president of the senate." In an article entitled "Not Chaos but Construction," Rauschning explained the Nazi program, which combined economic proposals with a promise to keep Danzig German. Rauschning promised that, as president, he would honor the constitution and existing treaties. He refrained from attacking Poland and restricted his fire to Ziehm and Hinz. For the *Vorposten,* the article was a masterpiece in studied moderation. No mention was made of Jews until two weeks later, when Rauschning discussed "world Jewry." In his typically "moderate" fashion, he explained (quite mistakenly) that "National socialism is not racial hatred, but the purging from the [German] people of foreign, destructive personalities." This article even implied that assimilated, patriotic German Jews were acceptable to the Nazis.[77]

Rauschning was not a racial anti-Semite in the *völkisch* tradition, although even his later attitude toward Jews remained ambiguous.[78] His idiosyncratic interpretation of his party's attitude toward Jews was a strained attempt to meet the Nazi program halfway, at the same time distorting it in a more moderate and less harmful direction. The same was true of all of Rauschning's efforts to interpret national socialism. The difference between Rauschning and the fanatical Gauleiter was such that the Danzig NSDAP appeared to one observer to have a "Janus head."[79] Confusing as this may have been, the Janus-like appearance of the party was most useful in the election campaign. Forster rallied the party faithful and the newly radicalized, while Rauschning appealed to the reasonable, patriotic, and concerned voter who feared Marxism and the Poles but who had no taste for SA pogroms or the provoking of foreign powers.

Still, Rauschning does seem an odd choice. His selection may have reflected Hitler's concern for international appearances. As early as August 1932, Hitler had told Rauschning that he had no intention of beginning his future government with a war, and that he was prepared to sign an agreement with Poland.[80] Given the international implications of the situation in Danzig, Hitler could not have an overzealous Nazi at the head of the senate. Rauschning, despite his history of activity on behalf of the German minority in Poland, was able to make himself acceptable to Warsaw as a reasonable, sincere advocate of German-Polish understanding. His Polish policies will be considered in detail in the following chapter.

Rauschning not only reassured the Poles, he also impressed the British with his manner and reminded the British consul of "an old-fashioned English squire" rather than a Nazi.[81] Since the British foreign minister, Sir John Simon, was responsible for reporting to the council of the League of Nations on Danzig questions, the British had a special connection with the free city, in which they also held certain commercial interests.[82] Rauschning's function was similar to that of the conservative German foreign minister, Baron Konstantin von Neurath—to serve as a moderate front for an ultimately aggressive German foreign policy.

Hitler had ample reason to approve of Rauschning's candidacy, but the Führer's approval alone was not sufficient. Albert Forster also had to concur in the choice. Hitler would not have forced Rauschning on Forster, any more than he would support Rauschning against Forster in 1934. Although no direct evidence exists, it may be assumed that Rauschning was, from the beginning, Forster's own candidate for senate president and was brought to Hitler's attention by the Gauleiter. For if Rauschning was useful to Hitler, he was also useful to Forster. This usefulness was based on his position in the party. His prestige in the party was great enough for him to accompany Forster and Linsmayer on a visit to Hitler in August 1932. As the successful organizer of the nazification of the Agricultural League, and as a speaker, he was widely respected in the rural districts. But he had no real source of personal power in the local party organization. Rauschning was active neither in the SA nor in the SS, he had no strong roots in any Ortsgruppe, and he belonged to no faction or clique. He presented no challenge to Forster's control over the Gau, as Greiser would have done and later did.

Just as Rauschning acted as a front for Hitler, so he acted for Forster. When it was necessary to take unpopular steps toward cooperation with Poland, Rauschning assumed most of the responsibility, in effect shielding his Gauleiter from the righteous anger of disillusioned party members. It was only after some time, when Rauschning began actively to interfere in Forster's own projects, that he became a hindrance. Since he had no political base in the NSDAP, he was easily removed in late 1934. But in the Nazi spring of 1933 all this lay in the future, and Rauschning and Forster, despite their obvious differences in style and character, fought the election campaign with a common single-mindedness.

The campaign lasted through April and May and was conducted with the excitement usual when the NSDAP was bent on victory. It featured speakers from the Reich, a radio message from Hitler, and liberal accusations of treason from all parties.[83] But although the senate fought tenaciously, Ziehm did not yield to the temptation to denounce the NSDAP to the high commissioner as a danger to public order. This possibility did exist, and the party could have been banned with the cooperation of Poland and the League. Indeed, this would have been the only way to prevent a Nazi victory. Instead, Ziehm continued the earlier pattern. When the Polish commissioner-general denounced Nazi attacks on the international status of the free city, and on individual Poles, Ziehm responded by informing the high commissioner that the only endangerment of public order during the campaign had come from the Polish side.[84] Ziehm obviously feared Polish intervention more than he dreaded a Nazi electoral triumph. In any case, Danzig's dependence on Germany seemed to make a banning of the NSDAP dangerous, considering the new conditions in the Reich.

The example of the March Reichstag elections, in which the NSDAP had won 43.9 percent of the vote, spurred Forster to try for an absolute majority. But despite Nazi pressure, the election of 28 May was still free.[85] The results are shown in table 2.

TABLE 2

DIVISION OF VOLKSTAG SEATS BY PARTY, 1930 AND 1933

Party	Year	
	1930	1933
Center	11	10
DNVP	10	4
KPD (Communists)	7	5
NSDAP	12	38
Polish parties	2	2
SPD	19	13
Other parties	11	0
Total	72	72

Source: Adapted from *Taschenbuch*, p. 159.

The NSDAP received 107,331 of the 214,128 votes cast, or 50.03 percent, and held an absolute majority of the Volkstag. A delighted Hitler telegraphed: "Forster! Magnificent!"[86]

The victory was impressive, but it should not be overestimated. It was achieved only after the establishment of full Nazi dictatorship in the Reich, with all that this implied to Danzigers aware of their dependence on Germany. Many voters doubtless felt that a vote for the NSDAP was a vote for a return to the Reich. The Nazis gained 74,874 votes between 1930 and 1933. The raw statistics available do not allow a precise determination of where these votes came from, but some estimates may be made.

Perhaps 15,500 were new votes, from those who had not cast a ballot in 1930 (there were over 11,000 more voters eligible in 1933 than in 1930). An insignificant number of Center voters shifted their support to the NSDAP, and the Center actually increased its popular vote, although not enough to make up for the increase in the total number of voters. The SPD and the KPD lost heavily, but they retained the core of their voter support. The Nazi gains came principally at the expense of the parties of the old Bourgeois Block, which were in a state of dissolution and had not even entered this election, and at the expense of the DNVP, which lost about half the votes it had received in 1930.[87]

The Center and the SPD, together with the Communists, had prevented a Nazi majority in the urban areas; only a large Nazi rural vote, where these parties were weak, had made the total Nazi majority possible. Most significant was the failure of Ziehm's DNVP to hold more than half of its previous constituency. By convincing Danzigers that the NSDAP promised the best guarantee of Danzig's German character, the Nazis had beaten the DNVP at its own game. In the free city the rhetoric of extreme nationalism was the obvious way to give political expression to economic distress, and the Nazis, in radical opposition to the entire system, free from the inhibitions of governmental responsibility and common decency, had done it best.

4

The Rauschning Period, 1933–34

During the first few months of Hitler's government in Germany, he ruled with a cabinet that represented at least a nominal coalition of NSDAP and DNVP. The circumstances of his assumption of power made this device unavoidable since he was awarded the chancellorship, not as the result of a revolution or an overwhelming election victory, but at the end of a series of rather ordinary political deals. The Danzig elections of 28 May 1933, however, gave a Volkstag majority to the NSDAP. It would have been possible for the Nazis to govern without taking any other party into the senate. Since the coalition government of the Reich was already in full dissolution, it would not have been surprising had the Nazis decided to go it alone in Danzig.

But Danzig was not Germany. Its constitution was guaranteed by the League of Nations, and the League council's attitude toward prospective Nazi "reforms" in the free city was still uncertain. The tense state of relations with Poland also had a sobering effect. If both the League and Poland were unduly offended by events in the free city, the high commissioner could make use of his undoubted right to request Polish military aid to restore constitutional conditions, or the council of the League could take such action.[1] While on the road to power, Hitler had privately welcomed the possibility of a Polish invasion of Germany's eastern territories, since it would drive an infuriated and patriotic electorate into the arms of the NSDAP.[2] But a Polish invasion of Danzig at the very beginning of Hitler's own regime would have been a disaster for the new Germany, both at home and abroad. The Nazis in Danzig had to tread carefully. It seemed wise to make the new senate as representative as possible, to avoid any appearance of the establishment of a dictatorship. In June 1933 it was not yet clear what attitude would be taken toward the new government in Danzig by Poland and the League, and no excuse could be provided by the Nazis that might serve as a cover for intervention in the free city.

The New Senate

Despite initial conciliatory speeches by Gauleiter Forster and President-elect Rauschning, the NSDAP made no serious effort to entice the DNVP into a coalition.[3] The German consul-general, Baron von Thermann, did his best to arrange a compromise, since he failed to perceive that the DNVP-NSDAP coalition in the Reich was already virtually defunct (on 27 June the Reich DNVP chose self-dissolution). Neither party responded positively to Thermann's initiative. Rauschning was far more interested in the ten seats held in the Volkstag by the Center. He has claimed that the formation of a coalition with the Center was entirely his own idea and "against the wishes of the [other] Nazis."[4] An NSDAP-Center government would have the backing of exactly two-thirds of the Volkstag, the majority necessary for constitutional amendments and enabling laws. Rauschning's effort to achieve a coalition with the Center was successful. The absence of evidence makes it impossible to determine the precise considerations that moved the Center to participate in the new senate. It was partly force of habit, no doubt—the Center had never been absent from a Danzig government. The party had found it possible to work with German Nationalists and Social Democrats alike, just as it had in the Reich. While other parties were tied to narrow economic groups, or hamstrung by devotion to political principles, the Center enjoyed complete maneuverability on questions unrelated to ecclesiastical affairs. As a sympathetic Catholic observer put it, Center policy was capable of an "astounding elasticity."[5]

Despite the forthright denunciations of Nazi anticlerical activity issued by Catholic sources in Germany prior to Hitler's assumption of power, the Center had seen its way to cooperation in the election of Göring as Reichstag president in 1932. Monsignor Kaas, the Reich party chairman, had attempted to arrange Center participation in the national government formed on 30 January 1933. This was prevented only when Hitler rejected Kaas's terms.[6] The Center supported the new government in the Reichstag, and the Catholic hierarchy muted its anti-Nazi rhetoric. As it happened, a Reich conference of bishops was scheduled to meet in Fulda from 30 May to 1 June, directly after the Danzig elections. Although the pastoral letter issued by this conference regretted certain Nazi excesses and insisted on church rights in education, it was marked by a positive attitude toward the new state.[7]

Under these circumstances, there was no reason for the Center to refuse the Nazi offer of a coalition in Danzig, especially since the NSDAP made no impossible demands. The new senate was elected on 20 June by a forty-nine-vote block of thirty-eight National Socialists, ten Centrists, and one member of the DNVP, Max Bertling, who now sat with the NSDAP parliamentary group. Bertling was elected a senator without portfolio, although he did not remain in the government for long. There were two Centrists in the new senate. Monsignor Sawatzki was elected senator without portfolio, and former Senate Vice-President Willibald Wiercinski-Keiser received the Department of Justice. The Department of Public Works and Employment went to Karl Hoepfner, an engineer and professor at the Danzig Technical College, who may not yet have joined the NSDAP. Julius Hoppenrath, senator for finance under Ziehm, continued in office. He joined the NSDAP shortly afterward, and there is some reason to believe that he had worked closely with the Nazis even while a member of the Ziehm senate.[8]

The remaining new senators were all Nazis. Rauschning, the senate president, also received the Department of Agriculture, and like his predecessors he headed the Foreign Department. Greiser was vice-president and senator for the interior. Wilhelm von Wnuck was named senator without portfolio, and Hans Albert Hohnfeldt emerged from obscurity as senator for social affairs. Adalbert Boeck, a school teacher and Kreisleiter of Danzig-town, was chosen senator for art, science, and church affairs. The Department of Trade and Industry went to an engineer, Wilhelm Huth, and the Health Department to a Nazi physician, Dr. Helmut Kluck.[9]

The new senate of 1933 was well-balanced. Hoppenrath, Sawatzki, and Wiercinski-Keiser, members of the old senate, loaned stability and respectability to the new. The presence of Bertling and Hoppenrath implied the reconciliation of the NSDAP with the old conservative forces in the free city, even though the DNVP was not a coalition partner. Hoepfner was an "expert" who would help the senate with technical economic problems while reassuring business and financial circles. Wnuck and Hohnfeldt represented the group of pre-1930 party members who had been somewhat pushed aside after Forster's arrival in Danzig, but who had cooperated with the new Gauleiter. Their appointment healed grievances and assured the "old fighters" that they had not been forgotten. At the same time, these men were not given important posts. Within two years, Wnuck and Hohnfeldt had left the senate. Boeck, Huth, and Kluck belonged to the group of party members who had joined about the time of Forster's appointment as Gauleiter. They had been active in organizing the party's affiliate organizations, Boeck among the schoolteachers, Huth among the students, and Kluck among the physicians. As senators, Boeck and Kluck would be responsible for the nazification (*Gleichschaltung,* or Nazi "coordination") of the schools and the medical profession, respectively.

Arthur Greiser, the new vice-president and senator for the interior, had been associated with radical national circles in Danzig since 1923 and was a power in the NSDAP. He had been a member since 1929, deputy Gauleiter since 1930, and Nazi Volkstag spokesman since 1931, and he was "next to the Gauleiter the most beloved leader and helper of the great National Socialist family in Danzig."[10] His appointment as senator for the interior, and therefore head of the police, assured him a key position in the government. His presence in this post satisfied the militant elements of the NSDAP, who appreciated Greiser's reputation for toughness.

Rauschning was by no means happy with his vice-president. He had originally had someone quite different in mind, an official in the Reich Finance Ministry. The plan fell through because a scheme could not be devised that would satisfy the high commissioner's likely objection to the election of a Reich official as vice-president.[11] The matter was pursued with utmost secrecy, through government rather than party channels, and it is possible that Greiser, and even Forster, never learned of it. It is apparent from Rauschning's reluctance to accept Greiser that the senate president understood clearly the distinction between his own policies and those likely to be followed by his Nazi colleagues. Rauschning failed to prevent Greiser from becoming vice-president, and party influence in the senate increased further when Bertling was replaced by Gau propaganda chief Paul Batzer, who created the "Department of Public Enlightenment and Propaganda," patterned after Goebbels's Reich ministry.

Worse yet, from Rauschning's point of view, was the growth of a conflict between NSDAP and Center, which began over the issue of labor organization. A precedent had been established on 12 May, before the elections. The Free Trade Unions in Germany, closely associated with the SPD, had been taken over by the Nazis. A Nazi labor organizer from the Reich accordingly demanded that the Free Trade Unions in Danzig, as a branch of the Reich organization, be turned over to his control. The courts granted his request.[12] On 26 June the Danzig Nazis moved similarly against the Christian Trade Unions, associated with the Center party. This was the first blow struck against Catholic secular organizations. The Center's youth group dissolved itself in September and recommended that its members join the Hitler Youth.[13] Pressure on the Center was increased by the self-dissolution of its parent Reich party and by the self-dissolution of the Danzig DNVP, announced by Ziehm on 6 September.[14] Although the DNVP was to reappear in the fall of 1934, in the fall of 1933 this could not be predicted. Non-Nazi political groups were becoming almost invisible.

In September, Centrist Wiercinski-Keiser revealed that he had gone over to the Nazis. He offered his resignation as senator for justice, only to be immediately reelected by the NSDAP voting alone. Disgusted by this parliamentary sham, a disillusioned Monsignor Sawatzki resigned permanently from the senate and took his party out of the by now fictitious coalition. He confessed to his friend Ernst Ziehm that "one couldn't believe a word that they, the Nazis, said." [15] For the first time since the founding of the free city, Sawatzki and the Center ceased to participate in the government. The Nazis ruled alone.

The Settlement with Poland

Nazis in Danzig and in the eastern German border areas held massive anti-Polish demonstrations during February and March 1933. In response, Poland's minister of war and de facto ruler, Marshal Józef Pilsudski, reinforced the Polish guard at the Westerplatte, while he attempted to form an anti-Hitler front in collaboration with France. These initiatives failed.[16] Most alarming to Pilsudski was Mussolini's proposal for a "Four-Power Pact" among Britain, France, Germany, and Italy, to secure peace in Europe through treaty revision. Fearing a deal at Poland's expense, Pilsudski decided to seek a direct understanding with Hitler.

Long before he came to power, Hitler had declared himself prepared to give up certain German nationalist aims for the sake of his own concept of a sensible foreign policy. He had even advocated the surrender of the Germans of the South Tyrol as a prerequisite for friendship with Mussolini.[17] In 1933, he was prepared to encourage the Polish approach, and Danzig "became his chosen instrument for German-Polish reconciliation." [18] Under orders, Forster pledged that the Nazi senate would abide by treaties and would enter into direct negotiations with Poland. To the Poles, this seemed a distinct improvement over the obstinate attitude of the Ziehm government, and Polish Foreign Minister Józef Beck was not long in expressing his appreciation to German authorities and in giving his blessing to Danzig-Polish talks.[19]

After the Danzig elections, local Nazi leaders were invited to Berlin for coffee and cake at the Reich chancellory, to celebrate their victory with the Führer. Hitler took advantage of the occasion to speak privately to Rauschning and Forster. He warned them that Danzig's struggle with Poland was henceforth to be carried on "silently and secretly," and that the long-term solution to the Danzig question was to be left to the Reich. Later public statements by the Gauleiter and the senate president reflected these instructions.[20]

After a state visit by Rauschning and Greiser to Warsaw on 3 July, negotiations began in earnest.[21] They were intended to replace the old procedure of League arbitration. In July 1933, thirty-five questions were pending before the high commissioner and the council.[22] Their removal from the League agenda was most welcome, but acting High Commissioner Helmer Rosting sensed a potential danger to League authority. He insisted that the negotiations take place under his auspices, so that the League could preserve its authority as arbiter. Rauschning may even have allowed Rosting to believe that the negotiations were taking place at the high commissioner's own suggestion.[23]

A document on the rights of the Polish minority in Danzig was initialed on 5 August and went into effect the following month. Danzig agreed to encourage education in Polish; a reversal of previous policy, although merely a confirmation of earlier agreements with Poland that Danzig had never fulfilled. The use of the Polish language in Danzig was to be protected. Polish merchants of Jewish origin were to be allowed to ply their trades unmolested, and Danzig agreed to recognize Polish educational and artisan certificates. Neither the senate nor Polish state agencies in Danzig would exert pressure on their employees regarding the language in which their children were educated.[24] This document on the rights of the Polish minority was paired with an agreement on the use of the port of Danzig by Poland, which was signed on 18 September. Poland undertook to ship through Danzig specified quantities of certain goods over the coming year and to lift customs regulations that discriminated against the free city. A bilateral commission was to settle all disputes arising out of the agreement.[25] It had formerly been the contention of the senate that Poland was obliged to make "full use" of the port of Danzig and to use other ports only after Danzig's facilities were working to capacity. The senate now recognized that the new Polish port of Gdynia had a claim to "equal participation," or "parity."[26]

To Rauschning, Danzig's concessions on minority rights and

harbor utilization were justified by his conception of what Germany's Polish policy ought to be. In retrospect, he drew a distinction between his own policy, which aimed at the creation of "a new, stable order in the form of a federation" in the East, and Hitler's policy of creating "half-sovereign" states under German "protection." Rauschning would have replaced the "fictitious order" of the League with a system of eastern alliances based on mutual advantage and respect, in which Germany would occupy a position of natural leadership. The system established at Versailles would become peacefully obsolete. Such a policy, Rauschning felt, could not have been carried out by the Weimar Republic, since the republic was not strong enough "to be able to guarantee security—and, of course, to overcome sterile opposition." [27] In 1933, he still believed that Hitler's Polish policy gave hope that the Führer might be moved "toward a moderate policy of economic and political penetration of central Europe." [28] While president, Rauschning completely failed to distinguish between Hitler's plans for conquest and his own desire "to overcome sterile opposition." Perhaps the difference was not as great as he later believed.

Danzigers were startled by the turnabout in government and Nazi policy, despite Rauschning's strained attempts at explanation.[29] No less startled were the officials of the German Foreign Office, who had followed an anti-Polish policy since the Treaty of Versailles and had worked for the return of Danzig and the corridor to the Reich.[30] They could not criticize Hitler, but they showed their displeasure by questioning Rauschning's judgment. A meeting between Rauschning and Richard Meyer, head of the eastern department of the German Foreign Office, was held in Zoppot on 2 and 3 August. It led to no agreement. From Secretary of State Bernhard von Bülow on down, Foreign Office officials expressed skepticism at Rauschning's policy of reconciliation through concessions.[31] Indeed, they had good reason to think Rauschning's concessions gratuitous. High Commissioner Rosting pointed out to Geneva that the Danzig-Polish agreements gave the Poles far more than they could possibly have gained through League arbitration.[32]

Whatever the Foreign Office thought, the general outlines of

Hitler's foreign policy were soon clarified. He aimed at cooperation with Italy and Britain and at the isolation of France. The League system of collective security and France's network of eastern alliances were to be destroyed by means of bilateral pacts. An immediate goal of German policy was to be friendship with Poland, eased by direct negotiations between Danzig and Warsaw. This tactic would simultaneously weaken the French alliances and the League system. In late September Neurath was able to report from the League assembly session that Polish Foreign Minister Beck had been unusually amiable. "He welcomed quite particularly the developments in Danzig." Neurath took advantage of Beck's approach to give assurances of German goodwill toward Poland, which were then repeated by Joseph Goebbels.[33] Beck was to be convinced that the new German policy represented the desires of the highest levels of government and party.

The friendship between Germany and Poland was soon strained by Hitler's withdrawal from the League and the disarmament conference in October. Once again, Pilsudski considered the formation of an anti-German front. Once again, the French response proved insufficient. Pilsudski and Beck turned back to Hitler's offers of friendship. The result was the German-Polish Non-aggression Pact of 26 January 1934.[34] Hindsight shows us that the pact was no reversal of German policy at all, but a heightening and extension of treaty revisionism beyond the "wildest dreams" of Neurath and Bülow.[35] In fact, the Poles never really trusted Hitler. Again, events in Danzig played a part. They made it obvious to Poland that Rauschning, with his plans for German-Polish and Danzig-Polish reconciliation, was not in control of the free city. His influence with the Führer was therefore open to doubt. Under these circumstances, Rauschning's Polish policy stood little chance of genuine success.

Whatever the official policy of senate and NSDAP, Polish citizens and members of the Polish minority were under considerable pressure as a result of the nazification of the free city. On 31 August 1933 Commissioner-General Kazimierz Papée submitted a memorandum to the senate, providing details of the mistreatment to which Poles in Danzig were subject.[36] His complaints fell into two categories: economic discrimination, and the threat or use of violence. The agreement on minority rights satisfied most of Papée's economic complaints when it went into effect in September, although it was never fully enforced. But the agreement did not cover the illegal use of force against Poles and Polish citizens of Jewish origin by members of the NSDAP. Members of the Polish minority were singled out, isolated, and treated badly by public authorities and private individuals alike.

Forster made some effort to hold his men in check, particularly after a highly publicized assault by a group of SA men on a prominent visiting Polish businessman who had failed to give the Nazi salute as the swastika flag was carried by. Objection to the policies of the government was declared to be a breach of party discipline, and those party members who refused to accept the official desire for "peace and understanding" with Poland were threatened with disciplinary action.[37] A serious split was developing between the leadership of the free city and the anti-Polish elements of the population, both within and outside of the NSDAP. The staging of public events, such as a visit by the Polish premier on 22 September, did little good so long as the population could "not yet perceive any practical effects of a lessening of tension." [38]

Danzig's relations with Poland were not proceeding quite as Rauschning had hoped. Forster may have had a better understanding of Hitler's plans, for he privately predicted that the German policy of "reconciliation" with the Polish "vermin" would soon be replaced by a policy of annihilation. In this prophecy he was of course correct, although somewhat premature. Rauschning still believed that Hitler's view of the reconstruction of eastern Central Europe was the same as his own. As early as October 1933, he was complaining directly to Hitler that the leadership of the Danzig SS and SA, and Gauleiter Forster personally, were making an agreement with Poland more difficult.[39] He had perceived that the incidents of which Commissioner-General Papée never ceased to complain were more than the unfortunate excesses of undisciplined SA men. There were, in fact, two Nazi Polish policies in Danzig, and Hitler allowed both to exist despite their apparently contradictory natures.

The Poles for their part also played a double game. Even after the September agreements and the displays of cooperation, the Poles failed to halt the economic warfare they had been carrying out against Danzig all year. The borders were still blockaded by discriminatory customs and other regulations that made it almost impossible for the free city to export to Poland or to be supplied with basic foodstuffs, such as grain, which Danzig's specialized agriculture could not produce. The Danzig-Polish trade war was simply a reflection of the tariff war between Germany and Poland, which lasted from 1925 until early 1934.[40]

This unsatisfactory situation moved Rauschning to visit Warsaw once again, on 11–12 December. Hitler approved the trip, for he wished Rauschning to sound out the Poles on the possibility of a Hitler-Pilsudski meeting. Rauschning stressed to Pilsudski Danzig's desire for agreements on the importation of foodstuffs and the removal of Polish customs inspectors. Danzig was willing to cooperate with Polish financial and economic policies, provided only that the German character of the free city was respected. Pilsudski's response was little more than a general expression of admiration for Hitler, with some reservations about the pace of the latter's "reforms." He agreed that a conversation with the Führer would be desirable but pointed to the innumerable "technical difficulties" in the way of a meeting. In January, Beck did accept Rauschning's December declaration as a basis for negotiations and held out the possibility of agreement on the foodstuffs question through mutual concessions. Danzig and Poland would agree not to use the League machinery in disputes. The two economies would be closely integrated. Danzig would have to guarantee once again the rights of the Polish minority, and both governments would influence their journalists in the direction of moderation. Beck also suggested that Danzig should recognize that Poland's right of access to the sea through the free city was not limited to the transport of goods and that more direct participation by Polish firms in Danzig's economy ought to be encouraged.[41]

On the whole the Polish reply was promising, although Beck's last suggestion touched on Danzig's sore point, the fear of Polonization. New negotiations on the basis of this exchange of views soon began. They were presumably encouraged by the signing of the German-Polish Non-aggression Pact, although agreements were not actually signed until 6 August 1934. They settled various technical details of the customs administration, and the quarrel over importation of foodstuffs and other essential articles was ended.[42] With this new set of agreements, the most irksome practical issues between Danzig and Poland were temporarily reduced to questions of administrative procedure. It could be said that Rauschning's policies had finally borne practical fruit. But the agreements did nothing to alter the dislike of the average member of the Danzig NSDAP for Poles and Poland. Rauschning did his best to popularize his policy, and in March 1934 he founded the "Danzig Society for the Study of Poland." His initiative may have pleased the Poles, but the leaders of his own party were significantly absent from the inauguration of the society.[43]

The German-Polish understanding meant that the League, hitherto the arbiter between Poland and Danzig, was to be largely excluded from that aspect of the affairs of the free city. But the League had another role to play in Danzig as the guarantor of the constitution. Here, too, Polish friendship would be useful to national socialism. Beck correctly coupled these two aspects of Nazi policy when he later wrote:

> The new senate, with the consent of Berlin, adopted a conciliatory attitude toward Poland, while defending itself bitterly against the efforts of Geneva to impose on the internal organization of the free city a rigid framework, in contradiction to the aspirations of national socialism.[44]

The Formation of a United Opposition

The legal basis for the nazification of Danzig was an enabling law, "for the relief of the distress of people and state," adopted by a fifty to nineteen vote in the Volkstag on 24 June 1933.[45] A similar law enabled Hitler to rule without the Reichstag. The new senate could now issue decrees having the force of law without obtaining the consent of the Volkstag. Since the Nazis enjoyed an absolute majority, the consent of the Volkstag to any law would in any case have been assured, but rule by decree enabled the government to dispense almost entirely with the calling of the Volkstag, thus depriving the opposition of a major public platform. One of the first of the decrees issued under the authority of the enabling law, on 30 June, provided that a person could be taken into protective custody and held indefinitely without legal remedy. Another decree, "for the protection of the good name of national associations," was published on 10 October. The national associations referred to were the NSDAP and its affiliates, which received special legal protection for their uniforms and insignia. The decree provided prison terms for "any person who intentionally makes or spreads an untrue or grossly distorted statement about facts calculated to do serious injury to the good name of the associations." [46] To these legal measures was added the de facto cooperation between Reich and Danzig police authorities.

The higher Danzig police officials had always been men from the Prussian police, a reflection of the pattern in the other branches of the Danzig civil service. Men arrested in Danzig frequently had served their sentences in the Reich,[47] and the deportation of undesirable Reich citizens wanted for crimes in Germany had been commonplace even without a formal extradition hearing. Now that the Prussian police had been nazified, the old practices took on a sinister political meaning. The Danzig police did not wait for the formal change of government in the free city. In early June, four Communists who happened to be German citizens, including the chief of the Danzig "Red Assistance" (*Rote Hilfe*) organization, were turned over to the Gestapo by the Danzig police at the bridge to the East Prussian town of Marienburg. This was the first use of informal deportation for political purposes, but it was not to be the last. The four Communists disappeared from view, presumably into German prisons or concentration camps. The Communist opposition was never a serious threat to the Nazis in Danzig, perhaps because the police began to roll up the KPD so early. The most interesting thing about the deportation incident is that it was brought to High Commissioner Rosting's attention by SPD leader Arthur Brill, not otherwise noted for his concern for Communist rivals.[48] The SPD very likely feared that its own members would be next. In any case, the high commissioner did nothing.

Attacks against the SPD had been a standard feature of Nazi operations before the May elections; they culminated in the "legal" seizure of the Social Democratic Free Trade Unions on 12 May. Bereft of their major organizations, with their newspaper, the *Volksstimme,* intermittently banned or confiscated, and with their members subject to attack in the streets, the Social Democrats did not give in even when the SPD was formally banned in the Reich on 22 June. The NSDAP decided on a spectacular move. Arthur Brill was placed in protective custody after the Volkstag voted on 23 August to revoke his parliamentary immunity. The SPD immediately protested to Rosting, who in turn approached Rauschning. Brill was eventually released, and the decree relating to protective custody was altered. The right of appeal to the courts was reestablished, but, as the high commissioner admitted, under the new version of the decree three-week terms of protective custody "could, in theory, follow one another indefinitely." [49] The intervention of League authority had hardly produced a major reversal of senate policy, but at least the smooth progress of *Gleichschaltung* had received a minor jolt.

Despite the fact that the SPD continued to exist as a political party, with some legal protection afforded its parliamentary leaders, the various subsidiary socialist organizations, such as the Workers' Sport Association, were rendered almost inoperative. The Free Trade Unions had been taken over because a court had ruled that they were branches of a Reich organization that had been subjected to *Gleichschaltung.* The Workers' Sport Association attempted to avoid this fate by swallowing its patriotic German pride, severing itself from its Reich parent body, and subordinating itself to the equivalent Polish socialist organization. Governmental discrimination made it impossible, however, for the association to function, as sports facilities were denied and assets were arbitrarily confiscated. The League was petitioned but provided no remedy.[50]

The campaign against the SPD was in the tradition of Nazi coalition-oriented policy and, by itself, could not create a united opposition. If handled well, it would have been an excellent means of isolating the leftists from other non-Nazis and thus reconciling the "bourgeois" parties to the Nazi victory. But the extension of *Gleichschaltung* to the Christian Trade Unions on 26 June and the pressure brought to bear on other organizations connected with the Catholic Center party demonstrated that the Nazis would not be content with the destruction of "Marxism." The key to the success or failure of political *Gleichschaltung* in Danzig was the behavior of the Center. Through September 1933, political developments seemed to be following, in a somewhat belated fashion, the pattern developed in the Reich between January and June. A coalition was formed, the Nazis increased their power at the expense of their partners, and the pretense of coalition was finally dropped. But when the Center party left the senate, it failed to follow the example of the DNVP or of the Center in the Reich. It did not dissolve itself. Its continued existence was an embarrassment to the Gauleiter, a clear sign that the coordination of the free city with the Reich was not moving as rapidly as had been hoped.

The Center in the Reich had been influenced in favor of self-dissolution by the negotiations for a concordat between Germany and the Vatican (initialed in early July), which appeared to guarantee the rights of the German Catholic church.[51] A Danzig concordat could not have been negotiated without involving Poland, which had official responsibility for the conduct of the free city's foreign affairs. It would have been unwise for the senate to have used the services of Polish diplomacy in this matter, since the Poles might well have interjected their own complaints about Catholic resistance to Polish penetration of the hierarchy in Danzig. Forster hit upon the notion of concluding a direct agreement with the bishop of Danzig. As an internal matter, an episcopal agreement would not have involved the Poles. The self-dissolution of the Center might have been encouraged by the conclusion of such an agreement.[52]

Had Forster's scheme been realized, it might have prevented the formation of a united opposition. But application of the plan required a certain amount of subtlety and restraint. The Gauleiter could not restrain himself, and he yielded to his personal anticlerical prejudices. Instead of waiting for the Center to dissolve itself, he determined to smash it. On 31 October the signal was given when Greiser announced that "Supporters of the Centre Party were no longer wanted in the Civil Service, since they were enemies of the State." This amounted to a declaration of a government intention to violate the equal-protection clauses of the constitution, and the high commissioner was disturbed.[53] Worse yet, the SPD's *Volksstimme* and the Center's *Danziger Landeszeitung,* which published Greiser's speech with critical commentary, were ordered to suspend publication by the chief of police. The editors and publishers protested to the high commissioner, only to find themselves in temporary protective custody.

Rosting intervened in favor of the arrested men, but he could not help the editor of the *Landeszeitung,* Heinrich Teipel, who had the misfortune to be a German citizen. Teipel was deported, into the custody of the Gestapo. The confidence of the opposition in the ability of the League to protect it was badly shaken. The Danzig population had no sympathy for the newspapermen, who had appealed to an international authority against their own countrymen. The political climate became so unfavorable that the Center felt obliged to deny any connection with the incident. The party lost its press organ, the *Landeszeitung,* which reappeared after its suspension as an "independent" Catholic newspaper under the control of Senator Wiercinski-Keiser and hostile to the Center. It seemed that Forster's frontal assault was working.[54]

The Center had been badly mauled by December 1933, but it was neither destroyed nor fully resolved to enter into active opposition. At this point, a great deal depended on the bishop of Danzig, Count Eduard O'Rourke, a Russian aristocrat who traced his ancestry to ancient Irish kings and Prussian noblemen.[55] O'Rourke had not been moved by the offensive against the Center, and he had favored the project of an episcopal agreement with the senate.[56] But once more, Forster could not restrain himself. Pressure from the NSDAP on the numerous Catholic secular and semireligious organizations, most of which had little to do with politics, stiffened the bishop's resistance. The bishop was particularly strong in defending Catholic youth groups and church influence in the schools. He even made use of the Center's replacement for the *Landeszeitung,* the new *Danziger Volkszeitung.* Under Nazi pressure, a united Catholic front was formed.[57] A clumsy attempt by Wiercinski-Keiser to form a "German Catholic" movement, sympathetic to national socialism, was a dismal failure.[58]

One-third of the population of the free city was Catholic.[59] Some degree of political expediency was called for. Instead, the Gauleitung launched a vicious campaign against the Catholic clergy, which coincided with and imitated a campaign in the Reich.[60] Typical was an article in the *Vorposten,* which appeared in April 1934, accusing the clergy of opening up a *Kulturkampf* against party and state and of using swindling, lying tactics.[61] As always, the Nazis projected their own faults upon their opponents. Some Catholics were frightened by Nazi tactics, but in April there were still approximately fourteen thousand young adults and children who belonged to Catholic youth groups. Both Bishop O'Rourke and his parish priests publicly protested every incursion into the church's domain. In August 1934, the parish priests petitioned the League, charging the unconstitutionality of decrees and orders directed against their youth organizations. In an impressive display of courage, forty-four of the fifty parish priests in Danzig reaffirmed their support of the petition in writing, when the authenticity of their original signatures was questioned.[62]

Attacks against the youth and charitable organizations, and against the clergy, disturbed the Catholic population far more than the original offensive against the Center party. It remained to be seen whether the Center, the traditional political defender of the rights of the church, could take advantage of the new militancy of the Catholic population and continue to function in an increasingly repressive political system. The Center did continue the fight and drew encouragement from contacts with anti-Nazi Catholic groups in Austria and among the German minority in Poland.[63] The non-Catholic opposition in Danzig was also contacted. These moves were conducted without public fanfare, in partial secrecy dictated by Nazi methods of reprisal. Only gradually did the results become visible.

Local elections were held in two rural Kreise, Grosses Werder and Danziger Niederung, on 18 November 1934. The purpose of the elections was to replace the old county assemblies (Kreistage) and community assemblies (Gemeindetage), which had been elected in 1930. For some time these bodies had been superseded for all practical purposes by Nazi "state commissioners," whose constitutional position was dubious at best. The results of the elections justified the Nazi gamble in holding them, since the NSDAP polled between 78 and 92 percent of the votes cast for the various assemblies. Both districts had already cast more than 60 percent of their votes for the NSDAP in May 1933. They were strongly Protestant, and the Center was correspondingly weak. The SPD, too, had never drawn a large vote from these rural areas. But the very high percentages won by the NSDAP were due to a campaign of slander, intimidation, chicanery, and outright violence directed against individual members of the opposition. No distinction was made between "bourgeois" and "Red" opponents. Again, Nazi policy promoted the unity of the opposition. The Center cooperated with the remnants of the DNVP to produce a "Christian-National" list of candidates, and the Christian-Nationalists and the Social Democrats campaigned against the Nazis, not against one another.[64]

A complete evaluation of the Danzig opposition must wait until the following chapters, which deal with its near triumph and its eventual destruction. A few preliminary observations may be allowed here. The Social Democrats continued in active opposition because, from the beginning, they were engaged in a struggle for personal as well as organizational survival. A small DNVP group that surfaced under the leadership of Gerhard Weise continued to fight primarily out of stubbornness and personal conviction. The Center, originally content to compromise with the NSDAP, was driven into opposition by the uncompromising tactics of the Gauleiter. The differences between the three parties did not disappear, but their common opposition to the Nazis brought them together.[65] While the organized anti-

Nazi opposition was being destroyed in Germany, it continued to exist in Danzig. Danzig at the end of 1934 was only a "semi-dictatorship." [66] Above all, the high commissioner was a channel to the outside world, and the League council represented a hope that the Nazi victory was reversible. That hope was to be destroyed, gradually, between 1935 and 1937.

The Forster-Rauschning Conflict

Hitler's policy of cooperation with Poland, and the limitations imposed by the League presence in Danzig, demanded that the Gauleiter exercise at least minimal restraint, even in purely domestic matters. This requirement kept Forster and Rauschning working together for a time. But Rauschning's policy was self-defeating. By preparing the way for German-Polish cooperation, he lessened the threat of Polish intervention in Danzig, and the threat of Polish intervention was his most powerful argument for keeping Forster under control. By furnishing a respectable front for the nazification of the free city, Rauschning reassured both Britain and the League and made serious outside interference with Danzig's domestic affairs increasingly unlikely. Rauschning, moved by considerations both of practical politics and personal morality, did his best to conduct the *Gleichschaltung* of the free city in a rational, responsible, and "humane" manner. But Forster never ceased to regard Rauschning's policies as mere covers for the brutal reality of *Gleichschaltung*. It is to Rauschning's credit that he penetrated this mystery rather quickly. In November 1933, High Commissioner Rosting noted the political nervousness caused by the developing conflict between president and Gauleiter.[67] It took Rauschning longer to realize that his whole effort was a tissue of contradictions, incapable of realization, and that he was doing no good at all by remaining in office.

One of the first disagreements between Forster and Rauschning concerned the economic reorganization of the free city. Before he became president of the senate, Rauschning had believed that a corporate reconstruction of the economy according to natural trade groupings was the best solution to the chaos that had supposedly been created by liberal laissez-faire economic policies.[68] An attempt at reorganizing the Danzig economy into "chambers" representing its several branches was made in July 1933. Rauschning soon realized that the plan invited Nazi corruption and was little more than a scheme by the Gauleitung to force party influence on the business community. He withdrew his involvement.[69] The problem of corruption greatly concerned Rauschning, and he correctly felt that a poor example was being set by Gauleiter Forster's widespread real-estate holdings and boisterous style of life.[70]

Rauschning's position was weak, and he took few steps to strengthen it. He could only have become effective within the NSDAP by compromising his high moral standards, and this he refused to do. An astonished East Prussian friend put Rauschnings' situation to him frankly: "Why, you have no real power at all." [71] But Rauschning's lack of power did not mean that he was ignored by political factions within the Danzig party. As president of the senate he was a potentially valuable ally, if he would allow his position to be used by others less scrupulous than himself. In November 1933, for example, he was drawn by Greiser into a running duel Greiser was having with SA leader Max Linsmayer. Rauschning believed that he was defending responsible government against the overenthusiasm of the SA, but he was in fact merely being used by Greiser as a front for an attack on Linsmayer.[72]

Even as Rauschning was entangling himself with Greiser and Linsmayer, he was involved in a continual argument with the Gauleiter over finances. Forster's innumerable "employment projects" included an indoor swimming pool, the rebuilding of the city theater, and sewer and road construction. Rauschning had a sensitive conscience in financial matters and refused to approve projects for which there were no available funds. The dispute went to Hitler, who decided in favor of the Gauleiter. Hitler would not hear of Rauschning's own proposal; an austerity program coupled with devaluation of the gulden. The Führer promised that clandestine Reich loans to the Bank of Danzig would make a devaluation unnecessary.[73] Rauschning was not satisfied, and by December 1933 he was telling his Danzig friends that continued interference from the party would make it impossible for him to continue as president.[74]

Rudolf Hess, the deputy of the Führer, intervened in December to arrange a four-point compromise between Forster and Rauschning. It was agreed that the senate was under the authority of the senate president, "according to the leadership principle." Party agencies would refrain from interfering in state administration. Rauschning was declared to be "responsible" to Forster for total government policy, but Hess was to decide in the event of a disagreement. Finally, Rauschning had to approve all party actions "that affect the prerogatives of the government." [75] The ambiguous wording of this "settlement" settled nothing, and confusion grew as Forster and Rauschning lobbied separately in the Reich for continued and increased subsidies to Danzig.[76] The finances of the free city degenerated rapidly under divided management.

Despite Hess's insistence on the leadership principle, by early 1934 it was obvious that Rauschning stood alone in the senate. The other senators, and Greiser in particular, testified at the highest party level to Rauschning's "alienation" from the NSDAP. Rauschning was still concerned with the future of his Polish policy, and he suggested that he be allowed to manage foreign affairs while Forster himself assumed full governmental responsibility as president. Forster responded: "I wouldn't think of ruining my career." In February, Rauschning dared to ask Hitler for a grant of plenary power in Danzig, but his position was far too weak to deserve Hitler's support.[77] Hitler was not yet willing to dispense entirely with Rauschning's services in relations with Poland and the League. He perhaps also recognized that Rauschning's respectability made easier the party's task of domestic rule in Danzig. But he had no intention of supporting Rauschning against Forster, who remained one of his personal favorites.

By April 1934, rumors of a split between Gauleiter and senate president moved both men to appear together in public and to engage in hypocritical mutual praise.[78] The ruse could not work forever. On 1 May, shortly before the Danzig delegation was to leave for Warsaw to discuss the trade conflict with Poland,

Forster told a large public gathering that the free city might return to the Reich if it were not treated justly by the Poles.[79] A furious Rauschning saw his entire program of cooperation with Poland endangered at a particularly sensitive moment, and he once again threatened to resign. This time, it was Max Linsmayer who arranged a temporary reconciliation. The SA leader feared that Rauschning would be replaced by Greiser, Linsmayer's enemy and a man with a real position of power. The new high commissioner, Sean Lester, also promoted the reconciliation by arranging a meeting between Forster and Commissioner-General Papée. Forster was apparently convinced of the dire consequences that might result from his speech. Since he was not prepared to accept responsibility for a major check to Hitler's program of friendship with Poland, he became more amenable to an agreement with Rauschning. The German consul-general, acting for the Foreign Office, also put pressure on the Gauleiter to compromise with the president.[80]

Rauschning was kept on until after the trade agreements with Poland were concluded in August 1934. The agreements ended his usefulness to both Forster and Hitler. In early September, he returned from a League council session in Geneva to be faced by a series of "unconstitutional" demands from the party, including the reduction of League influence, the resumption of the fight against Poland, and the crushing of the opposition.[81] Rauschning took his case in person to Berlin, as all power in the free city passed to Forster and Vice-President Greiser. The Rauschning period in the history of the free city ended in September 1934, although Rauschning did not tender his formal resignation until two months later.

5 A Year of Crisis, 1935

The year 1935 began in the shadow of Hermann Rauschning's resignation. It seemed certain that Forster would now be able to clear up what remained of the Danzig opposition. Appearances, as it developed, were deceiving. Chapters 5 and 6 trace the development of the crisis of 1935, a situation that challenged Nazi rule in a manner inconceivable in the Reich. In Germany, it had been possible for Hitler to create an almost closed system in which there were no visible alternatives to his own rule. This had not been possible in Danzig. By an odd paradox, the increasingly self-contained nature of the Third Reich created special difficulties for the Nazis in Danzig. In particular, the necessities of Germany's economic situation prevented the transfer of Reich funds abroad, and the effects in the free city were disastrous. The economic catastrophe in turn created new opportunities for the opposition, which still existed thanks largely to Danzig's international status.

Danzig in 1935 was still a relatively open society. Economic and political standards still existed by which the population could measure the performance of their Nazi rulers. Propaganda alone could not hold oppositional tendencies in check as long as non-Nazi avenues of political expression could be kept open. The hopes of the opposition were ultimately to be disappointed, but in the midst of the struggle the end was neither predictable nor inevitable. In the free city, the NSDAP was forced to continue being what it had already ceased to be in the Reich—a fighting party. Significantly, the techniques that had led to power were not sufficient to hold it. Only the failure of the League council to exercise its responsibilities prevented a reversal of the Nazi triumph of 1933. This failure by the League had nothing to do with developments in Danzig itself, but was caused by the determination of Britain and France to reach an understanding with Hitler on armaments and future treaty revision. The western powers were forced by the League guarantee to consider Danzig's affairs, but when it came to practical action the free city was regarded by them as a matter for Poland and Germany alone.

Exit Hermann Rauschning

While Rauschning remained away on "sick leave" in late September 1934, Forster and Greiser moved to destroy what remained of his position in Danzig. They found a useful instrument in the person of Theodor Loevy, a Latvian Jew and Danzig resident arrested on 20 September. Loevy was the editor of a business periodical and of a newspaper, the *Danziger Echo,* which served the Jewish community. He was charged with violation of press regulations and possession of Communist pamphlets. In the course of his defense, Loevy claimed that he had worked in cooperation with two of Rauschning's closest associates, Georg Streiter, director of the Senate Press Department, and an engineer named Bechmann who acted as the president's agent in economic matters. These claims were correct. Rauschning had found in Loevy a good contact with both the Jewish and the business communities. Two days after Loevy's arrest, the *Vorposten* called for an investigation of "Jewish influences" in the government. Streiter and Bechmann were taken into custody and suspended from government service.[1]

Slim as it was, Rauschning's only hope was intervention from the Reich. On 28 September he asked Foreign Minister von Neurath to forward a memorandum to the Führer and to obtain a rapid decision on the situation in Danzig. In his memorandum, Rauschning summarized and justified his policies. As long as the Reich was unable to intervene forcefully to aid Danzig, he wrote, it was absolutely necessary for the free city to cooperate with Poland. Complete dependence on Poland could be avoided only by respect for the position of the League as guarantor of the constitution. Forster's interference with matters of state, according to Rauschning, threatened this entire, delicate structure.

Neurath recommended to Hitler that Forster be reprimanded and ordered to refrain from interference with the senate and that Rauschning, who was waiting in Berlin, be granted an interview. Greiser meanwhile appeared in Berlin and presented Rauschning with Forster's latest demands. These included the permanent banning of the two major opposition newspapers, the *Volksstimme* and the *Volkszeitung,* the arrest of Catholic priests, the deportation of Theodor Loevy, and the dismissal of three senate employees (including, presumably, Streiter and Bechmann). Forster also refused to agree to Rauschning's proposed financial reforms, which depended on a general cutback in government spending and a lowering of government salaries.[2] It may be assumed that Forster concocted these demands with the expectation that Rauschning would reject them.

Rumors of Forster's initiative soon reached High Commissioner Sean Lester, who requested an explanation from Greiser. Greiser assured Lester, with a straight face, that there could be no question of a conflict between the Gauleitung and the senate—after all, he himself was both vice-president and deputy Gauleiter. There was, in particular, no thought of any change in policy toward Poland. Greiser returned to Berlin after this interview and informed Rauschning that the Führer had left all decisions on Danzig affairs to the Gauleiter. The latter desired that Rauschning resign, preferably "for reasons of health." Neurath was away on a hunting trip, but Secretary of State von Bülow made a last effort to save Rauschning's position. He was urged on by Consul-General Otto von Radowitz. Rudolf Hess was contacted in the hope that he could patch together a compromise, as he had done the year before. In Danzig, Radowitz worked together with Max Linsmayer, who still feared the accession of Greiser.[3]

The German Foreign Office had decided that whatever its disagreements with Rauschning regarding Poland, his presence in Danzig was necessary to the smooth conduct of German foreign policy. Rauschning used the Foreign Office to direct his last appeal to Hitler. He requested that the Führer order him to resign, instead of leaving the decision up to Forster. Hitler refused to intervene.[4] Despite all further efforts on the part of the

Foreign Office, Rauschning handed in his resignation on 23 November. He had obligingly waited until after the local elections of 18 November. This surprising gesture of cooperation may be explained by Rauschning's sense of his own honor and good name. He did not wish to be accused of timing his resignation to harm the Nazi election effort. It would seem that he had not yet determined to go into open opposition to the NSDAP. But he did refuse to allow the Gauleiter to ease him out gently. He forced Forster to poll the members of the National Socialist parliamentary group for a secret vote of no confidence.[5] The outcome of the vote was a foregone conclusion, but Rauschning insisted on following the formalities of parliamentary government. He wanted it to appear that he was yielding responsibility for the government of the free city, not because of unconstitutional pressure from the Gauleiter, but because he had lost the confidence of the majority of the Volkstag. He did not achieve complete frankness in his public announcement, but he did drop all pretense of illness. He explained that he was resigning for "special reasons." Since Greiser had been circulating an official story that he was ill, the reference to special reasons, rather than to illness, would be plain enough to intelligent observers.[6]

These hesitations and maneuvers may have done something to assuage Rauschning's feelings, or his sense of honor, but they did nothing to alter the facts. Forster had won. On 28 November Greiser was elected president of the senate by the Volkstag, and Lothar Rettelsky, who had carried on Rauschning's work with the farmers, became senator for agriculture.[7] The vice-presidency remained vacant for the time being. It was eventually filled by Wilhelm Huth. With Rauschning gone, a major domestic obstacle to the complete political *Gleichschaltung* of Danzig had been removed.

The Elections

The November elections in Danziger Niederung and Grosses Werder proved to be the high point of Nazi success at the polls. They began a chain of events that led directly to the only dubious Nazi election victory recorded anywhere after March 1933.

The session of the League council held in January 1935 considered two petitions from Danzigers: a petition of the parish priests objecting to decrees prejudicial to the Catholic youth organizations, and a petition of the Center party detailing the atrocities committed during the recent electoral campaign and demanding the restoration of constitutional conditions.[8] The rapporteur, Britain's Anthony Eden, recommended to the council that the petitions be tabled until the next session, on the understanding that negotiations between the senate and the petitioners would take place. Negotiations were begun, but they were accompanied by public statements by President Greiser—accusations of treason and the like—which the Centrists and the priests rightly considered insulting. Greiser obviously did not intend the talks to succeed, and they broke down within a month despite the best efforts of High Commissioner Lester.[9] On 12 February Greiser ordered the Nazi parliamentary group to present a petition to dissolve the Volkstag. It was decided to hold new elections on 7 April. Greiser gave as his reason the necessity of demonstrating the falsity of the Center's claim that the NSDAP did not have the support of Danzig's population.[10]

Lester was extremely annoyed at this turn of events, which seems to have surprised him.[11] He correctly blamed Forster for the decision, but he may not have understood that there was more behind it than the impetuous whim of the Gauleiter. The elections seemed necessary in order to close the growing gap between the government and the population. As has already been shown, the Nazi policy of Polish reconciliation had deeply alienated some segments of the Danzig population. There had been no change in policy after Rauschning's resignation, and Forster and Greiser could no longer hide behind the man they had chased from office. Other elements of the population, particularly the business community, had been far more worried about Danzig's growing economic instability than about compromises with the Poles. Danzig's businessmen had trusted Rauschning, and they were shocked by his resignation. Danzig was not sharing in the apparent prosperity of the Third Reich. Growing lack of confidence in the government gave renewed courage to the opposition. Forster and Greiser sensed that there was a crisis of confidence, and they assumed that it could be papered over with a new election in which all the tricks of National Socialist propaganda could be employed.

But Danzig was not the Reich. Would Nazi propaganda techniques have their hoped-for effect in an election in which the opposition was still able to participate? Even in the Reich, with no alternative visible, the old ballyhoo approach was wearing thin, and Germans were responding with growing indifference to the never-ending series of marches and speeches.[12] The very crisis that made a new election desirable also contained the risk of Nazi failure. Some encouragement must have been derived from events in the Saar, where on 13 January over 90 percent of the voters had elected to return to Germany. This, to be sure, was a vote for Germany rather than a vote for national socialism. But the positions of the Saar and the free city were clearly analogous, since both areas had been separated from Germany against the will of their inhabitants. Forster made sure the point was not lost on Danzigers.[13]

The elections in Danzig were intended to be a repetition of the Saar plebiscite, an indication to the world that national socialism represented the freely expressed will of the German people.[14] But direct references to the Saar plebiscite had to be avoided during the Danzig campaign, since Berlin did not wish it to appear that Germany had designs on the free city. The international situation was delicate. On 16 March, the very day chosen by the Danzig NSDAP to begin active campaigning, Hitler announced the beginning of German rearmament. Negotiations soon began on Anglo-German naval and air pacts—pacts that would amount to tacit British recognition of Hitler's repudiation of Versailles.[15] Sir John Simon and Anthony Eden visited Hitler on 25 March, in the middle of the Danzig election campaign.[16] The German Foreign Office was most anxious that nothing give an impression of aggressive German intentions. Forster was advised to keep the Saar out of the campaign and to avoid stressing connections between the NSDAP in Danzig and the Reich party.

Forster replied to German Consul-General von Radowitz that in an election campaign "a party must deploy its full strength." The slogan he chose to attract the voters was "Fight the separatists—Danzig stays National Socialist." The term "separatist" made no sense save as a reference to the Saar plebiscite, where it had been used by the Nazis to label those who were working against a return to Germany. The voters could be relied on to discount the official statement by the senate that the elections were not a plebiscite on Danzig's international status.[17] Forster made no attempt to deemphasize the connections between the party in Danzig and the party in the Reich. Despite the objections of Radowitz, speakers for the NSDAP in Danzig included Göring, Hess, Goebbels, and Josef Bürckel, Gauleiter of the Saar-Palatinate and newly appointed Reich commissioner of the Saar.[18]

The campaign was marked by violence and the election by fraud. The Nazi elements of the population behaved as if the election would be a great turning point followed by a general reckoning with Jews, Poles, and "traitors." The houses of anti-Nazis were vandalized and there was occasional shooting, although no one was killed. Opposition newspapers were intermittently confiscated, and the state radio was reserved for the NSDAP. Since all solicitation other than for the officially sanctioned Winter Aid charity was forbidden, the opposition had difficulty obtaining funds. The Polish list, however, received aid from the commissioner-general. The Nazis seem to have drawn only 5,000 gulden directly from the Reich, as compared with the 81,000 gulden dispensed by the commissioner-general to the Polish candidates, but more was not needed. Campaign expenses arising in the Reich (e.g., printing costs, and travel costs for speakers from Germany) were met by the Reich. The Nazis drew freely on Danzig state funds, in addition to local party resources, and they made liberal, if illegal, use of public employees in the posting of election propaganda. Municipal firemen, for example, swathed the famous town hall with slogans and swastika banners. The stage was set for a well-managed Nazi triumph.[19]

In addition to the Poles, the Center, and the SPD, the NSDAP faced three smaller opponents, the least significant of which was the Free Front Soldiers' list formed by a disgruntled war veteran.[20] A Communist list was also entered, even though the KPD had been banned in March 1934. The DNVP had likewise officially ceased to exist. This was attested to by three prominent former members in a public statement, but Gerhard Weise considered himself the Danzig chairman of the party. He entered a list for the elections, under the name "National Front Black-White-Red." The senate refused to register the list, using as an excuse the prearranged protest of the German consul-general at this supposed abuse of the Reich colors. Undaunted, Weise submitted the list again with no title but his own name.[21]

Forster was certain that the elections would bring a great victory for the NSDAP. At the very least, he expected a two-thirds majority.[22] Given the Saar precedent, the terror-ridden and propaganda-filled election campaign, and the fact that the Nazis could exercise great influence on the election machinery, these expectations did not seem unreasonable. Danzigers went to the polls on Sunday, 7 April. That night, Forster prepared to announce the results on the state radio: "The results of the vote of German Danzig in the election of the Danzig Volkstag are . . ." Here Forster broke off as he looked at the election returns on the paper handed to him. After a moment's silence, the radio announced, "We now present marching and dance music." Forster retired from the studios. It is said he suffered from uncontrollable fits of weeping that night.[23] The election had yielded an embarrassing distribution of seats in the Volkstag, as shown in table 3.

The NSDAP, more than two years after Hitler's takeover of power, had won not quite 59 percent of the vote, and that in an election that could barely be described as free.[24] Since three "guests" had already joined the National Socialist parliamentary group, bringing it to a total of forty-one before the dissolution of the Volkstag in February, the practical effect of the election was to increase Nazi strength in the Volkstag by only two votes.

The statistics available for the 1935 election, as for the voting in 1933, do not permit a precise description of the origin of the increased Nazi strength. Once again, it may be assumed that the Nazis captured a large number of new voters, particularly young people voting for the first time. On the other hand, the Communists did not come to the polls in large numbers. The KPD had done little in Danzig after the Nazi takeover beyond distributing "subversive literature" and maintaining some contact with the Communist party in Poland. Police pressure had been constant, particularly after the official banning of the party in March 1934. Known Communists were special targets for Nazi assaults, and many had doubtless been afraid to go to the polls, if they were not already in jail or exile. They had not been able

TABLE 3

Division of Volkstag Seats by Party, 1933 and 1935

Party	Year	
	1933	1935
Center	10	10
DNVP (Weise list)	4	3
Free Front Soldiers	—	0
KPD (Communists)	5	2
NSDAP	38	43
Polish parties	2	2
SPD	13	12
Total	72	72

Source: *LNOJ* 16 (1935): 824–25.

to mount much of a campaign, in part because the other opposition parties shunned cooperation with them, for "tactical reasons."[25] As a result, the Communists alone of the opposition groups showed a sharp drop in voting support. Some persons who had voted Communist in 1933 may have switched their support directly to the NSDAP, but it seems more likely that they voted for other opposition parties, making good in part the defections to the Nazis that these parties had suffered.

Of special interest was the failure of the Nazis to absorb all of the "nationalist" vote, to which they had devoted special effort. They had succeeded in persuading Max Bertling and Paul Kindel, two DNVP deputies elected in 1933, to switch their allegiances.[26] Weise and Ziehm, the two remaining DNVP deputies, had resisted all threats and promises. Ziehm retired from political life and was not a candidate in 1935. He had courageously refused a place on the NSDAP list, and in an open letter to Forster he had supported Weise.[27] Rauschning, who had remained on his farm in the Grosses Werder, also wrote an open letter to the Gauleiter. In it he attacked Nazi terror, the economic policies of the government, and Forster's personal dictatorship. The issues of the *Volksstimme* and the *Volkszeitung* which printed Rauschning's letter on the eve of the election were confiscated, but the Weise group managed to circulate it as a handbill.[28] Weise benefited from the declarations of both former presidents, and he was able to elect three deputies. The "nationalists" actually increased their representation by one mandate, as compared with the Volkstag immediately before dissolution.[29]

The "national" issue seems to have backfired somewhat for the NSDAP. The Danzig public, continuing what was by now an old tradition, blamed the economic distress of the free city on Poland. This may be one reason why the Communists, who largely ignored this explanation for Danzig's depression, did not do well. In comparison with Nazi concessions, the old SPD policy of moderate cooperation with Poland seemed like outright jingoism. Nor did the opposition fail to make full use of this fact against the NSDAP in a manner that could only be described as scurrilous if it had been aimed at any other opponent. Despite the support Rauschning gave the opposition, every aspect of his understanding with Poland was attacked, as was Hitler's general policy of cooperation. The Nazi charge of "separatism" was weakened by opposition countercharges. An SPD handbill put it: "The Nazis promise 'Back to the Reich!' But what has happened? Hitler guaranteed to Poland the maintenance of the boundaries of the Treaty of Versailles in a ten-year treaty."

Similarly, the opposition turned against the NSDAP the old charges of corruption, bossism, and system politics that had been used so successfully by the Nazis before their takeover of power. Thus another SPD handbill: "New autos and gold braid! The people have forgotten neither." Forster and Greiser became the "Brown Bosses," as their enjoyment of the fruits of power was described in lurid detail. Danzig politics, like German politics, had not been precisely clean before the Nazi challenge, but it appears that the opposition had absorbed a few lessons since 1933.[30] And one element of the old politics was conspicuously absent. The opposition parties entirely refrained from attacks on one another.

The election was seen abroad as a Nazi defeat and a challenge to Hitler's claim that the German people were united behind his regime.[31] The NSDAP was privately most embarrassed, despite some forced public efforts to claim a victory.[32] The harshest, most complete judgment came from Erich von dem Bach-Zelewski, at that time SS leader of East Prussia and Danzig (SS-Oberabschnitt Nordost). In a telegram to Heinrich Himmler, he reported: "After yesterday's 60 percent election success a deep depression reigns in Danzig." Bach-Zelewski suggested that the underlying cause of the Nazi failure was a fear on the part of Danzigers that a return to the Reich might cut them off from the Polish economy and complete their economic ruin. This notion missed the point. The Nazis seemed not to realize that the Danzig population had lost hope in a quick return to the Reich, since official policy appeared to be leading in the opposite direction. More perceptive were Bach-Zelewski's other observations. He suggested that the corruption and "bosslike" (*bonzenhaftes*) behavior of party officials had hurt badly. The voters had also been alienated by Greiser's recent divorce and remarriage and by a slander campaign against him engineered by Linsmayer.[33] Bach-Zelewski warned that the enemies of national socialism still survived "in their old strength." The elections had proved it. In Danzig, League supervision allowed the opposition to fight openly, but in the Reich it continued to fight in secret.[34] The impression the election gave foreign observers was thus confidentially confirmed by a high SS officer close to the Danzig scene. The anti-Nazi opposition still survived, and if in Danzig, then why not in the Reich as well?

Financial Disaster

The Danzigers who went to the polls in April 1935 may not have realized the full extent of the free city's economic and financial crisis. The immediate cause lay, not in Danzig, but in Germany. Credit from the Reich was drying up. The Reichsbank's gold reserves, which had already been badly drained, had amounted to 991 million marks in December 1932. By 1939, they were to be reduced to 78 million marks.[35] Rearmament and "full employment" cost money, and Germany's balance of payments presented a dismal picture. The Reich government refused to consider devaluation, as too reminiscent of the inflation of 1923; instead, it instituted total currency control under the authority of Reichsbank President Hjalmar Schacht. As early as June 1934, Schacht attempted to cut off all transfer of credits from the Reich to Danzig. Only Hitler's direct intervention kept up a minimal, insufficient flow of credits.[36]

Danzig's need was great. The projected budget for fiscal year 1934–35 showed a minimum deficit of 26 million gulden for the free city and 18.2 million for the Danzig municipal government. Danzig authorities estimated in February 1934 that 79 million marks would have to be transferred from the Reich between 1 April 1934 and 31 March 1935 to cover the normal expenses of government. Although the figures are uncertain, nothing close to this sum ever transferred. A further 4 million marks would have been necessary just to begin the special projects desired by the party, with the final cost conservatively estimated at 20 million marks.[37] With internal sources of revenue drying up because of continued depression, a major financial crisis in 1935 was inevitable.

Forster's attitude toward money was childishly irresponsible. The deficit spending possible in Germany, or in the United States under Roosevelt, was not possible in the tiny free city, absolutely dependent as it was on international trade and confidence in its currency. Forster's fear of austerity programs and devaluation was understandable from the political point of view. Since most classes of consumer goods in Danzig were imported, a devaluation drastic enough to be effective would predictably lead to a sharp rise in the cost of living. Forster must have been aware that much of the Nazi vote in the early thirties, in both Danzig and the Reich, had been a protest vote against the inability of other parties to deal with the depression without creating more misery for those already suffering the most. Even Rauschning had publicly denied the possibility of devaluation, while secretly planning just that. Greiser may have been more honest when, on 28 November 1934, he assured the Volkstag that the gulden would not be devalued.[38]

Perhaps Greiser believed that Forster's high Reich connections would strengthen the flow of German marks into the free city. But Reich support stopped completely in 1935, as the rearmament program picked up speed. A devaluation could not be avoided. Most foreign and domestic observers blamed the crisis, when it surfaced into public view, on irresponsible Nazi economic policies such as Forster's building program and the anti-Semitism that drove some Jewish businesses to Gdynia and elsewhere. Forster was hardly in a position to defend himself and his policies by confirming the correct suspicion of a few international financial experts, who realized that the direct cause of devaluation was the cessation of Reich subsidies, most of which had been kept secret all along.[39] Forster could not inform his constituents that Hitler's regime was the first German government that had failed to pay its share toward keeping Danzig German.

At the end of April 1935, after the elections, Forster met with Schacht, Göring, and Hitler, and a devaluation of the gulden to 57.5 percent of its previous value was agreed on. This devaluation would bring the gulden down to the level of the Polish zloty. At the insistence of the German Foreign Office, no mention was to be made of this fact. Instead, the devaluation of the gulden was to be publicly related to the devaluation of sterling in 1931—the gulden had previously been linked to sterling, and the present devaluation would restore that connection.[40]

On 30 April the newly chosen Volkstag met and reelected the old senate, with Wilhelm Huth to fill the post of vice-president. No mention was made of devaluation. Two days later, Danzigers were shocked by the announcement that the gulden had lost more than 40 percent of its purchasing power. Despite the appointment of Wilhelm von Wnuck as price commissioner, prices soared out of control. Long lines appeared in front of the shops, as Danzigers made a desperate effort to spend their gulden before prices rose still further. A freeze on wages added to public concern. Runs on the banks forced bank holidays and limitations on withdrawals. The panic lasted through May and into June.[41] It soon affected Nazi circles, as confidence in the regime disappeared. Even Forster admitted privately that a popular referendum at that moment would have resulted in a Nazi defeat.[42] Public confidence was further undermined by the strong suspicion that certain Nazis, especially Wnuck, had exploited their prior knowledge of devaluation for their personal profit by purchasing real estate.[43]

The reserves of the Bank of Danzig had already shrunk from 35 million gulden in August 1933 to 13.5 million in April 1935.[44] The value of these reserves, expressed in gulden, was increased by devaluation. But obligations of the bank continued to fall due. The Nazis attempted to ease their emergency banking regulations in early June, only to face a new run on the banks. By mid-June the reserves of the Bank of Danzig amounted to only 5 million devalued gulden. The situation of the bank was far worse now than it had been before devaluation, and state bankruptcy seemed a real possibility. The Reichsbank helped with a secret and fraudulent transfer of funds. These bogus reserves were for display purposes only, to keep the extent of the disaster hidden from potential sources of new loans and from the Polish members of the Bank of Danzig's board of directors. (Almost half of the bank's stock was in Polish hands.) Reichsbank President Schacht's cheerful estimate of the Bank of Danzig's situation, given to the Polish ambassador in Berlin, was an outright lie, based on a phony balance sheet. The Reichsbank funds could not have been used to meet obligations.[45] The Danzig leadership panicked. Greiser began negotiations with the Polish commissioner-general, behind the back of Consul-General von Radowitz and the German Foreign Office, with a view to gaining Polish support for the gulden. Greiser may even have been prepared to introduce the zloty into the free city and to surrender control of Danzig's economy to Poland.[46]

Once the German Foreign Office discovered Greiser's desperate move toward Poland, it was impressed with the need for quick action. The Ministries of Economics and Finance agreed that Danzig should be helped, but Reichsbank President Schacht and

War Minister Werner von Blomberg refused to approve genuine credit transfers, on the grounds that they would endanger the rearmament program. Hitler, perhaps encouraged by Göring and Hess, intervened to save the Danzig situation. It was agreed in early June that the Reich would resume minimal transfers to Danzig. The local Nazis would have to sacrifice their pet building projects and the entire employment-creation program. The unemployed in Danzig would be put to work in the Reich. Supervision of a drastic government austerity program was given to Dr. Helferich, a Prussian financial administrator who was to function as a financial dictator in Danzig.[47]

As part of the agreement that was to rescue the gulden, the senate introduced complete control over transactions in foreign currency, including the zloty. The controls caused speculative discounting of the gulden in Poland and were probably in violation of the agreements of 1920 and 1921 that defined Danzig-Polish relations. The Polish government claimed that Danzig economic policies were illegal and were endangering the value of Polish customs receipts collected in the free city. The Danzig Customs Office exchanged all gulden it collected for zloty, at par, before transferring receipts to Poland, but Poland had no guarantee that this practice would continue if the gulden suffered further disaster. On 21 July the Danzig Customs Office (a branch of the Polish Customs Service staffed by Danzigers) was directed by Warsaw to cease collecting duty on goods destined for Poland. These duties could now be paid only in Gdynia. Overnight, trade in Danzig's harbor came to a halt. The Polish case was a complicated one, but the potential danger to Polish customs receipts hardly justified the drastic nature of the customs ordinance of 21 July. It is no wonder that the Danzigers suspected that the Poles were simply taking advantage of Danzig's weakness in an attempt to strengthen their hold on the economy of the free city.[48]

The crisis nicely illustrates the complex nature of the economic-political relationship between Poland and the free city. Under the cover of an amicable political settlement, neither side abandoned its ultimate aim of revising Danzig's status. The

Poles continued to discriminate against Danzig, in favor of Gdynia. This was partly a public and partly a private matter. Polish exporters, particularly Jews, who were numerous in the field, often preferred to do business through the Polish port. Many Polish export-import firms made the move from Danzig to Gdynia after the customs ordinance of 21 July 1935, and they would not return. In 1935, the total tonnage passing through Danzig was lower than it had been in 1933, whereas tonnage passing through Gdynia had risen consistently. Danzig's share of Poland's sea-going trade dropped from 47 percent in 1934 to 37 percent in 1935. It may be argued that over the entire period from 1933 to 1939 Danzig did not come off badly in regard to her share of Polish trade. But what is most important at this point is the fact that, at their moment of greatest weakness, the Danzig Nazis believed with some justification that they were faced with a full-scale Polish economic offensive. The effect of the July customs ordinance was catastrophic.[49]

At the suggestion of the German Foreign Office, Greiser instructed the Danzig customs officials not to carry out the ordinance.[50] Practically speaking this was an empty gesture, since goods intended for Poland had already ceased to flow through Danzig, but Greiser's order challenged Polish control over the Customs Office, an integral element of the free city's international status. A diplomatic deadlock developed, as Danzigers gazed anxiously at their quiet wharves. Schacht, Greiser, and Helferich produced a plan for declaring Danzig a "free port," or joining the free city economically to Germany. They were probably speculating on the rapid return of Danzig to the Reich, perhaps as early as the spring of 1936.[51]

Forster remained in the background, but the Gauleitung encouraged rumors that a return to the Reich was imminent, presumably to improve the Nazis' general political standing.[52] The German Foreign Office objected that the time was not yet ripe for a permanent solution to the Danzig question, since any action in Danzig would destroy the German-Polish understanding desired by the Führer and might mean the end of claims on the corridor. The Foreign Office called for a resolution of the crisis through direct Danzig-Polish negotiations, but it could not assure the adoption of its view without the help of some source more influential with Hitler than it was itself.[53]

On 1 August the senate announced that eight categories of goods (pigs, rye, feed, butter and eggs, fruit, medical supplies, solid fuel, and all goods arriving by post) would be allowed into Danzig duty free, as a result of the emergency created by the Polish customs ordinance. The measure had been agreed on at a meeting in Berlin on 30 July. But there had been no understanding about the purpose of the move. Greiser saw it as an escape valve for the political and economic resentments that had been building up in Danzig since the election and the devaluation. Helferich saw it as a means of "stuffing Danzig full" of goods without burdening the Reich's balance of payments. To the Foreign Office, it was only a means of putting pressure on the Poles to negotiate for a rapid settlement. So great was the confusion that the Foreign Office and the Danzigers could not even agree on what had actually been said at the meeting of 30 July. The Poles responded to the Danzig initiative by refusing to allow any goods whatever from Danzig into Poland. There is no telling how far the situation might have deteriorated had not Hermann Göring suddenly entered the dispute.[54]

Göring, who cultivated good relations with the Polish ambassador in Berlin, Józef Lipski, was told by the latter that the action of the Danzig Senate was endangering the entire Polish-German understanding. Göring telephoned Greiser and demanded that a negotiated settlement with Poland be reached quickly. This intervention sent both the Foreign Office and the senate scurrying, and Greiser was most upset. He protested that he had always been willing to negotiate.[55] There could be no foot-dragging in this matter, since Göring and presumably Hitler, in whose name he spoke, had made up their minds that a basic element in Germany's foreign policy had been threatened. On 6 August Forster and Greiser met with Göring in Berlin. The two Danzigers were told that the Führer and the Polish government had agreed that a special ambassador would be sent from Warsaw to Danzig to achieve a settlement. On 9 August a joint Polish-Danzig communique announced the lifting of the offending customs ordinance, as well as Danzig's countermeasures. The entire matter was arranged by Göring, who gave exact instructions to Greiser and completely superseded the authority of the Foreign Office as well as the commission given to Helferich. His intervention was much resented, but his orders were followed. On 11 October an amicable settlement was reached. Only one load of duty-free goods had entered Danzig from Germany.[56]

The first eight months of 1935 certainly did not provide an impressive record of Nazi achievement in Danzig. The elections had been a fiasco, the financial and economic situations were desperate, and the opposition was stronger than ever. Ill-considered efforts to hurry Hitler along the road to annexation had led to the lowering of Danzig's stock among party notables in the Reich. The false rumors of an early return to Germany had worsened the crisis of confidence in government and party. The situation of the Danzig NSDAP would in any case have been difficult in 1935, but the one man most responsible for the extent of the difficulties was undoubtedly Albert Forster. Excitable and impulsive, he lacked the political balance necessary at such a time. Forster was fortunate in having Greiser as a scapegoat. It was no accident that the posts of Gauleiter and senate president were never combined. But all things considered, it is surprising that Forster was able not only to maintain but even to strengthen his control over his Gau.

Forster Retains Control

After the takeover of power in Danzig, Forster gradually built up his personal political position, largely by getting rid of individuals whom he disliked or whom he felt were disobedient. The two categories tended to coincide. One example will suffice. In March 1934, Hans Albert Hohnfeldt ran afoul of the Gauleiter. The senator for social affairs and former Gauleiter was accused by Forster of disobedience in a minor matter, involving Hohnfeldt's attachment to a crackpot "Germanic" religious sect. It is likely that Hohnfeldt had never been forgiven by the Gauleiter for representing in his person the "old fighters" of Danzig, such as they were. Forster railroaded a conviction through the

Gau party court and forced Hohnfeldt out of his party and state posts, and out of Danzig. He refused to reverse himself, even when the chief of the Supreme Party Court advised him to do so. So great was Forster's hatred of Hohnfeldt that he persecuted him even after his departure from Danzig and helped others to destroy the minor career he attempted to pursue in the Reichsleitung.[57]

Forster's defeat of Rauschning was more widely noted, but it did not, in itself, solidify the Gauleiter's position in Danzig. As has been indicated, Rauschning occupied no post of importance and had no strong following within the party. The matter of picking a successor presented Forster with a series of dangers. At no time did he consider taking the post himself. As for other possibilities, he confessed to Radowitz, "It will probably have to be Greiser, since I don't have anyone else." [58] As a matter of fact, there was another candidate—Wilhelm Huth, senator for economic affairs. Huth's candidacy was put forward by a mixed group of Greiser's opponents, the most important member of which was Max Linsmayer, head of the Danzig SA.

The SA had been a factor in Gau politics since the Fricke revolt of 1930. Linsmayer, a long-time associate of Forster, had been appointed Fricke's successor to insure that the SA would remain under the Gauleiter's control, but he had gradually developed a more independent position. It is not possible to trace the effects in Danzig of the purge of the SA conducted by Hitler in the Reich on 30 June 1934, but it seems likely that Linsmayer was connected with the clique around the murdered SA leader Ernst Röhm, although unlike Röhm's immediate companions, he probably was not homosexual.[59] The party did its best to convince the public that no purge of the SA was conducted in Danzig. On the other hand, it was reported in the foreign press that Linsmayer had been threatened with expulsion from the party and that two of his subordinates had been forced to resign. This cannot be confirmed, but the bitterness left by the purge deepened Linsmayer's earlier dislike of Greiser. The SA purge had been carried out in the Reich by the SS, and Greiser was an honorary SS officer who took the honor seriously.[60]

After the purge, the SA retained an unusual amount of influence in Danzig, and SA men occupied some key posts in the party and government. This was noted with concern by the local SS, which suffered from the desultory and corrupt leadership of Dr. Alexander Reiner (replaced in October 1934) and failed to develop an independent position of power.[61] Despite initial difficulties, Linsmayer got on well with Rauschning and favored retaining him as president. He worked with Radowitz to this end and instigated a smear campaign against Greiser that may have delayed Rauschning's resignation and Greiser's election.[62] Once it became obvious that Rauschning could not be saved, Linsmayer supported Huth's candidacy in cooperation with Wilhelm von Wnuck, now Hohnfeldt's successor as senator for social affairs as well as president of the Volkstag. They were joined by one of Rauschning's protegés, the head of the Senate Personnel Department.[63]

Forster may have seen Huth's candidacy as a dangerous combination of forces. Greiser was in any case the obvious choice for senate president, since he was the best-known Nazi in Danzig aside from the Gauleiter and Rauschning. Rauschning's removal inevitably shook public confidence, and it would have been unwise to replace him with a relatively unknown party member. After Greiser's election, he and Forster arranged to have Linsmayer recalled to the Reich. As for Wnuck, he tendered his resignation on 28 November 1934, the very day that he supervised the election of Greiser (in his capacity as Volkstag president).[64]

Forster at first refused to accept Wnuck's resignation, and he retained his offices. Greiser and certain of Forster's subordinates, however, continued to conspire against him. When Wnuck was suspected of having profited from the devaluation of 1 May 1935, he resigned all his offices and left Danzig for a post in the Supreme Party Court. He was the last of the pre-1930 Danzig Nazis to hold an important post, with the exception of Greiser himself, who had joined the NSDAP in 1929. But Wnuck was more fortunate than Hohnfeldt. He got on well in his new Reich position, and Forster made no move against him.[65]

The political situation within the party was now much simplified. There remained only two individuals around whom factions could form—Forster and Greiser. Forster took immediate steps to check the new president. Rauschning's man in the Senate Personnel Department was replaced by the Gauleiter's own adjutant. Greiser was thus denied independence in patronage matters and was hindered in his later efforts to build a strong party for himself among the state officials. Forster may have refused to accept Wnuck's resignation when it was first offered because he wished to keep an enemy of Greiser in the senate. It was only when Wnuck had been publicly slandered beyond repair that Forster let him go. Most interesting in this respect was the further career of Wilhelm Huth. Huth was not harmed by the political shipwreck of the faction that presented him for the presidency. On the contrary, he was elected vice-president of the senate by the new Volkstag on 30 April 1935. He now enjoyed a close personal association with Forster, which lasted until 1945.

Forster was thus in firm control when Helferich arrived from the Reich, charged with the reform of the finances of the free city. Helferich quickly concluded that nothing could be done to improve the financial situation of Danzig without the dismissal of two "incompetent" officials: Wilhelm Huth and Finance Senator Julius Hoppenrath. Greiser was sympathetic. If Huth and Hoppenrath were removed, the president would be free of two senators who had special relationships with the Gauleiter.[66] Their replacements would presumably be professional civil servants from the Reich, without local ties. Forster, not surprisingly, refused to consider these personnel changes.[67] Helferich's superiors turned to Göring for help, since the latter had taken personal control of Germany's involvement in Danzig affairs. On 16 October officials concerned with Danzig, including Göring, met in Berlin to plan further implementation of Helferich's economy measures. In particular, it was agreed that Hoppenrath and Huth should be replaced.[68]

Forster simply refused to ask for the resignations of his friends. He sensed a grave threat to his political position. Göring, who had already picked Hoppenrath's successor, was furious at Forster's defiance and vowed to carry the dispute to a "higher place."[69] There is no record of Hitler's decision, but both Huth and Hoppenrath continued in their posts. It is entirely possible that the Führer evaded the responsibility for making a decision, a favorite technique of his, until the quarrel blew over.

Forster's influence continued to grow. Details are not available, but it is known that Greiser's situation deteriorated to the point where Forster arranged party proceedings against him. In November 1935, he had to deny rumors of his impending resignation.[70] In 1936, Greiser's supporter Dr. Helmut Kluck, senator for health, attempted to strike at Forster by circulating a memorandum on Danzig's unfortunate situation to party and state officials in the Reich. Kluck was replaced by one of Forster's men, Dr. Erich Grossmann.[71] Greiser did continue in office, perhaps because of sympathy for him in SS circles. The SS resented Forster's efforts to separate the SS in the free city from its divisional headquarters in Königsberg.[72] But Forster always retained the upper hand, and Greiser's chances for independent action were strictly limited.

Forster's insistence on control in Danzig was in accord with the leadership principle on which the entire party organization was supposed to rest. The leadership principle, when combined with Forster's personal relationship with Hitler, gave the Gauleiter a sometimes astonishing degree of independence. This was demonstrated in his dispute with Rauschning and again in his successful defiance of Göring. Forster's independence was of course always limited by the will of his Führer. Forster, Greiser, and all other Nazi leaders in Danzig were absolutely dependent on Hitler. Rauschning had been no exception, so long as he had remained within the party. Hitler tolerated, even encouraged, factionalism and personal rivalries, but he never tolerated disobedience on matters he had reserved for his own decision.[73] Forster was powerless to return Danzig to the Reich prematurely, and he could not expect unlimited financial support, given the more important demands of the German rearmament program. But on a lower level of decision-making he could rule almost unchecked.

6 The Nazification of Danzig, 1935–37

The campaign preceding the elections of May 1933 had been well covered by the foreign press, and the notion that Danzig was already Nazi had taken firm root. The *Manchester Guardian* had reported:

> Picturesque, medieval Danzig looks like a Nazi fortress today, thirty-eight hours before the elections. . . .
>
> The Nazis on bicycles and in decorated motor-cars and aeroplanes give the impression that the Nazis are taking the city by storm.[1]

This was, of course, precisely the impression that the Gauleitung had been striving to create. As we have seen, the elections of 1935 corrected the belief that Danzig had been totally coordinated by the Nazis, and even led some foreign commentators to the opposite conclusion. The truth lay somewhere between.

Even after the elections of 1935, it could still be said that Danzig seemed to be "to all intents and purposes a miniature Third Reich." [2] Events in the free city did proceed along the same lines as in the Reich. But the pace was slower, and the achievement of total *Gleichschaltung,* or coordination, was uneven, especially in the political sphere. The process of political *Gleichschaltung* was only completed in 1937, after which time Danzig was indeed only a "miniature Third Reich," although the introduction of anti-Semitic legislation was put off for another year.

Gleichschaltung in Danzig before 1935

It is necessary to take a brief backward glance at the progress *Gleichschaltung* had made in Danzig before the crisis year of 1935. The glance will be brief because the process did not differ greatly from that which took place in the Reich, although the results were somewhat different.[3] A scarcity of source material also prevents a more complete examination of this period.

The first institutions in Danzig to be coordinated were those with direct connections with the Reich, such as the German Consulate. The consul-general at the takeover of power, Baron von Thermann, had not previously demonstrated any sympathy with national socialism, but he "coordinated" himself with admirable speed by joining the SS cavalry. In late 1933 he was appointed German minister to Argentina, in which post he was to be instrumental in the *Gleichschaltung* of the local German community.[4] His successor in Danzig, Radowitz, was already a member of the SA, although he used his party position only to further what he believed to be Foreign Office policies.[5] Nazi party credentials were not, of course, any guarantee of success in Danzig. Neither Radowitz nor those who followed him as consul-general got along with the Gauleiter, and all preferred to deal with the senate president. Forster resented them as meddlers in his Gau, particularly dangerous because they were in regular communication with Berlin. In fact, the German Foreign Office gradually lost control of Danzig affairs after 1933, just as it lost control over German foreign policy in general. The German consul-general no longer represented the Reich—he was the agent of a declining political faction in Berlin. Under these circumstances, relations between the Foreign Office and the senate president were reduced to the level of a political intrigue.

The Consulate-General was an important agent for dispensing Reich subsidy funds, and those organizations that were dependent on it naturally felt obliged to coordinate themselves. The records show that many organizations such as Catholic and youth groups, which had received assistance from the Reich in 1931 and 1932, no longer received aid after the Nazi takeover. Coordinated institutions continued to receive help. But as with the consulate itself, coordination was not a sufficient guarantee of success. The *Danziger Heimatdienst* ("Homeland Service"), for example, was the major "nonpartisan" propaganda organization in the free city. It coordinated itself quickly, but it was soon embroiled in internal party feuds and came close to dissolution. When the

Reich was forced to cut off its subsidy in 1935, it moved its base of operations to Berlin.[6]

Although the records of senate subsidies are not available, it may be assumed that, like Reich funds, they were administered in a discriminatory fashion. But the cultural and social life of Danzig was not completely coordinated in the first years of Nazi government. All public employment was denied to Jewish and oppositional artists, scholars, performers, and writers, but many private organizations continued to lead an uncoordinated existence. They were normally affiliated with the opposition parties, the Catholic church, or the Protestant oppositional "Confessing church" (*Bekennende Kirche*).[7] These groups found their public activity increasingly circumscribed, but the fact remains that it was possible for a Danziger to engage in artistic efforts, book study, choral singing, sports, or youth activities without joining a Nazi organization—a possibility that hardly existed in the Reich.[8] Naturally, the uncoordinated groups became centers of thinly disguised political activity and helped to keep the spirit of opposition alive in the free city.

The internal life of the Polish community in Danzig really falls outside the range of this study. A strict separation existed between the Poles in Danzig and the non-Nazi or anti-Nazi Germans, except among the persecuted Communists. But it is significant that the full range of Polish professional, political, cultural, and social organizations was preserved, although pressures were sometimes exerted by the Nazi authorities on individual members. The Polish commissioner-general, armed like his German colleague with the power of the purse, and with a great deal more money to spend on a much smaller community, attempted fairly successfully to coordinate the activities of Danzig's Poles in accordance with policies adopted in Warsaw. His greatest success was the merger in 1935 of the two Polish political parties, which weakened the influence of those local Polish leaders who had opposed the Warsaw government.[9]

The reorganization of the business life of the free city along corporate lines, which occasioned a dispute between Rauschning and Forster, was, on paper, identical to the system adopted in the Reich.[10] From the limited evidence available, it seems that the restructuring was more apparent than real and had little influence on such major branches of the economy as the export-import trade and shipbuilding.[11] This may be partly explained by the close connection between the economies of Danzig and Poland and by the economic barriers that existed between Danzig and the Reich.

The system of "economic chambers" was absorbed in 1934 into a larger organization known as the "Danzig Labor Front" (with the same initials as the equivalent Reich organization, the DAF). The DAF was planned to take in every "working" (*schaffender*) person in the free city, including even foreigners and Jews. In practice, the DAF drew most of its membership from the coordinated professional associations (of teachers, lawyers, physicians, and so forth), from agricultural laborers, and from white-collar workers; that is, from segments of the population that had not been thoroughly organized by the old Free Trade Unions. The socialist trade union leaders attempted to continue their activity through the "General Workers' Association," which survived until it was banned by the chief of police in December 1935. Given the political situation, it could not function as a normal union, but it did serve as a center of opposition among the workers. As for the DAF, it proved unable to attract large numbers of working-class members until after 1935.[12]

The Nazis did attempt to take advantage of Danzig's unemployment problem for purposes of *Gleichschaltung.* Since 1931, various groups in Danzig had organized "labor services" (*Arbeitsdienste*), all more or less state subsidized and intended to provide work for the unemployed. The first Nazi effort came in April 1932. In July 1933, the Nazi senate banned all non-National Socialist labor services. In 1934 the senate announced a one-year labor service obligation for all Danzigers between the ages of seventeen and twenty-five. By January 1935, 950 Danzigers had been called up, and a compulsory state labor service had been organized, even before the equivalent steps had been taken in the Reich. Danzig's unemployed, both inside and outside the labor service, were frequently sent to work in the Reich. The primary motive was to ease the support burden on the free city, but labor in Germany was also used as a means of political "education."

Danzigers who refused to go to the Reich to work were denied unemployment assistance payments, on the grounds that they had turned down available employment.[13] But despite all these pressures, the *Gleichschaltung* of Danzig's working class, employed and unemployed alike, was far from completed by 1935.

The failure of *Gleichschaltung* in Danzig to keep up with the rapid pace set by the Reich was not due to unusual lack of enthusiasm for national socialism among Danzig's population. The NSDAP in Danzig totaled 9,519 members in December 1932 and 21,861 in June 1934. Although the growth rate of the party in Danzig between 30 January 1933 and 1 January 1935 was only 140.3 percent, as compared with 194.1 percent for the entire NSDAP, the number of party members in Danzig remained relatively high. At the beginning of 1935, 1 out of every 18.6 citizens was a party member, and 1 out of every 11.1 eligible voters was a party member. In the Reich, only 1 out of every 26.4 citizens and 1 out of every 18.5 eligible voters was a party member.[14] These figures, as well as the electoral majority won by the NSDAP in 1933, suggest that the party proved unusually attractive to the Danzig population, although enthusiasm may have waned somewhat after 1933.

If *Gleichschaltung* was slow in the first two years of the Nazi regime, this slowness was due to a greater capacity for resistance on the part of the non-Nazi and anti-Nazi elements in Danzig. Resistance was made possible and was strengthened by Danzig's peculiar relationship with the League of Nations. The most important symptom of this special situation was the continued existence of opposition political parties.

The Nazis, the Opposition, and the League

After the dubious Nazi election victory of April 1935, the opposition parties united in an attempt to force new elections, to take advantage of the crisis created by the devaluation of the gulden. The Nazis resisted desperately. The NSDAP was informed by the director of the Danzig Bureau of Statistics that it could hope for only 18 to 35 percent of the vote in a new election.[15] A motion by the SPD, the Center, and the DNVP to dissolve the Volkstag was accordingly rejected by the NSDAP on 26 August 1935. The Volkstag voted at the same time to revoke the parliamentary immunity of four of the opposition's leaders. Greiser used amazing frankness in speaking against the motion for dissolution. Ziehm, he said, had eased the Nazis' takeover of power by dissolving the Volkstag. The present senate would not make the same mistake. This was a public admission that the NSDAP feared a new election would not give them a majority.[16]

The leaders of the Communists, the SPD, the Center, and the DNVP had meanwhile filed suits in May before the Danzig Supreme Court (*Obergericht*), requesting that the April elections be declared void. It was claimed, correctly, that the fraud and terrorism practiced by the NSDAP and the government had made a free vote and a fair count impossible.[17] The court's decision was not announced until 14 November. It declared the vote in eighteen rural precincts invalid. One seat was taken away from the NSDAP and given to the SPD. But the court refused to invalidate the elections as a whole, despite its finding that widespread fraud had indeed existed.[18] The opposition thus failed to gain its main point—the holding of new elections under a court order. This peculiar decision, which granted the plaintiffs' allegations yet reached a verdict relatively favorable to the defendant, illustrates the difficult position in which the supreme court found itself.

The president of the supreme court, Dr. Walter von Hagens, had occasion to describe the painful situation of Danzig's judges in a letter to Gauleiter Forster. Hagens defended the judges of the criminal courts against the Gauleiter's public charges that they lacked the proper National Socialist attitude, since they had proceeded against a number of Nazis accused of breaking up a meeting of the SPD. Hagens pointed out to the Gauleiter that the constitutional and legal position in Danzig was very different from that in the Reich, since "a criminal action of the sort in question is impossible in the Reich, if only because 'legal' meetings of the SPD do not exist there." He implied that he would have no objection to enforcing a new set of laws, if the Nazis were able to change the constitution. But so long as meetings of the SPD were permitted by law, they would have to be protected by law. Clearly Forster was correct. Most of Danzig's judges did not possess a proper National Socialist attitude. A leading Nazi legal theorist had already proclaimed that a judge could not be "bound by a law" when applying the law.[19]

The decision on the opposition's charges of election fraud presented a clear contradiction between the demands of the law and the demands of the NSDAP. The prehistory of the decision is instructive. The judicial commission that considered the charges was placed under great pressure. In early July some prominent Danzig officials, both active and suspended, attempted to found the "League of Patriotic Officials." They were acting in concert with Gerhard Weise. After the first, and last, meeting, eleven of the founders were arrested. They included two prominent judges. The two were soon released, thanks to the intervention of Hagens and the high commissioner, but the independence of the Danzig judiciary was at least questionable thereafter.[20] Hagens informed Radowitz on 29 August that the judicial commission had completed its hearings on the opposition's charges and the NSDAP would probably lose two or three seats. The date set for formal court proceedings was 30 October. On 28 October Forster summoned Hagens and attempted to discuss the matter. The judge defended his judicial integrity and threatened to leave if Forster insisted on discussing a pending case. The Gauleiter desisted, although he continued publicly to make known his contempt for the judicial process and the independence of judges. Hagens himself was especially vulnerable to Nazi attack, since it was well known that he had had a Jewish grandfather.[21]

Hagens and his colleagues attempted in their final decision to strike a compromise between the demands of the law and the demands of the party. The verdict failed to satisfy anyone, and it did not save Hagens. He resigned from the supreme court on 31 December 1936. His successor was Dr. Walther Wohler, an ardent and "idealistic" Nazi who had worked closely with Greiser in the Senate Department of the Interior.[22] From that time on the Danzig courts may be considered completely coordinated, although Forster's influence on them was perhaps weaker than Greiser's.

The opposition parties approved of the supreme court's findings regarding the prevalence of terror and fraud during the election campaign but did not accept the court's verdict as final, since it did not allow for new elections. On 26 November the representatives of the DNVP, the SPD, and the Center therefore petitioned the League council, through the high commissioner, requesting that the supreme court be overruled and the elections be declared invalid.[23] This petition was added to a host of others relating to the unconstitutional state of affairs in Danzig.[24] But in this latest case of oppositional appeal to Geneva, the senate reacted with unusual vigor, probably at the urging of Forster. In a government declaration on 27 November, Greiser accused the opposition of placing itself "beyond the pale of the German national community" and added that Danzig's present suffering was due to its separation from Germany. Since "this separation was willed by the League of Nations," any appeal by a Danziger to Geneva was treasonous. Greiser even suggested that, had it not been for the 19.9 million gulden that Danzig had allegedly been forced to expend on the League presence since the founding of the free city, the recent devaluation might have been avoided. (According to the confidential calculations of Geneva officials, the true sum was 1.5 million gulden.) Greiser also included a threat. The Danzig constitution, he pointed out, had been written at a time when Germany was powerless. It was time the League realized "that the distribution of political power in Europe has been fundamentally changed." [25]

High Commissioner Sean Lester was not only disturbed by the political implications of Greiser's speech, he was deeply offended by what he considered to be a personal attack. He denied Greiser's insinuations and complained to Viktor Böttcher, Greiser's deputy for foreign affairs, that the senate was not fighting "cleanly." In early December the high commissioner traveled to Warsaw, Berlin, and Geneva to gather support.[26] The threat to Nazi Danzig implicit in this unusual journey may have led Greiser to moderate his formal response to the opposition petitions. The reply took a hypocritically constitutional stand, denying the League's right to support the wishes of a minority against the decision of Danzig's properly constituted courts.[27] But it was obvious that the issue between Danzig's Nazis and the guarantor of the constitution, the League of Nations, had finally been joined. On the course of the conflict would depend the prospects for success and the very existence of the Danzig opposition.

It is now necessary to retrace our steps somewhat. In September 1932, on the sudden death of High Commissioner Manfredi Gravina, the post was filled on a temporary basis by Helmer Rosting, who headed the department of the League secretariat concerned with minorities questions and administrative commissions, including the Danzig High Commission. Rosting never intended to stay for long in Danzig,[28] but the appointment of a successor was delayed by political arguments in Geneva. The Germans desired that the post be given to an Englishman, who, it was felt, would be able to stand up to Polish pressure. The Poles insisted on a citizen of a small, neutral European state. The British, who already provided the rapporteur on Danzig questions to the council, did not care to become further involved. They therefore proposed Sean Lester, League representative of the Irish Republic. The Germans were not pleased, but eliminated themselves from the negotiations when Hitler withdrew from the League. The British insisted on Lester despite objections from Colonel Beck, who feared that the Irishman would be a British agent. Sir John Simon forced the issue by threatening to resign as rapporteur and publicly to blame Polish obstructionism. The Poles finally yielded. Lester was named to his post on 26 October 1933, the appointment to become effective the following 15 January.[29]

His initial reception in Danzig was good. Fortunately, the German Foreign Office was able to scotch rumors that this son of an old Irish Protestant family was actually a Jew, or of Jewish origin.[30] Lester was a cultivated, conservative, rather formal man, who got on well with Rauschning. He was no rigid antifascist, but he had a strong respect for the terms of his mission, as he saw them. Since he was rarely called upon to adjudicate Danzig-Polish disputes, thanks to Rauschning's detente with Warsaw, his mission consisted of the two closely related tasks of supervising the constitutional life of Danzig and maintaining the League's prerogatives in the free city. He was possessed of a strong personal sense of his own position, and he always insisted that he be treated with the respect due him as the representative of the League. Under normal circumstances this respect was not denied him. He impressed all those with whom he dealt in Danzig as an honorable and serious official, sincerely concerned with the well-being of the free city. Although he was not initially competent in German, he strove to improve his ability in that language, and he soon familiarized himself with all the peculiar strands that made up the fabric of Danzig politics.

About the time of Rauschning's resignation Lester became increasingly unpopular in party circles, not only because he had backed the losing side in the intraparty struggle, but because he was serving as a channel for the complaints of the opposition. The high commissioner always encouraged would-be petitioners to exhaust every constitutional avenue of redress before taking their complaints to Geneva, but reports that his visitors from the opposition were being closely questioned by the police aroused his anger and determination.[31] He correctly viewed the right of access to the high commissioner, and the right to petition the League freely, as essential elements of the League's position in Danzig.

The events of 1935 only worsened Lester's relations with the Nazi leaders. During the election campaign, Greiser publicly attacked him for associating with members of the opposition.[32] Despite his best attempts to be impartial, the high commissioner was inevitably more useful to the opposition than to the government. His principal contact with the SPD was Erich Brost, editor of the *Volksstimme.* The Center party also used his good offices, particularly in its negotiations with the government in February 1935. Only Gerhard Weise was reluctant to take the "un-German" step of consulting the high commissioner. The July arrests following the meeting of the "League of Patriotic Officials" made him enter the offices of the high commissioner for the first time.[33] In the second half of 1935, Lester was in constant contact with all three major opposition parties. But he did not encourage the parties to continue or to increase their opposition. All his efforts in 1935 were directed toward bringing about a compromise within the constitutional framework of the free city. Lester even discouraged the opposition leaders from presenting their petition on the elections.[34] But the attacks of the senate and the Gauleiter on the League, and the continued persecution of the opposition, naturally drove Lester away from the government and closer to the anti-Nazi forces.

It was clear to Gauleiter Forster that the high commissioner and the League were major obstacles to the *Gleichschaltung* of the free city. The climate of opposition kept alive in Danzig was dangerous not only to the local dominance of the NSDAP, but to the international image of national socialism. As we have seen, the Nazi failure to sweep the 1935 elections was widely noted abroad. So was the oppositional activity which filled the remainder of the year. Sir Horace Rumbold, former British ambassador to Germany and a prophet of Hitler's aggressive intentions, suggested to the British Foreign Office "that Danzig might be regarded as a barometer for the scale of public opinion and party feeling in the Reich." [35] It is no wonder that Forster was anxiously awaiting an opportunity to strike at the League.

Lester himself provided the first opening. The German warship *Admiral Scheer* made a visit to Danzig at the beginning of September. Lester gave the usual formal reception for the ship's officers, to which he invited the members of the senate and other prominent Danzig officials. For reasons that are not entirely clear, he also invited some well-known members of the opposition. When these men, including Hermann Rauschning, arrived, all the Danzig officials, following Greiser's lead, made their excuses and departed. Lester took this painful scene as both a personal insult and a demonstration against the League.[36] He was quite right. The action resulted in a virtual rupture of relations between Lester and the government and made it easy for Forster to push Greiser into giving the offensive government declaration of 27 November, with its references to German might and to the gratuitous expense of the League presence in Danzig.

The moment chosen for the attack must have seemed particularly favorable. In early October, Italy had invaded Ethiopia. The League was faced with the gravest crisis since its foundation. The matter of sanctions against Italy, no matter how carefully it was handled, created new tensions between Italy and the western democracies, and brought Hitler and Mussolini closer together. With the political climate in Europe, and particularly in Geneva, so disturbed, events in Danzig might well pass unnoticed. Just before he delivered his government declaration, Greiser told Lester that Eden, the League rapporteur on Danzig questions, would certainly be far too concerned with the problem of prospective oil sanctions against Italy to worry about the domestic situation in the free city.[37]

When Lester left Danzig in early December for Warsaw, Berlin, and Geneva, he intended to secure the institution of a League committee to investigate the situation in Danzig. He also wished to secure the removal of Forster, whom he recognized as the man behind the attack on the League. Lester's reception everywhere was polite, even in Berlin, but he received nothing beyond vague assurances. The British were involved in Lester's quest through their legation in Warsaw, but the British Foreign Office was unwilling to do anything more than to ask Poland to bring pressure on Berlin. No British interests, it was felt, were involved in Danzig. The Poles promised, in a general way, to support the League in the free city, and Papée did present Greiser with an official Polish note to that effect. But the Polish government was even less prepared than the British government to confront Hitler on the matter. Lester spoke with Neurath in Berlin and complained of Forster's activities, especially his continual references to the approval of the Führer and to the growth of German power. Neurath answered soothingly, and Forster actually was called to Berlin by Hitler to report. Only one month later, however, Neurath supported Forster's campaign against Lester by complaining to the British ambassador that the high commissioner was not suited for his post. Neurath also gave the Polish government a clear warning that it could expect a worsening of relations with Germany if it participated in harsh League measures against Danzig. Germany's new strength, both military and diplomatic, was making itself felt in Danzig matters.[38]

Late in 1935, the opposition parties submitted a plan to Lester that called for new elections, to be held under the supervision of the League. They felt that free elections could be guaranteed if the Danzig police were placed under temporary League control, and that foreign troops would not be needed. At this point two members of the opposition, Hans Lazarus of the DNVP, and Ernst Künstler of the SPD, decided to attempt to see Eden and other influential persons in London. Lester and the leaders of the SPD and the Center tried vainly to prevent the trip, which they felt would do more harm than good. Weise, however, was persuaded to give Künstler and Lazarus a letter addressed to Eden. The two Danzigers did not meet Eden, but they were interviewed, in January 1936, by R. C. Skrine Stevenson, an adviser on League affairs in the Foreign Office. Stevenson listened sympathetically, promised little, and offered no advice. The Foreign Office was not eager to deal with members of the opposition, for fear that this might compromise Eden's efforts to reach a quiet settlement with Greiser in Geneva. The claim made by the Social Democratic visitor that the opposition would rise in revolt if it were abandoned to the Nazis was discounted on the evidence of socialist behavior in Germany in 1933. Lazarus and Künstler may have been able to prove to the British that the opposition parties existed, but they could not prove that they were, or ought to be, important in considerations of British foreign policy.[39]

Given these preliminaries, the results of the council's deliberations on Danzig in late January were predictable. Events in Danzig were allowed to resume their course without substantial League interference. But there was some token slowing of the pace of *Gleichschaltung*. It proved to be "the lull before the storm."[40]

The Final Phases of the Struggle

At the council meeting in January 1936, Greiser took a conciliatory stand. He got on well with Eden, thanks partly to the good offices of Colonel Beck, and was willing to promise that the senate would institute reforms in government practice that would restore constitutional conditions. Eden informed Greiser that the council would be satisfied with new senate regulations to improve freedom of the press, and with compensation for two state employees who had been dismissed for political reasons. Greiser at first asked the German Foreign Office, by telephone, to arrange a decision by Hitler on the course to be taken in the negotiations with Eden. When Hitler's decision was typically delayed, Greiser went ahead on his own responsibility. Not even Forster was consulted. Greiser's willingness to compromise was welcome to the British, not least because it was mistakenly assumed that, since he had telephoned Berlin, he was following direct orders from Hitler.[41]

Greiser was playing a complicated game. Back in Danzig from Geneva, he justified his moderate behavior in speeches that ridiculed the League and the opposition and minimized the importance of his concessions.[42] In this he was justified. The new press regulations adopted by the senate did little to relieve the pressure on the opposition newspapers, and the question of compensation for dismissed state employees was not a vital one. Greiser had yielded on these matters merely to preserve the appearance of compromise, thus allowing Eden and Beck to table the major question—the validity of the elections.

It was plain fact, difficult though it was for the Danzig opposition to grasp, that neither Britain (through the League) nor Poland wished to involve itself in the complex sort of international action that would have been necessary to force the holding of new elections in Danzig. To the opposition the demand for new elections was a matter of simple justice, and desperate personal importance. To Eden and Beck it was a can of worms, the opening of which would have been both dangerous and gratuitous. Greiser's willingness to allow a formal compromise provided the way out.

Forster was doubtless displeased with the results of the council meeting, which cheated him out of a confrontation by temporarily defusing the conflict with the League that he had been encouraging. Greiser could claim the support of Göring for his policies.[43] Forster paid the penalty for having made himself unpopular with Reich officials, and especially with Göring, because of his truculent behavior during the recent Danzig financial crisis. Hitler was, in any case, better served by Greiser's policy than by Forster's. The Führer was not ready for the confrontation over Danzig that Forster desired. It was necessary to prepare for the remilitarization of the Rhineland and the renunciation of the Locarno Pact, both of which occurred in March. This was not the time for an additional conflict over Danzig, which would have run the risk of antagonizing Poland and Britain. Beck had done a great service in helping to arrange the Greiser-Eden compromise, and Eden had accepted the public responsibility for treating Nazi Danzig gently. They would have felt themselves ill-served by an immediate renewal of tension in Danzig. It was time to move slowly.

Although Greiser freely attacked the League after his return from Geneva, he carefully abstained from any direct attack on Lester. Lester found Greiser's homecoming speeches satisfactory. Relations between the senate and the high commissioner became quite cordial. Greiser and Lester renewed their social contacts, suspended since the *Admiral Scheer* incident, and Lester abandoned earlier thoughts of leaving Danzig. He was aware that Greiser had received new support in Berlin, and he hoped that Forster's influence would now decrease. At the same time, Lester's relations with members of the opposition began to cool, since he insisted on "deflating too optimistic views" concerning a far-reaching change in the Danzig situation. Lester had no illusions about the real state of affairs in Danzig and was now content to concentrate his efforts on amelioration rather than thorough reform.[44]

Lester was mistaken in believing that Forster might be seriously checked in the drive toward total *Gleichschaltung*. In the first half of 1936 the thrust of Nazi foreign policy was toward the West. Hitler did not wish to risk a serious confrontation with Poland, nor to add to his difficulties by exasperating Britain in Geneva. Forster was accordingly denied an open conflict with the League, for the time being. But *Gleichschaltung* continued unabated. Danzig officials and teachers were subjected to continuing pressures, and the line between party and state almost disappeared. Non-Nazi or anti-Nazi officials were suspended or retired. The senate was willing to continue paying full salaries to suspended officials, to avoid new confrontations with the high commissioner. Assaults on anti-Nazis also continued, although arrests of opposition members became rarer.[45] The senate and the party only refrained from actions the formal content of which would force the high commissioner to intervene. Lester seems to have been content with this arrangement, as long as it lasted. In his reports to Geneva, Lester confirmed that the government was implementing the recommendations made by the council in January. He even referred to a "spirit of co-operation between the Government and the High Commissioner." No Danzig dispute was brought before the council in its May session, and the opposition petitions remained tabled. At the same time, Lester agreed to a year's extension of his appointment, which was due to expire on 15 January 1937.[46]

Just as no firm evidence exists to explain precisely why the lull in the Danzig-League confrontation began in late December 1935, it is uncertain why it came to an end in June 1936. It has been suggested that Hitler and the Nazis were encouraged by the failure of the democracies to react forcefully to the reoccupation of the Rhineland, and by the powerless state of the League as revealed in its inability to halt the Italian conquest of Ethiopia.[47] This general explanation is likely enough, but it does little to explain the timing of events in Danzig. Since no record of a Reich decision exists, the most that can be said is that Hitler lost interest in controlling his more aggressive followers in Danzig. What is certain is that the Danzig SS and SA suddenly became more active in early June, as cases of assault against members of the opposition, Jews, and Poles increased.

The situation exploded on 12 June, with a particularly brutal attack by members of the SA on a meeting being held by the DNVP. Many of those attending were injured in the melee. The attacking SA men used clubs, and their victims fought back with chairs and other improvised weapons. The death of Storm Trooper Deskowsky during the fight helped to attract international attention to the incident. The Gauleiter gave Deskowsky a hero's funeral, at which both Himmler and Viktor Lutze, head of the SA, spoke. Nazi martyrs were now rare in the Reich. Vengeance was vowed for the dead man and for two other Nazis who were killed when a Social Democrat whose house they shot up chose to return their fire. The Gauleiter refused to accept the report of Senator for Health Kluck, which showed that Deskowsky had died from a heart attack caused by a syphilitic condition, rather than from some dastardly blow struck by an anti-Nazi.

Kluck, a supporter of Greiser, was forced out of office after he sent a report to the Reich criticizing Forster's "almost Bolshevist terroristic methods." [48]

The change in Danzig's domestic climate was also reflected in renewed attacks on the high commissioner. On 25 June the German warship *Leipzig* paid a visit to Danzig. The commander, when reporting to Greiser as protocol required, told the startled senate president that he had been instructed, at Hitler's orders, to omit the customary courtesy call on the high commissioner. The embarrassed Greiser hurriedly sent a subordinate official of the foreign department to Lester—the high commissioner was already in formal dress, waiting to entertain his expected guests from the warship. Not unnaturally, Lester was highly insulted.

Lest the significance of the snub be missed, Forster drove home the attack in an article under his own byline, which appeared in the *Vorposten* on 27 June. The high commissioner, he claimed, was "superfluous." Lester had allegedly continually tripped up the government and had favored the opposition at every possible opportunity. By encouraging the opposition, Lester had made himself responsible for the three recent Nazi deaths. Forster also recalled the incident that had occurred during the visit of the *Admiral Scheer* the previous year. These considerations, he suggested, were the real reasons for the omission of the visit to the high commissioner by the commander and officers of the *Leipzig*. The article was, in effect, given Reich approval in the organ of the German Foreign Office, the *Diplomatische Korrespondenz*, which was already able to comment on it the day it appeared in Danzig. Forster was correct when he later claimed that Hitler had reviewed and corrected the piece before publication. The article had actually been written on the very day of the incident, or perhaps even earlier. It is entirely possible that Forster knew of the planned insult to Lester, whereas Greiser was kept in the dark until the last minute.[49]

The *Leipzig* incident and the renewed violence, which included many attacks on Polish citizens and Polish-speaking Danzigers, were called to the attention of the League by Lester.[50] The council placed the matter on its agenda for 4 July and invited Lester and Greiser to attend. The latter found time to stop in

Berlin and to prepare, with Göring's help, the speech he was to deliver in Geneva. The Führer approved the text, telling Greiser he wanted the speech to be a "bombshell." [51] It was made clear to Greiser that the policy of reconciliation with the League, which he himself had initiated in December, had outlived its usefulness. It no longer had the approval of the Führer. Greiser altered his posture toward the League with commendable speed and tried to make up for lost time.

Greiser's performance in Geneva lived up to his master's expectations and may even have surpassed them. The speech attacked the right of the League to interfere with Danzig's domestic affairs. Greiser suggested that the present high commissioner be replaced, or even better, that the post be abolished. The general tenor of the speech was offensive enough, with its hypocritical appeals to democratic principles in the name of an alleged majority of Nazi Danzigers, with its aggressive nationalism, and with its complaints against a "torn and divided" opposition that was somehow able to maintain a reign of terror against National Socialists. The arrogant manner of delivery made matters worse. To cap all, Greiser ended by treating the members of the council to the Nazi salute. This proved too much for some of the journalists present, who laughed out loud. Greiser, passing the press gallery on his way out of the room, avenged himself by thumbing his nose. According to some reports, he also stuck out his tongue. He may or may not have waggled his fingers. Having thus made himself internationally notorious, he was given a hero's welcome by the local Nazis on his return to Danzig.[52]

It may be assumed that Greiser's extraordinary behavior, although not the speech itself, was entirely his own idea, an attempt to outdo Forster at the Gauleiter's own game. Forster himself was with Hitler at the time. He later told Lester's successor, Carl Burckhardt, that Hitler had been upset by Greiser's actions. Forster, acting out of simple jealousy, did his best to reinforce the Führer's bad impression of the incident. He was probably angry that he had not had a similar opportunity himself.[53] Because of Hitler's desire that Nazis exposed to international publicity behave in a dignified manner, and because of Forster's intrigue, Greiser's action did not have the expected effect of strengthening his position with the Führer. But in Danzig the more militant party members were pleased to see the old, vituperative Greiser, of the days before 1933, back among them. In any case, Greiser's experiment of cooperation with Lester was definitely over.

From this time on, Lester had no influence on events in Danzig. On his return from Geneva a police guard was posted at his door. Everyone visiting him was questioned and sometimes detained. Lester thus lost all direct contact with the intimidated opposition.[54] The Polish government was requested by the League council to obtain an explanation of the *Leipzig* incident from the German government. Beck was seriously disturbed by the incident, and by Greiser's speech, because he feared a change in the status of the free city might be planned by Germany. He accordingly warned Berlin that any change in Danzig's status would cause a conflict between Germany and Poland. In the face of this vigorous reaction, the Germans were quick to assure the Poles that there had been no such intention on their part, and the *Leipzig* matter was closed when the League council accepted a formal German statement to Poland, dated 24 July 1936, that there had been no intention of acting in violation of Danzig's international status or of diminishing Polish rights in the free city.[55]

A Committee of Three—consisting of representatives of France, Britain, and Portugal (later replaced by Sweden)—was appointed by the council in July. It was to follow events in Danzig and report back to the council at the next session. The committee's report, in October, recommended that Poland be charged with improving the situation in Danzig.[56] Poland had repeatedly demonstrated its indifference to the deteriorating Danzig situation, save for instances when Poles, direct Polish interests, or the international status of the free city were involved. Beck was no more prepared to intervene to protect the opposition in Danzig than were the British. The opposition had frequently shown itself far more anti-Polish than the Nazi senate. It would have been strange indeed had Beck decided to jeopardize his understanding with Germany for the sake of Danzig's anti-Nazis, once he had been satisfied that a German coup was not imminent.

The council, in accepting the recommendation of the Committee of Three, washed its hands of Danzig without any serious expectation that matters there would improve. Germany and Poland could settle the Danzig question between themselves. As for Lester, he asked to be relieved of his post. He was appointed deputy secretary-general of the League on 5 October. He returned only occasionally to Danzig thereafter, although he formally remained high commissioner until he was succeeded by Carl Burckhardt on 15 January 1937. During the Second World War, Lester was to be the last secretary-general of the League, a caretaker until the organization's official dissolution in 1946.

The mandate given to Poland and Lester's resignation were the public expressions of an opinion widespread in the League secretariat that the League ought to give up entirely its guarantee of the Danzig constitution and allow Poland and Germany to decide between themselves whether or not they desired League arbitration in case of disagreements over the free city. A resident high commissioner would no longer be necessary.[57] Although the council decided that it would be awkward, particularly in view of anti-Nazi opinion in Britain and France, for the League formally to withdraw from Danzig, a de facto withdrawal did take place. Sean Lester later commented, in his new capacity as deputy secretary-general, that "the League's guarantee was virtually abandoned in Sept. 1936." [58]

The Nazis did not wait until September. As soon as Greiser returned to Danzig in early July, the senate abandoned itself to a veritable orgy of *Gleichschaltung*. A number of decrees of 16 July provided the "legal" basis. The term of protective custody was increased from three weeks to three months. Police measures of a political nature were removed from the jurisdiction of the courts and placed under the direct jurisdiction of the senate. The execution of civil judgments against the senate was effectively prevented. It was made easier for state employees to be dismissed for political reasons. Members of the Volkstag were forbidden to edit newspapers (this affected the two Centrist editors of the *Volkszeitung*). Members of the opposition parties were, in effect, made liable to arrest by mere reason of their membership. Finally, the kosher slaughtering of animals was forbidden by new veterinary regulations allegedly designed to prevent cruelty to animals, after the pattern of Reich ordinances.[59]

A wave of arrests followed. The opposition press was completely silenced, and the opposition itself was driven underground. Once the League proved its impotence to the Nazis, the climate of dissent that had flourished so uniquely in Danzig ceased to exist. On 14 October 1936, the SPD was banned. The DNVP, unable to affect events, nonetheless held out under Weise's leadership until May 1937, when it announced its dissolution. The Center was rendered similarly impotent, but it refused to dissolve itself "voluntarily," and it was finally banned on 20 October 1937. In November 1937 the formation of new political parties was forbidden. Danzig had finally reached the stage of political *Gleichschaltung* reached by the Reich in 1933. These later events had no significance except as mopping-up operations. By late 1937 most of the opposition leaders were in exile or in jail.[60] Gerhard Weise, his resistance broken at last, submitted and voted with the NSDAP in the Volkstag, his personal survival merely a trophy of the Nazi victory.[61]

Particular pressure during the cleanup of the opposition was exerted against those anti-Nazis who had the misfortune to be members of the Volkstag. The deputies were arrested, maltreated, bribed, and otherwise persuaded to join the NSDAP or to vote with it. Those who refused, or fled Danzig, were declared incapable of fulfilling their duties and were replaced by those next on the lists that had been submitted by the parties for the elections of 1935. These new deputies were then subjected to the same treatment. The rather sickening details of the process were fully reported in the dispatches of the British consul-general, but nothing was done to halt it. The enabling law of 1933 was extended on 5 May 1937 by a vote of forty-seven to twenty, a two-thirds majority of those present, and one short of a two-thirds majority of the entire house. With the self-dissolution of the DNVP on 14 May, the NSDAP gained an absolute two-thirds majority, and it continued to increase its numbers in the Volkstag.[62] By this time the two-thirds majority had lost its original significance. It was no longer necessary to amend the constitution and to trouble the council with the task of dealing with amendments, since the constitution had long since ceased to operate.

By mid-1937, the only important source of public opposition left in Danzig was the Catholic church. Bishop O'Rourke continued to issue his pastoral letters condemning the unconstitutional pressure on Catholic organizations, especially youth groups, and the groups themselves continued to exist. In May, O'Rourke carried his complaints to the Vatican, where he told the pope that he was ready to resign if it were thought desirable.[63] In June 1938, O'Rourke finally gave up. He announced his resignation and his appointment as titular bishop of Safena (in Mesopotamia).[64] The new bishop of Danzig, Karl Maria Splett, had previously been administrator of the cathedral in Danzig-Oliva. The senate was initially displeased with the appointment but discovered to its delight that Bishop Splett was willing to fight all efforts by the Poles to penetrate the church organization in Danzig and was at the same time prepared to accept the dissolution of most of the Catholic schools. This put a virtual end to Catholic education in Danzig and to the Catholic youth groups as well.[65] It also ended all public opposition to the NSDAP.

The NSDAP in Coordinated Danzig

In late 1937, the Gauleitung of Danzig grew concerned over a certain flabbiness evident in party organization, and especially over the large numbers of party members who did nothing beyond paying their dues. A statistical study was therefore made of the party and the general population. This was intended to give party officials an accurate picture of the Gau Danzig as of 31 December 1937 and was not for general publication.[66] The information contained in the survey has a greater claim to accuracy than most Nazi published statistical material. Similar statistics for the earlier, and more significant, periods in the development of the Gau are unfortunately lacking.

The survey was based on a census of the general population undertaken by the Ortsgruppen of the NSDAP on 1 November 1937. This census showed 375,972 Danzig residents, as compared to 407,517 shown in the last official census, taken in 1929. The earlier census had included about 7,000 visitors (mostly tourists). The remainder of the difference was largely accounted for by approximately 17,000 Danzigers working in the Reich, and by 2,000 fulfilling other obligations in Germany. Most of these were probably students or members of the German armed forces. Two thousand may have been absent on ships at sea. It may be assumed that the unprofessional census undertaken by the party missed a certain number of people. But despite this, the material may be considered accurate enough for our purposes here.

The party had barred new members from June 1934 to September 1936. The membership was 21,861 in June 1934 and jumped to 29,819 as soon as new members were again accepted.[67] By December 1937, 36,465 people (including 5,357 women), or 9.7 percent of the entire population, belonged to the NSDAP. The party members were proportionaly distributed between town and country. The membership was organized into three rural and six urban Kreise, which were further divided into forty-six rural and forty-two urban Ortsgruppen. The greater number of Ortsgruppen in the rural Kreise was made necessary by the separation of the inhabitants into many small villages. Urban Ortsgruppen had a far larger number of officials and staff workers. The proportional distribution of party members between urban and rural districts was not repeated within the urban area. The two Kreise of Innenstadt and Neufahrwasser, with the greatest concentrations of working-class people, contained 39.2 percent of the urban population within their boundaries and provided 32.5 percent of the urban party members. The class differences cannot be analyzed precisely, because the Kreise were too large and included neighborhoods of widely varying character. Unfortunately, no figures are available for the Ortsgruppen.

The figures at least suggest that the party was less popular with the working-class population, which had previously been most influenced by the SPD and the KPD. Industrial workers provided 11.5 percent of the party membership, a relatively low figure. This is particularly interesting when it is considered that all non-Nazi workers' organizations had been destroyed and that party organizers in Danzig "were specifically encouraged to promote membership among workers." [68] Although not many industrial workers were interested in joining the NSDAP, public and railway laborers contributed more, proportionally, to the party membership. They had early been subject to Nazi influence because of the special conditions of their employment. Rural laborers, who had been little organized by SPD and KPD, were also more inclined to join the NSDAP.

Occupational statistics must be dealt with rather freely, since

TABLE 4

ANALYSIS OF THE GAU DANZIG BY OCCUPATION, DECEMBER 1937

Occupation	Percentage
Industrial laborer	11.5
State and municipal laborer	1.5
Agricultural laborer	3.7
Railway laborer	2.2
Total laborers	18.9
Nonindependent artisan (*Handwerker*)	17.4
White-collar worker (*Angestellte*)	15.1
Official and manager (*Beamte*)	8.0
Farmer	7.9
Independent merchant	7.5
Housewife	5.9
Independent artisan	5.4
Professional	4.1
Teacher	3.1
Policeman (*Schupobeamte*)	2.1
Student	1.5
Retired	1.2
Without occupation	1.9

Source: Gauorganisationsamt Danzig, "Statistik des Gaues Danzig der NSDAP," December 1937, HA/30/587.

a basis for comparison with other statistical sources is lacking.[69] An analysis of the membership of the Gau Danzig in December 1937 by occupation gave the results shown in table 4. Not indicated in the table is the fact that civil servants of all ranks and types provided 21.2 percent of the membership. Almost all of the regular police force belonged to the party.[70]

Despite certain occupational imbalances, the party at this late date could not be regarded as representative of certain economic groups to the exclusion of others. The situation was comparable in the Reich.[71] Nor was the party particularly youthful: 55.7 percent of the members were between thirty-one and fifty years of age. The party had come to include most of the elements of Danzig society. This was even more true of the many National Socialist auxiliary organizations, which included nonparty members. The overlapping memberships of selected party organizations and affiliated associations in December 1937 (many Danzigers belonged to several of these groups) are listed below:

SA	12,851
SS	2,155
NSKK (Motor Corps)	1,290
NSFK (Flying Corps)	453
DAF (Labor Front)	77,352
Peasant League	23,000
Women's groups	29,279
Civil Defense	46,000
NSV (Popular Welfare Association)	40,000

By 1937, all normal avenues of public expression and social and economic activity were connected in one way or another with the NSDAP. The churches were only partial exceptions.

The all-inclusiveness of the party did not increase its effectiveness as a political force. Neither did its rapid growth. A breakdown of the membership in December 1937, by the date of party entrance, is given below:

Entered before Forster's arrival (24 October 1930)	1.2%
Entered between 24 October 1930 and 1 February 1933	20.5
Entered between 1 February 1933 and 1 May 1933	27.7
Entered between 1 May 1933 and 1 January 1938	50.6

The "old fighters" were heavily outnumbered. This may explain why 39.7 percent of the members participated in no way in party activities and were accounted members only because they continued to pay their dues. Interestingly enough, the percentage of active members in the party varied widely from one Kreis to another, from 75 to 51.2 percent. The three rural Kreise had the highest percentages of active members. The two working-class Kreise and the lower-middle-class suburb of Langfuhr had the lowest percentages. Some of the Kreise contained both rural and urban areas. There was a strong correspondence between the percentage of active members and the extent of the rural character of the Kreise. This correspondence suggests that the greater enthusiasm for the NSDAP shown in the rural areas during the elections of 1933 and 1935 (the worst Nazi excesses occurred in the country) continued through the later period. The traditionally greater force of social pressure in the villages, as compared with the city, may also explain the results.

Local variations not withstanding, it is plain that the NSDAP was not a fighting, dynamic political force in Danzig in December 1937. Although this fact may have disturbed some party leaders, they should have reflected that the party's period of struggle against domestic opposition was over. Secure in its control of the state, the Nazi movement could rely on the powers of the state to carry out its policies. The high-level feud between Greiser and Forster only rarely affected ordinary political life. The party organization existed primarily to involve the population in appropriate political activity to assure its loyalty, and to encourage productive participation in whatever tasks were set by the leadership.

7

The "Final Solution" of the Danzig Question, 1937–39

The free city now began the final phase of its de facto existence, which coincided with the last strained years of peace in Europe. Despite all Hitler's own uncertainties, and despite the best efforts of European statesmen to give him what they believed he wanted, the Führer moved the Third Reich toward the war that would lead to its destruction. The historical revisionism of A. J. P. Taylor has failed to alter significantly our picture of Hitler as bent on unlimited expansion beyond the remotest dreams of more conventional German patriots, and it does not seem necessary or desirable to enter the dispute Taylor provoked.[1] The major events that preceded the outbreak of the Second World War are too well known to require retelling here. The international role played by the Danzig question has also been discussed elsewhere.[2] This chapter will be concerned primarily with domestic matters—the destruction of the Jewish community, the continuing feud between Forster and Greiser, and the remilitarization of the free city. But in this period of growing international tension, which was to end with a German-Polish war, events in Danzig had a wider significance. They influenced, and were influenced by, the coming of the European catastrophe.

The Jews

In our discussions of the various stages of *Gleichschaltung,* we have so far barely touched on one of its most notorious aspects —the persecution and destruction of the Jewish community. The "Jewish question" in Danzig is best treated here as a separate subject with a history continuous from before 1933. Its ultimate solution coincided with the final stage in the development of the free city and does much to illuminate the nature of Danzig politics in this period.

The Jewish community included both German and "eastern" Jews (*Ostjuden*). Most of the latter had settled in Danzig after 1920. With few exceptions, the native Danzig Jews were liberal in matters of religion and politics and German in their national convictions. Zionism among them was limited to a few enthusiastic intellectuals. The creation of the free city, which opened the way for a strong immigration from Poland and other eastern European countries, changed the character of the Jewish community. It grew in size from 2,717 in 1910 (0.8 percent of the population) to 9,239 in 1924 (2.4 percent). The increase then slowed, and there were 10,488 Jews in Danzig in 1929. The newcomers, who spoke Yiddish rather than German, had little in common with the older group. Zionist, Orthodox, and socialist opinions were frequent among the eastern Jews, who were also much poorer on the average than the German group. The native Jews were disturbed by a noticeable growth of anti-Semitism in Danzig after the First World War and tended to blame the increase on their eastern coreligionists.[3]

The Nazi victory in the Reich in 1933, and the concurrent nazification of Danzig, naturally produced early fears of anti-Semitic measures, and some Jews may have left Danzig even before the elections of 1933.[4] But despite Nazi boycotts and other measures on the Reich pattern, an intolerable situation did not develop immediately on the Nazi takeover. Many members of the Danzig Jewish community, particularly the *Ostjuden* among them, doubtless thought of anti-Semitic activity in terms of the traditional eastern European pogrom. The pogrom, although it might initially be organized or incited by public authorities, depended for its effectiveness on the deep-rooted anti-Semitism of the Slavic, Baltic, and Romanian populations. Once popular violence ran its course in an orgy of drunkenness, looting, and sometimes murder, life would return to normal, and the social and economic position of the Jews would reemerge unchanged.[5] Since Nazi anti-Semitism did not follow the pogrom pattern, Jews were slow to recognize the danger of their situation. The notion that they might permanently be excluded from Gentile society rarely occurred to them, since there was little in recent European experience to suggest it. Only certain Zionists and extremely Orthodox Jews were prepared to accept exclusion when it finally came —a small minority even welcomed it.

The Nazi anti-Semitic program could not be carried out along lines similar to the pogrom. Spontaneous anti-Semitic violence, particularly in urban areas, had been very rare in Germany after the mid-nineteenth century. Cases of genuinely spontaneous attacks on Jews were also rare in the Third Reich, and the population sometimes resisted Nazi incitement.[6] Furthermore, the pogrom model did not suit the goals of the Nazi movement, which aimed at a systematic, total, and permanent exclusion of Jews from German society, a goal that led eventually to the "final solution."[7]

Danzig's Jews may have been comforted by the many official assurances given them that they were fully protected under the constitution. The Polish-Danzig agreement of 18 September 1933 specifically guaranteed the rights of Jewish merchants,[8] and similar guarantees were given repeatedly by Presidents Rauschning and Greiser. Unfortunately, the performance of the Nazis did not match their promises. No anti-Semitic ordinances were issued, but administrative measures were adopted that "would lead to the same result," as Senator for Justice Willibald Wiercinski-Keiser admitted in a cynical moment. Jewish officials, professionals in public employ, teachers, and cultural figures found it increasingly difficult to make a living in Danzig. Merchants also faced discrimination from time to time, especially if they were of eastern origin.[9]

A particularly interesting series of incidents occurred in June and July 1935, at the height of Danzig's financial and economic crisis. The National Socialist Organization of Artisans and Tradesmen (NS-Hago) started an anti-Semitic campaign led by the proprietor of a sporting goods and clothing store, "who apparently wishes to fight competition in this way." This motive was attributed to the store owner by Radowitz in the draft of a telegram to the German Foreign Office, but the phrase was struck out in the version actually sent.[10] Radowitz must have decided that it was unwise to impugn the pristine idealism of a Nazi anti-Semite. In any event, the clothing retailer and his friends made themselves conspicuous. On Sundays, when the summer crowds were greatest, groups of Nazis, some in uniform, entered three of the free city's public bathing beaches. There they displayed anti-Semitic placards with standard slogans such as "The Jews are Our Misfortune," and they made short speeches. The Gentile bathing public openly expressed its disapproval of these displays, either because they sympathized with the Jews or because they resented the interruption of peaceful Sunday excursions. A similar event occurred in late July. Nazis from Elbing, just across the East Prussian border, held an anti-Semitic demonstration in front of a café in Zoppot that caused most of the customers to leave. These demonstrations were made the subject of a petition to the high commissioner by Jewish organizations whose members also complained of an organized assault on Polish Jewish merchants during a trade fair.[11]

The Gauleiter refused to interfere. Senator for Propaganda Paul Batzer, who had jurisdiction over promotion of tourism, was furious, as were Greiser and Radowitz. The incidents, combined with the public display of Julius Streicher's anti-Semitic paper, *Der Stürmer,* could only hurt Danzig's tourist trade, and at a time when the economy was in desperate trouble. It may seem odd, but many of the tourists who visited Danzig and patronized the beaches and other attractions such as the casino and the Wagner festival in Zoppot were Jewish. Most of them came from Poland and were used to the annoyances of living in an anti-Semitic country, but there was a limit to what they could be expected to tolerate during their vacations. Germans were virtually prevented from visiting Danzig by Reich regulations forbidding the export of large numbers of marks, and so a drop in Jewish tourism could not be made up from the Reich. The senate, unable to convince the Gauleitung to call off the campaign, turned to Radowitz and the German Foreign Office to request that pressure be put on Forster through Reich party channels.[12] The campaign soon died down. The lack of a positive response from the general public may also have discouraged the effort.

The economic factor kept the lid on the anti-Semitic kettle for some time. It was only in 1937, after the *Gleichschaltung* of Danzig was otherwise almost complete, that pressure to "solve the Jewish question" began to build again. The force behind the new campaign was the Gauleiter, not Greiser. It was the Jews' misfortune that Greiser was weaker in 1937 than in 1935. He had lost two of his allies in the senate, Kluck and Batzer, and Radowitz was no longer consul-general. Radowitz's successors, although they did not work well with Forster, lacked their predecessor's strong personality and showed little desire to play an important role in domestic affairs. Greiser felt the weakness of his position, despite his good relations with Göring and the Foreign Office. Whatever his misgivings about the usefulness of Forster's anti-Semitic policies, there was a limit beyond which he would not go in opposing them.

TABLE 5

Citizenship of Jewish Population of Danzig, 1937

State	No. of Citizens
Danzig	1,226
Germany	376
Poland	3,724
Others (primarily Russia and Lithuania)	2,153
Total	7,479

Source: Burckhardt, *Danziger Mission*, pp. 205–6.

By 1937, perhaps three thousand Jews had left Danzig. Table 5 divides the Jewish population remaining, according to citizenship. The Jews still provided slightly under 2 percent of Danzig's population.[13] This community was now subjected to a concentrated attack that was to end in its destruction. At the end of April 1937, Forster announced that the Nuremberg laws, introduced in Germany in September 1935, would soon be enacted in Danzig. Forster's failure to realize his proclaimed anti-Semitic program at this point was apparently due to the direct intervention of the new high commissioner, Professor Carl J. Burckhardt, a Swiss historian.[14] But anti-Semitic propaganda continued to prepare the public for the eventual promulgation of the Nuremberg laws in the free city.

Typical was the handling of an incident that allegedly occurred on 1 May 1937. According to the Nazi press, a Polish Jewish woman seized a five-year-old boy on the street and dragged him screaming into her house. The boy's mother obtained his release and then called the police. The Jewish woman explained that, because it was the Sabbath, she had wanted the boy to light her fire, a task forbidden to Orthodox Jews on that day. Whatever the facts, the incident would have passed unnoticed if the Nazi newspapers in Danzig and the Reich had not branded it as "Jewish insolence" and an insult to the entire German population of Danzig. It was even hinted that the Jewish woman might have had some sinister purpose in mind, a suggestion reminiscent of the age-old ritual murder charges made against the Jews.[15]

On 20 September 1937 High Commissioner Burckhardt had an interview with Hitler. Burckhardt flattered the Führer by appealing to him as a "practical politician" (*Realpolitiker*) and managed to obtain a further delay in the issuance of the Nuremberg laws in Danzig.[16] This did not improve the position of the Jews. On 23 October mobs smashed the windows of about three hundred Jewish businesses and dwellings, with damage to other property and isolated cases of assault. The party denied all connection with the rioting, claiming that the NSDAP had better means than the breaking of windows for the reduction of Jewish influence.[17]

There is no proof that the Gauleitung directly instigated this "pogrom." All observers, however, agreed that it was the result of an inflammatory speech given by Forster on 10 October. The matter remains puzzling, since it fits neither the pattern of normal public behavior in the free city nor that of Nazi policy at this time. Burckhardt suggested that Forster's renewed emphasis on anti-Semitism was an attempt to distract attention from the rising cost of living. This seems reasonable. It is likely that some of Forster's followers reacted rather more enthusiastically to his speech than he had intended. He made no attempt to keep the rioting going, and Burckhardt and the Polish commissioner-general, now Marian Chodacki, easily persuaded the senate to end the disturbance. On 27 October eighteen people arrested during the rioting, including one SA man and two other party members, were given sentences ranging from one week to seven months.[18] The severity of the official reaction insured that there would not be a repetition of the rioting in the near future.

The Jewish issue was a sensitive one for all parties. The League had been effectively eliminated as an influence in Danzig's domestic affairs, but the League guarantee still existed. Those governments that participated in the League's Committee of Three (Britain, France, and Sweden) were subjected to pressures from international and native Jewish organizations, which had the sympathy of the political Left. It was therefore possible that the Jewish question would force the League to intervene in Danzig or to withdraw the high commissioner. A withdrawal by the League might seriously disturb Polish-German relations, and for this Hitler was not ready. These factors may explain why Burckhardt was for a time so successful in getting anti-Semitic actions halted or delayed. Both Forster and Greiser had to tread very carefully. Neither could afford to appear to the Führer as "soft" on the Jewish question, even though it was obvious that Hitler desired no international fuss over Danzig.

The riots placed Commissioner-General Chodacki in a difficult and somewhat embarrassing position. Poland had had a long record of persecuting its three million Jewish inhabitants, and anti-Semitism was a major Polish political issue between 1936 and 1939. The senate had often delighted in answering charges of anti-Semitic activity by pointing to similar happenings in Poland.[19] Chodacki, in protesting the riots to Greiser, assured the latter that he had not turned suddenly philo-Semite (*Judenfreund*), but that he was obliged by his official position "to protect the economic interests of Polish citizens, even if they are Jews." Poland's economic relations with Danzig were in good part in the hands of Jewish merchants and agents. If they were excluded or discriminated against, Poland would lose much of its economic position in Danzig. Chodacki's efforts to protect Polish Jews by threatening economic retaliation by Poland were important in delaying or ameliorating the anti-Semitic actions of the Gauleitung.[20]

As for High Commissioner Burckhardt, he has claimed that his attitude toward the Jewish question was motivated by a desire to gain enough time to allow the Jews to emigrate in good order. He believed that their eventual exclusion was inevitable, and he resented the interference of the international Jewish organizations, which loudly protested events in Danzig and demanded that the League take immediate action. The events of 23 October Burckhardt regarded as of little importance, and he tried to prevent the League from taking any action at all. At the same time, he worked hard to prevent any repetition of the riots.[21] Burckhardt's general position will be discussed shortly, but we may note here that the sources provide no reason to doubt his humanitarian motives, whatever the judgment may be on the correctness of his course.

As harassment increased, Danzig's Jews spent 1937 and most of 1938 waiting for the other shoe to drop. That it did not drop for a time was due only to Danzig's international position and to the temporary requirements of German foreign policy. But the omens were ominous by mid-1938. As early as May, Forster announced that Jews would be segregated in the Zoppot resorts and beaches. During the bathing season the police carried out raids on Jewish hotels and rooming houses. Even Jewish tourists from Britain were held and searched.[22] It is worth a passing note that Jewish tourists still came to Danzig, not realizing how much the climate there had deteriorated. The old considerations were no longer working to hold Forster in check, and he began to give freer rein to his anti-Semitic impulses. Autumn brought additional restrictions, particularly on Jewish professionals. Jewish doctors were prevented from practicing, with the exception of two who were to treat Jewish patients only. In November, the members of the association of movie theater owners closed their establishments to Jews. Jews had already been similarly barred from all other public performances and cultural events, without the formality of legislation.[23]

Even more serious than these restrictions on the professions of a few and on the amusements of the many were the repeated attempts made by the Gauleiter to remove the ordinary legal protections still enjoyed by Danzig's Jews. Forster was quite set on introducing the Nuremberg laws and a law banning Jews from the civil service. The planned date was 15 October, the day of the Gau party rally, when the announcement might be made with maximum propagandistic effect. Once again, Burckhardt managed to get the action postponed, but he could do little else. In October there were at least two arrests for the "crime" of "race pollution" (*Rassenschande;* association of Jews with "Aryans" of the opposite sex), which was punishable under the Nuremberg laws, but not yet under Danzig law. As has already been shown, Forster did not like to depend on the courts, no matter how coordinated. The police treated these cases as political matters, outside judicial jurisdiction. The arrested persons were denied the right to counsel on the grounds that the proceedings against them were political rather than criminal. Fines of five thousand gulden in one case and two thousand in another were assessed and paid directly to the police. The victims were then released.[24]

Events outside Danzig came to the aid of the Gauleiter. On 7 November 1938 a young Jew named Herschel Grynszpan attempted to assassinate the German ambassador in Paris. He mistook his man and instead shot the third secretary, Ernst vom Rath. The victim died on 9 November, the anniversary of the Munich Putsch. That night, the "night of broken glass" (*Kristallnacht*), synagogues, Jewish shops, and Jewish residences all over Germany went up in flames or were systematically wrecked. Special anti-Semitic measures were issued on 12 November, and the Jewish community was forced to pay a one billion mark fine. Thirty-five Jews were killed; thousands were temporarily or permanently confined in concentration camps.[25]

Between 12 November and 15 November, Danzig's Nazis imitated their brethren, burning and otherwise damaging synagogues and Jewish stores and residences. On 13 November the Gauleiter declared that the Jewish question would be "thoroughly solved," although he disavowed responsibility for the rioting, much as the party in the Reich had done.[26] On 23 November the Nuremberg laws were published, in part, in Danzig. The "Law for the Protection of German Blood and German Honor" was taken over almost verbatim. This law, passed in the form of a senate decree, forbade sexual relations between Jews and those of "German or related blood." Situations that might lead to such relations, such as the employment of Aryan female servants under forty years of age in Jewish households, were also forbidden. To prevent misunderstanding, the German news agency explained that Poles were Aryans, as defined by the law, and were therefore "protected" equally with Germans from the horrors of miscegenation. Jews now received orders to close their businesses. The solution of the Jewish question moved into its final stages.[27]

On the occasion of the final announcement of the Nuremberg laws, Burckhardt did nothing more than exchange prearranged letters with Greiser. The League's Committee of Three, under the chairmanship of Britain's foreign secretary, Lord Halifax, likewise did nothing.[28] Burckhardt, Halifax, and the League officials in Geneva were not unconcerned with the fate of Danzig's Jews. They simply felt themselves to be powerless. In this they were probably correct, given the general deterioration of the League's position. They considered ways of aiding the Jews but could do little beyond helping a few individuals.[29]

The Jewish community had shrunk by about fifteen hundred people over the preceding year, to a total of six thousand. Most of those who had left were Polish citizens. The two thousand Jewish Polish citizens who remained still enjoyed some protection thanks to the commissioner-general and could in any case return to Poland with little difficulty. There were perhaps one thousand additional Jews, some of whom had the wealth and personal connections to emigrate privately, and the rest of whom were too old or sick to leave, whatever happened. This left three thousand Jews who desperately wanted to emigrate, albeit with regrets, but who had no place to go. The Jewish community at first expected that it would be easy to find room somewhere for such a small group with a special claim on the attention of international authorities.[30] Jewish hopes were disappointed. Ways and means were considered and reconsidered, but neither the League nor any member state of the Committee of Three made any move to help. The Jews began to panic and with good reason.

Over two thousand Jews gathered in the Great Synagogue on 17 December. They were addressed by one of their number,

Hermann Segall, who informed them that the Danzig authorities demanded immediate emigration. Were this demand rejected, worse treatment would surely follow. To Danzig's Jews, the choice was clear. Either emigrate or face total impoverishment, physical attack, and the concentration camp. The congregation gave unanimous approval to a resolution announcing their willingness to emigrate. Hermann Segall took over all arrangements.[31]

Segall was a strange choice. He was a "Revisionist," a member of a Zionist splinter group that had finally left the Zionist organization in 1935, after several years of internal combat. The international leader of the Revisionists, Vladimir Jabotinsky, preached immediate and massive immigration to Palestine, particularly from eastern Europe, regardless of British and Arab objections. Jabotinsky's radical disregard for legality, his role in forming armed "defense" groups in Palestine, and his declarations that "class warfare" had no place in Zionism, offended both conservative and Labor Zionists. The Revisionists were widely regarded as militarists and fascists by other Zionists and by non-Zionist Jews.[32] Most of the Jewish leaders in Danzig had this same reaction to Revisionists. They felt Segall was a "dangerous international crook" who had visions of himself as the fascist leader of a Jewish state in Palestine. But Segall enjoyed a good relationship with the police, who agreed with him that Jews ought to leave Danzig as soon as possible. He acted as liaison between the police and the Jews, and he cooperated actively with the police in organizing the meeting in the Great Synagogue on 17 December.[33]

That the leaders of Danzig's Jewish community allowed themselves to be guided by Segall is an indication of their desperation. Dr. Itzig, the president of the congregation, had gone to London. Instead of aid, he had received a Home Office decision that Danzig Jews would not be given special treatment in immigration to Britain. The international and British Jewish organizations offered no assistance.[34] The Jews of Danzig were tainted. Danzig did not come under the jurisdiction of the League high commissioner for refugees, since a widening of that official's competence would have meant a public admission that the League had failed in Danzig. The British wished to help but had their hands tied by considerations of foreign policy and domestic immigration politics. The efforts of Segall only made matters worse, since they involved the Jews in a plot to force entry into Palestine, and since they assured the noncooperation of the more established Jewish organizations that had influence in London.

Burckhardt seems at this point to have written off the Jews. On the other hand, the British consul, Gerald Shepherd, grew quite frantic. It was his duty to do everything possible to dissuade his contacts in the Jewish leadership from carrying out Segall's plan for illegal immigration to Palestine, a British mandate. But considering the probable consequences to the Jews if they should break their agreement with the Danzig police, Shepherd did not see how he could, in good conscience, advise them to do so. Despite a sharp reprimand from his superiors, he fulfilled his duty unenthusiastically at best. Relations between Shepherd and Burckhardt grew strained, partly because of the Jewish question, and partly because Shepherd became convinced that Burckhardt was more concerned with keeping his post than with serving a useful function. The Foreign Office tended to place greater trust in Burckhardt than in its own man in Danzig.

But neither Burckhardt nor Shepherd could much affect the situation. The police and Segall continued their close cooperation. The police did behave very well, under the circumstances, and there was no brutal treatment of the helpless Jewish population. On 3 March, the first transport of almost five hundred Jews left Danzig bound for Palestine via Romania. There were no incidents, and the group left, in rather good humor, before dawn. After considerable hardship and delay, the Danzigers were landed in Palestine on 1 July. The authorities apparently allowed them to stay. For these Jews, a grim story had a happy ending. Fortunately, it was not necessary for all the Jews in Danzig to leave in this manner. Some, mostly children, were finally admitted to Britain and Palestine legally, for "educational purposes." Others found other ways to various places of refuge.[35]

In the meantime, the senate concentrated on making life as difficult as possible for those Jews who still remained, and on making as much profit as possible out of their emigration. The situation of Danzig Jews was not now notably different from that of Jews in the Reich. Only the position of the Polish Jews was exceptional. For a time, many Polish Jews were exempted from discriminatory economic ordinances if their activities were important to Danzig's export-import trade.[36] In the Reich, thousands of Jews with Polish citizenship were simply pushed across the border at intervals after October 1938, despite Polish attempts to keep them out. In Danzig the senate, out of consideration for Polish feelings, did not at first effectively prevent Polish Jews from taking up residence. Even though more Polish Jews left Danzig than arrived, a certain influx continued. Many of these people did have interests in Danzig, and the situation for them in Poland was difficult in any case.[37] Only as relations with Poland deteriorated were Polish Jews kept from settling in Danzig and eventually subjected to the same pressures as their coreligionists.

There were approximately seventeen hundred Jews remaining on 1 September 1939 when their fate seemed sealed by the opening of hostilities. Some five hundred of them did manage to leave in a mass transport in August 1940. They reached Palestine in 1945, after internment in Mauritius. Almost all of the rest were thrown into concentration camps or deported into the rump Polish reserve run by the Nazis as the "Government-General of Poland." Several hundred old and sick Jews remained in a "ghetto," an ancient grain elevator converted into an old people's home. In March 1941 the majority were transported to the Warsaw ghetto or murdered near Lublin. In early 1943, the last of the ghetto Jews were sent to Theresienstadt. Only about one hundred Jews remained, married to Aryans. Perhaps fifty of these were still living in Danzig at the end of the Second World War.[38]

Danzig Politics in the Climate of Approaching War

The unhappy story just concluded provides some insights into the way Danzig's politics were conducted in the last years of the free city's existence. A much smaller matter is also rich in implications. On 1 May 1938 Gauleiter Forster announced that the Volkstag would convene on 20 June. This rare session was to celebrate the fifth anniversary of the formation of the first Nazi government in Danzig. All seventy German deputies would appear in brown shirts to symbolize their allegiance to the NSDAP. The British objected, through the high commissioner, and the French and British press wondered what measures would be adopted at the forthcoming meeting—constitutional amendments, alterations in the election law, the introduction of the Nuremberg laws? The Gauleitung did in fact intend to have the senate introduce new laws against the Jews and adopt a new swastika flag for Danzig. But these intentions were foiled by the German Foreign Office and by Burckhardt. Bülow's successor as secretary of state in the Foreign Office, Baron Ernst von Weizsäcker, conferred with Greiser and Forster. The new foreign minister, Joachim von Ribbentrop, had Forster personally promise that the planned laws would not be introduced. Burckhardt obtained permission from the British Foreign Office to warn authorities in Danzig and the Reich that the laws would embarrass the chairman of the Committee of Three, Lord Halifax. At the same time, Burckhardt promised the Germans that he would do everything in his power to insure that Halifax would remain friendly to Danzig.[39]

The meeting of the Volkstag on 20 June was purely ceremonial. A number of deputies had just laid down their mandates after subjection to the usual pressures, and two had fled abroad. Their places were taken by Nazis. As instructed, all the deputies, with the exception of the two Poles, appeared in brown shirts. In his speech, Greiser castigated the international press for mistakenly reporting that certain laws would be passed in the session.[40] The Gauleitung thus had its formal celebration of the political *Gleichschaltung* of the free city but was prevented from making legal changes that might have forced the League council to take up the Danzig question once again.

The Volkstag meeting provides an excellent illustration of the manner in which Danzig's affairs were conducted in 1938. The initiative in political matters came from the Gauleiter, who was secure in the knowledge that he held the favor of the Führer, and who had a strong hold over the senate as head of the party. Greiser had to give way in any disagreement with the Gauleiter, unless pressure could be brought to bear from outside the free city. In the case of the brown-shirted Volkstag session this pressure was forthcoming, and Forster had to modify some of his plans.

As the hapless Gerald Shepherd put it, the political atmosphere in Danzig at this time "would sometimes justify the use of a gas mask." [41] Greiser, pushed to the wall by Forster, resorted to every trick he could think of to strengthen his position in the party. Forster found that Hess, Göring, and Ribbentrop regarded him as a meddlesome troublemaker, and Himmler for the moment remained aloof. But Goebbels was with the Gauleiter and so was Hitler. This last was of course what mattered most. Under the circumstances, the only real hope for Greiser was Forster's possible transfer away from Danzig. Early in 1938, Forster was mentioned as Papen's successor as German ambassador in Vienna. Both Burckhardt and Greiser took these rumors seriously, and Greiser was full of plans for a new regime in Danzig. But the matter came to nothing, and Forster was denied any important role in the *Anschluss of* Austria. Embittered by his failure to have any influence on Nazi politics outside Danzig, Forster became even more intransigent on domestic matters. Somewhat shaken in his political confidence, he outdid himself in the anti-Semitic sphere, and the greatest efforts by Burckhardt and Greiser were needed to hold him even formally in check. Danzig, at least, was his, and he was determined to mold it after his own image.[42]

The course of events in Danzig depended on the general international situation and particularly on Hitler's intentions. Until the final destruction of Czechoslovakia in March 1939, Forster's control over Danzig's policy was limited, although with decreasing effectiveness, by those in Danzig and the Reich who still hoped that war could be avoided. Thereafter, when Hitler turned his attention fully to Poland and Danzig, Forster took control of affairs in the free city, in cooperation with German military authorities, to prepare for its return to the Reich. Those circles in Germany and Danzig interested in the preservation of peace were faced with a delicate situation, both before and after March 1939. Events in Danzig could, in general, be allowed to follow the lines desired by the Gauleiter. The opposition would be rooted out, and national socialism would continue its penetration of every aspect of public life. On the other hand, Forster had to be denied any move, no matter what its uplifting propagandistic effect within Danzig or the Reich, which would indicate an imminent change in the international status of the free city. League involvement particularly had to be avoided, given Britain's predominant role in that organization. After the Munich agreement, the British government faced mounting pressure from domestic groups demanding strong action against Hitler's aggression. Britain's League responsibilities in Danzig made the free city an important factor in the development of Anglo-German relations during this crucial period.

Poland was much more directly affected by Hitler's conquest of Austria and Czechoslovakia than was Britain. Foreign Minister Beck, in following a policy of cooperation with Germany, hoped to divert German pressure from Poland and at the same time share in the benefits of Hitler's diplomatic victories by annexing portions of Czechoslovakia. In regard to Danzig, Polish policy at first concentrated on defending existing rights in the free city and on obtaining a specific German guarantee of those rights.[43] Beck, like the British, faced powerful domestic pressure from those leftists and nationalists who disagreed with any policy that smacked of "appeasement." If war was to be avoided, it was vital that Forster and his cohorts not be allowed to provide the British and the Poles with additional evidence of the futility of cooperation with Hitler.

A key role in the process of keeping Forster under control was played by Carl J. Burckhardt, a Swiss professor of history who had assumed the post of high commissioner in March 1937. Burckhardt has been attacked as a Nazi sympathizer.[44] It would be better to say, with William Strang of the British Foreign Office, that Burckhardt was "not a strong anti-Hitlerite." [45] The picture that emerges from the documents and from Burckhardt's *Meine Danziger Mission* is that of a conservative, a believer in authoritative, but not authoritarian, government. Burckhardt, while genuinely horrified at Nazi atrocities, nonetheless "collaborated" with the Nazis in trying to convince both Britain and Poland to be cooperative toward the Third Reich. At the same time, he attempted to encourage moderate forces within Germany.[46]

The circumstances of Burckhardt's appointment have been described in his book, which relies heavily on League of Nations files.[47] His instructions from Eden, French Foreign Minister Yvon Delbos, and Secretary-General Joseph Avenol were that the high commissioner was no longer to be unduly concerned with Danzig's internal affairs. Instead, he was to keep Danzig-Polish relations running smoothly. The free city was to be kept off the agenda of the council as much as possible. Burckhardt's mission was further defined for him by R. C. Skrine Stevenson of the British Foreign Office. Stevenson explained that the high commissioner ought to so cultivate relations with the senate that the League guarantee of the constitution would not be called into dispute.

> His main object in so doing would be to protect as far as lay in his power the Opposition in Danzig. The establishment of a full National-Socialist régime was probably inevitable, but he might be able to moderate the pace at which it was carried through.

In short, the new high commissioner was to carry out a policy already decided upon, in its essentials, in the last months of Sean Lester's tenure. It was implied by Stevenson that the council would withdraw from the Danzig situation entirely if Burckhardt could not succeed in keeping Danzig off the council agenda.[48]

Burckhardt viewed his mission in these terms, and it cannot be said that he failed to carry out his instructions, insofar as they could be carried out. The only alternative left to him was resignation, and he chose not to resign. Certainly, the victims of national socialism would not have been materially helped by such an action. There is no doubt that the League was prepared to terminate its guarantee if Burckhardt resigned, or if the Danzig situation became an impossible liability. This further weakened Burckhardt's position in Danzig. He had no serious threats to work with—only bluffs.

Burckhardt had already formed a close personal relationship with Baron von Weizsäcker, who had been German minister to Switzerland prior to becoming secretary of state.[49] Weizsäcker informed Burckhardt, soon after the latter's appointment, that it would be arranged for the German consulates in Danzig and

Geneva to forward only the most positive reports on the new high commissioner, reports designed to attract the favorable attention of Hitler. In fact, all documents dealing with Burckhardt in the files of the German Foreign Office present him as sympathetic to Germany and to national socialism, as an admirer of Hitler, and even as an anti-Semite.[50] The authors of these documents, Weizsäcker, the German consuls in Geneva and Danzig, Greiser, and Viktor Böttcher, head of the senate foreign department, were building up Burckhardt's reputation in Berlin in order to forward their common goals—German-British cooperation, at least temporary avoidance of conflict with Poland, and a slow evolution of *Gleichschaltung* in Danzig. Burckhardt's authority was also used by the German Foreign Office and Danzig officials in attempts to discredit Gauleiter Forster.[51]

In Berlin, Burckhardt worked most closely with Weizsäcker, but he also found Göring helpful in keeping a rein on Forster.[52] In 1938, at least, Himmler seemed willing to cooperate in putting pressure on the Gauleiter.[53] In Danzig, Burckhardt had the cooperation of the German consuls, whose relations with Forster were very poor, and who in any case regarded Weizsäcker as their superior. Greiser cooperated wholeheartedly with Burckhardt and supported him vigorously in Berlin. Burckhardt's explanation of Greiser's conduct was simple: "he liked being the President of a Free State and felt that his position would be one of complete insignificance in the event of any further changes." Burckhardt, for his part, compared Greiser favorably with Forster at every opportunity. He even hinted to London that more positive British press coverage of Greiser's activities (and of his own) would be appreciated.[54]

As has been indicated, political opposition in Danzig ceased almost entirely by 1938. Burckhardt did nothing to halt this process, and there is little that he could have done, given the demonstrated unwillingness of the Poles and the League council to interfere.[55] Opposition may well have continued underground, despite the emigration or disappearance of most of the former opposition leaders. In August 1938 the British press reported that a secret "freedom transmitter" was broadcasting from Danzig. There were also reports of opposition leaflets being distributed on the eve of Hitler's birthday, 20 April 1939.[56] Available sources do not permit a thorough evaluation of these and similar reports. But there is no question that Burckhardt and other interested foreigners could not rely on non-Nazi forces to bring about a change for the better from within Danzig. One former leader of the socialist opposition, in exile in Warsaw, informed Burckhardt that his comrades in Danzig lacked the will to resist further.[57] Burckhardt placed all his hopes on Greiser.

Within the senate, Greiser controlled the Department of Foreign Affairs until the very end. Its officials, headed by Viktor Böttcher and his subordinate, Dr. Blume, formed part of the "conspiracy" to slow down Forster. Tenuous as it was, Greiser's remaining hold on power gave Burckhardt reason for optimism. In September 1938, he informed the members of the Committee of Three that Himmler's support had somewhat strengthened Greiser, that the senate president was far more popular in Danzig than the Gauleiter, and that Danzigers were weary of Forster's Nazi enthusiasms. Burckhardt foresaw "the evolution of a stable little authoritarian state with a disposition to cooperate with the League." [58] His wishful thinking had lured him into absurdity.

The weakness of the Greiser-Burckhardt-Weizsäcker combination against Forster was shown by the introduction of anti-Semitic legislation in November 1938—precisely the formal breach of the constitution that Burckhardt had tried so hard to avoid. The reasons for this failure are not to be sought in Danzig. A resistance circle in the Reich, led by General Ludwig Beck, had planned to overthrow Hitler in early September. It was expected that a strong British stand against Hitler's demands on Czechoslovakia would convince the German people that Hitler was headed for war. The German Foreign Office group around Weizsäcker accordingly urged the British to take such a stand. Among other intermediaries, Weizsäcker used Burckhardt. But this plan, which had the approval of Beck and other high military officers, failed when Neville Chamberlain decided to make his famous series of visits to Hitler, culminating in the Munich conference of 29–30 September. The Foreign Office group now successfully concentrated all its efforts on bringing about a peaceful solution to the Czech crisis.[59]

Despite Prime Minister Chamberlain's belief that he had finally reached an understanding with Hitler, the latter strongly denounced British interference in Germany's affairs, in a speech at Saarbrücken on 9 October.[60] The Munich conference had apparently only increased Hitler's contempt for the British. A major weapon was torn from the hands of Burckhardt and his friends in Germany and Danzig. Weizsäcker realized this and no longer attempted to hold Forster in check with arguments based on possible British disapproval of the Gauleiter's activities. He appealed to Ribbentrop to control Forster on the grounds that impending negotiations with Poland over Danzig and the corridor would be endangered if Forster had his way. But the tactic was unsuccessful. In November, Ribbentrop simply told Forster that no attention need be paid to Lord Halifax or Britain in introducing the new anti-Semitic laws. Forster had his way. In despair, Burckhardt announced to the British and the Danzigers that he planned to resign.[61]

But there was still the matter of Polish feelings. On 24 October 1938 the Germans first proposed to the Poles that Danzig be returned to the Reich and that an extraterritorial highway and rail corridor be granted to Germany across the Polish corridor. These suggestions were flatly rejected by Foreign Minister Beck. Beck himself suggested that the time had come to replace the League mandate with a direct Polish-German agreement, but that agreement would have to guarantee the continued existence of the free city and uphold all present Polish rights. German pressure against Poland was slow in mounting, largely because of continued concern with Czechoslovakia. In early December a remarkable thing happened. Forster, who had continually snubbed the high commissioner, informed him that his further presence in Danzig would be desirable. The Germans wanted Burckhardt to remain, at least until a total solution to the Danzig-corridor question was ready.[62]

Hitler had not yet resolved on a war with Poland, and he had not yet given up the idea that the Poles might be useful allies in an eventual war with the Soviet Union. Both Poland and Germany were growing nervous about the situation in the free city. It seemed to Burckhardt that he could perform a valuable service by remaining high commissioner. He could assist in keeping domestic affairs in Danzig under control by advising both Greiser and Forster, since the latter was now under the restraint of higher orders. Burckhardt could help to ease the relations of the two major powers concerned by functioning as an intermediary between Warsaw and Berlin. He was also convinced of the essential reasonableness of Hitler's demands, and at first he may have entertained hopes of using his knowledge of German-Polish negotiations to convince the British of Hitler's good intentions. It does not seem to have disturbed him that his continued tenure in Danzig in fact only served German policy, the ends of which he possibly misunderstood. We may have some sympathy with Consul Shepherd, who angrily denounced Burckhardt to London. Shepherd felt that Burckhardt's continued presence in Danzig did little beyond making the League appear "ludicrous." [63] But it was well known in London that Shepherd had been suffering from an acute attack of conscience since the revival of anti-Semitic persecution, and his views were no longer heeded.

The Germans proceeded cautiously. Ribbentrop continued negotiations in Warsaw in January. Outwardly at least, German-Polish relations remained harmonious until March 1939. Ribbentrop evidently believed that the Poles would eventually give in to the German demands.[64] He therefore continued to put pressure on Forster to prevent any provocation of the Poles. The Gauleiter had to moderate the aggressive tone he had adopted toward Poland just after the Munich conference, and he had to postpone such projects as the official introduction of the "German salute" and the swastika flag.[65]

On 15 March 1939 the Germans occupied Prague and destroyed the rump Czechoslovakia that had been left after Munich. On the twenty-first, Hitler's demands on the Poles regarding Danzig and the corridor were renewed. On the twenty-second, the Germans occupied Memel. The Poles may have been reluctantly considering a minimal territorial compromise, but if so, Hitler's new surprises encouraged them to abandon the notion.[66] After the German occupation of Prague, the British grew worried about apparent Nazi threats to Romania and were further concerned by the renewal of German demands on Poland. Halifax in particular gained the impression that Hitler's plans were very far-reaching and that they could only be stopped by a strong Anglo-French stand. On 31 March Chamberlain announced in the House of Commons that Britain and France would support Poland should a situation arise "which clearly threatened Polish independence, and which the Polish Government accordingly considered it vital to resist with their national forces." Beck then visited London, and a more detailed agreement was reached on 6 April. At this point, German-Polish relations were at complete stalemate. There was no longer any possibility of compromise. This may not have been clear to all parties. Despite the British guarantee to Poland, Chamberlain, along with High Commissioner Burckhardt and Burckhardt's friends in Germany, continued to assume that a peaceful settlement could be worked out that would give Danzig back to Germany and eliminate the city as a potential cause of war. This prognosis was invalidated only by the Polish government's refusal to yield to Hitler.[67]

On 28 April Hitler told the Reichstag of the "generous" offers he had made to the Poles, and he added, "Danzig is a German city and wishes to belong to Germany." [68] This sentence became the theme for German propaganda, as all former consideration for Polish feelings was dropped. In Danzig, propaganda turned viciously anti-Polish, in a manner reminiscent of the days before the Nazi takeover of power.[69] Germany's policy against Poland was now clear. It remained only for Danzig's Nazis to do their part.

Military Preparations in Danzig and the Final Conflict with Poland

Linguistically, Danzig was a German city. We shall never know what percentage of the population wished to return to Nazi Germany, especially since Forster decided not to hold the elections that constitutionally were due in the spring of 1939. By mid-March of that year, Polish-German relations had lost even their surface friendliness. The Polish political forces in the free city may have planned to run more than two candidates for the Volkstag. With all the German opposition parties dissolved, a percentage of the Danzig opposition would certainly have voted for Polish candidates, with unpredictable results. A totally fraudulent election would have been difficult to manage under the eyes of Commissioner-General Chodacki, who was alert for a chance to increase Polish influence in Danzig and to win a victory for Poland in the international battle being waged over Danzig and the corridor. Any increase in the number of Polish mandates over the two already held would have been a propagandistic disaster for the Reich and might have weakened Forster's internal party position. On 22 March the senate accordingly announced that, since the present Volkstag represented the will of the population perfectly, the needless expense of an election would be avoided, and the terms of the deputies would be prolonged for an additional four years. The decision casually destroyed the last vestige of constitutional government in Danzig, as the League's legal experts pointed out. But Geneva was by now too paralyzed to take any action whatsoever.[70]

Since the elections were not held, public opinion in Danzig remains a mystery. German patriotism may have been so strong that even union with Hitler's Third Reich appeared attractive to non-Nazis. But there was a snag. By the spring of 1939 it was apparent that a Danzig *Anschluss* could be accomplished only by war. Should this occur, the city itself would be a strategic area of considerable importance and might well become a battlefield. Reunion with the Reich might be accomplished only at the cost of major physical destruction and loss of life, a prospect no Danziger could contemplate with indifference. Forster was no exception. In 1938 and 1939, a large portion of the Nazi domestic effort went toward bolstering the defense capability of the free city and toward contributing to German war preparations. By encouraging this activity, Forster did more than protect his city and his Gau. He insured himself a continued position of influence as the emphasis of German policy shifted from the political to the military sphere.

Prior to 1935, the best-trained and best-equipped "military" force in the demilitarized free city had been the territorial police (*Landespolizei*). In that year, War Minister Werner von Blomberg declared that he was no longer interested in its maintenance, since the German funds used for its support could be better used for the rearmament of the Reich. It was accordingly decided to disband the *Landespolizei* and to transfer its personnel to the German army.[71] This did not mean that patriotic young men would in the future be denied the opportunity to serve their fatherland. The arrangements whereby Danzig citizens could serve as volunteers in the German army without losing their Danzig citizenship (and thus becoming ineligible for a possible future election or plebiscite) were settled by July 1935. The police then set up recruitment centers for volunteers. A certain Major Besser, a retired German army officer, was put in charge of recruitment. The police in each district sent out "invitations" to eligible young men, who then reported to recruitment meetings and were addressed by Major Besser. Poles and Jews who had been invited by mistake were excused, and pressure of various kinds was applied to the young German Danzigers who remained. Major Besser frequently implied that those who failed to volunteer would have employment problems. His tactics caused some stir in the Polish press in March 1936. Lester's subsequent inquiries were met by Greiser's assurance that the Danzig authorities had no part in such actions.[72] There the matter rested, and recruitment for the German army was allowed to continue undisturbed, although Besser was replaced.

In August 1937, President Greiser, who had himself taken several weeks of military training in the Reich, ordered all Danzig officials of the appropriate age to "volunteer" for two years of German army service before 1 January 1938.[73] In some respects, then, conscription existed in the free city. In general, the senate cooperated fully with the Reich military authorities on all matters affecting Danzig's place in a future conflict. In particular, the potential military roles of Danzig's harbor, shipyards, and merchant fleet were analyzed so that quick use could be made of them in case of war.[74]

In the last year of peace, the emphasis shifted away from the supply of German army manpower. As early as September 1938, Army Commander in Chief Walther von Brauchitsch informed Forster that recruits from Danzig were no longer needed in the Reich.[75] Instead, military efforts concentrated on the defense of the free city and its preparation as a possible staging area for an invasion of Poland. This was no easy matter. The military installations that had once existed in and around the city had been dismantled or converted to other uses under the provisions of the Treaty of Versailles. The authorities had at their disposal only a few former cavalry barracks that had been used by the police. On the other side, there was the fortified Polish munitions dump on the Westerplatte, which commanded the entrance to the inner harbor. Polish railway and post office employees were being organized into an irregular military force, with some professionally conducted training. The main railway station and the harbor post office were potential Polish fortresses in the heart of the city. The railways themselves, with the exception of the narrow-gauge local spurs, were in Polish hands.

Natural and political geography added further problems. There was no bridge over the Vistula north of the town of Tczew (Dirschau) on the Polish-Danzig border. Thanks to the decision of the Paris Peace Conference, the entire span of the Tczew railway bridge was in Polish territory. As the event later proved, the bridge had been mined and could easily be blown up to halt any German advance across the river from East Prussia through Danzig territory. Under these circumstances, both the Poles and their British friends had good grounds for believing that the Polish army could beat the Germans in a race for the city of Danzig itself.[76] Rumors of an impending coup in Danzig could be safely disregarded, since the Germans did not possess the military force and position in the area to back it up.

This weakness remained through early May 1939, despite the ever-present possibility of German naval support for a coup. But from mid-May until the beginning of the war, there was a steady flow of German military men into Danzig, and the free city was thoroughly fortified. The German army was preparing for a total solution to the Polish question—a solution that would involve far more than the return of Danzig to the Reich. Military cooperation between the Reich and the free city became almost open. An "SS Home Defense Force" (*SS-Heimwehr*) was formed and armed. Officially it was a party organization, but in practice it functioned as part of the German army. Most of its members mates of increasing German strength in Danzig to their papers, and foreign consulates were in a position to send back very complete reports. Most open of all was the construction of a pontoon bridge across the Vistula in Danzig territory so that troops from East Prussia could bypass Tczew. Another pontoon bridge was built across the Nogat River between East Prussia and the free city near Elbing, to supplement the older bridge at Marienburg. Poland's initial advantage of local position was destroyed. Very soon large stocks of ammunition and other military supplies were arriving nightly at the docks and across the border with East Prussia. When the fighting began, Danzig was militarily prepared.[77]

Beginning in May, the Nazi propaganda campaign in Danzig was turned on full blast. The principal subjects of the attack were the Polish customs inspectors who supervised the work of the Danzig Customs Office. They were boycotted and mobbed, targets of insults and bricks. On 21 May in the aftermath of an attack on the building housing Polish customs inspectors in the border village of Kalthof, a Danziger was shot to death by a chauffeur of the Polish commissariat-general. Negotiations on the issue of customs inspectors were conducted in an atmosphere of increasing tension and violence. Danzig's legal case against the powers of the customs inspectors, who had frequently used their position to increase Polish control over the economy of the free city, was rather a good one. Had an amicable settlement been desired, it could easily have been reached. But this was not the point. The dispute had the practical effect of disorganizing Polish supervision of customs, so that German military shipments could slip in uncounted. Furthermore, the attacks on the customs inspectors were Danzig's contribution to the German diplomatic offensive.[78] The Germans used this issue as they used the issue of alleged mistreatment of the German minority in Poland to prepare their own people for war and to isolate the Poles internationally.

Events in Danzig played little part in the diplomatic negotiations that preceded the outbreak of the war. Like people everywhere in Europe, the inhabitants of Danzig waited nervously for the Führer to make his decision. Since their city might well be the scene of considerable military action, they were perhaps a little more nervous than most. In late August, it was reported that Danzigers were sending their wives and children to the Reich for safety.[79] Foreign visitors tended to stay away from Danzig in the summer of 1939, and the natives had the beaches all to themselves. But despite the absence of foreigners and the inconveniences occasioned by military construction in and around the city, life continued in a more or less normal fashion. The city waited for others to decide its fate.

On 19 August German Consul-General Richard von Janson was sent a sealed envelope by his superiors in Berlin, with instructions to open it when he received a telegram with the code word "Fishing" (*Fischen*).[80] On 23 August Hitler set the attack on Poland for 4:30 A.M., 26 August.[81] Also on the twenty-third the senate named Gauleiter Forster the head of state (*Staatsoberhaupt*) of Danzig.[82] Greiser's feelings may be imagined. Even before the return of Danzig to the Reich, Forster won his long struggle with the president of the senate. When the union of free city with Reich was proclaimed, it would be Forster, not Greiser, who would have the honor of signing the appropriate pieces of paper.

In mid-May, the German consulate had been informed that the cruiser *Königsberg* would arrive in Danzig on 25 August to participate in a ceremony honoring German naval war dead. On 24 August the consulate learned that the *Königsberg* was having engine trouble and that the training ship *Schleswig-Holstein* would arrive instead.[83] At 8:50 P.M. on the twenty-fifth, Janson received a telegram that read: "26 Fishing 4:30." The sealed envelope was to be opened at 4:30 the following morning. But not quite one hour later, a second telegram arrived, canceling the first.[84] The British Parliament had finally ratified the Polish

with [illegible]
than helpless [illegible]
another telegram: "I Fishing [illegible]
1 September, the consul-general learned [illegible]
captains of German vessels not to leave port, and to requ[illegible] senate similarly to inform neutral ships, since "military operations must be reckoned with in the entire Bay of Danzig." In the harbor, the *Schleswig-Holstein* turned its guns toward the Westerplatte. At the borders of the free city, the *SS-Heimwehr* and their German army comrades pushed over the red-and-white boundary posts of the Republic of Poland and machine-gunned the buildings of the Polish frontier guards. Within the city, police and army units surrounded the Polish post office and the main railway station, which had already been garrisoned by their small Polish contingents. Shooting soon began. Later in the morning, Forster turned up at the League High Commission and ordered Burckhardt to leave. After a little hasty packing, Burckhardt and his small staff departed by automobile for East Prussia, headed for neutral Lithuania. As a small crowd watched, the swastika flag was raised over the high commission building, which had once been the headquarters of the German army command in West Prussia. And so came the moment for which Danzig had waited for over nineteen years. Back to the Reich, for better or worse.[86]

8 Epilogue: The War Years, 1939–45

Danzig returned to the Reich as soon as the Second World War began.* The political struggles that had marked the history of the Gau Danzig of the NSDAP did not cease, but they were transformed in the wartime context. The change in formal political authority posed an old question in a new form: What was to be the precise nature of the relationship between the Gau leadership and the central organs of the Third Reich? It was certain that, now as ever, the will of the Führer would be obeyed. But the content of the Fürer's will was by no means clear. Equally uncertain were the channels through which it would be expressed. Hitler's primary interests during the war were defined by the crucial diplomatic, economic, and military factors that determined the course of the conflict. He had little time or energy left for affairs in Danzig, which now seemed to have a purely local significance. Since Hitler could not make every decision himself and was often not even consulted, the field was left open for continual conflict among those individuals and agencies interested in the area.

The local winner in these struggles was Gauleiter Albert Forster. It has already been made abundantly clear that Forster's position within the NSDAP did not depend on the standard that might be used in an efficient, achievement-oriented state to measure political success or failure. Forster had misjudged the political situation in the free city and had helped to create and to keep alive a united opposition. He had hastened the ruin of Danzig's economy with foolish financial measures. He had

* With permission, use has been made in this chapter of material contained in my article, "Local Authority and the SS State: The Conflict over Population Policy in Danzig-West Prussia, 1939–1945," published in *Central European History* 2, no. 4 (December 1969): 331–55.

lowered the prestige of the local party by allowing and participating in corrupt practices. He had raised Polish suspicions and had obstructed German foreign policy. But despite all these blunders, he had never lost control of his Gau. His continued success depended, not on his ability to produce objectively verifiable achievements as a regional administrator, but on his skill as a National Socialist politician.

After the outbreak of war, Forster's entire political effort was aimed at retaining and expanding power already won, in a markedly altered situation. But although the war changed much in Danzig and in the neighboring "former Polish territories," it did nothing to alter the basic structure of Nazi politics. At the most, the tensions of war accentuated tendencies already present before 1939. But now there were more pawns in Forster's game —the 1.5 million inhabitants of the annexed Polish province of Pomorze.

On 1 September 1939 the "head of state" of the Free City of Danzig exchanged telegrams with the Führer of the German Reich. Hitler and Forster, in accordance with preconcerted arrangements, declared the territory of the free city to be part of Germany. This declaration was soon confirmed by military events. The pitifully small Polish garrisons in the Polish post office and the railway station surrendered during the first day of the war. The Westerplatte could hold out only a little longer. With virtually no damage done to the city, German forces from East Prussia swept beyond and around Danzig, to join with units from Pomerania and Silesia in the rapid conquest of Poland.[1]

On 8 October Hitler announced the new organization of the "former" Polish western provinces. The pattern of administration remained essentially unchanged until 1945.[2] The bulk of the old Prussian province of Posen (Poznan) was incorporated into the Reich as the Warthegau (officially changed in 1940 to Reichsgau Wartheland), the territory of the River Warthe (Warta). Further north, the Führer created the Reichsgau Danzig-West Prussia. The new Reichsgau was not entirely identical with the old Prussian province of West Prussia as it had existed before the Treaty of Versailles. It included two Kreise that had once been part of Russian Poland, and one, the Kreis Bromberg (Bydgoszcz), that had been part of the province of Posen. The West Prussian Kreise that had been left to Germany on the western edge of the corridor were not included, but the Reichsgau did gain five West Prussian Kreise that had been administered as part of East Prussia between 1920 and 1939. Danzig-West Prussia now comprised three distinct elements: the former free city, areas that had never been separated from the Reich and had been part of the Gau East Prussia, and former Polish territories.

The greater part of the Reichsgau, including the city of Gdynia, was formed by the Polish province of Pomorze, the northern segment of the corridor. The port of Gdynia was now jointly administered with Danzig's harbor, and the old competition between the two cities came to an end, although the reorganization had little practical significance during a war that brought commercial shipping to a virtual standstill. For symbolic reasons Gdynia was renamed Gotenhafen, after the Germanic Goths who had allegedly frequented the area. The change of name could not alter the fact that the city, with the rest of Pomorze, was almost entirely Polish in population. Gdynia felt the effects of German occupation with particular severity, and the population declined by as many as fifty thousand people during the first two years of the war.[3]

The administration of the "incorporated territories" required an enormous number of officials, who were hard to come by under wartime conditions. At first, the only German civilian officials in the former Polish areas were the newly appointed Kreisleiter of the NSDAP, who received civil appointments as district governors (Landräte). Most of the new Kreisleiter were men who had risen in the Danzig party organization and had served as Ortsgruppenleiter and staff officials.[4] They were Forster's men. Native members of the German minority in the former Polish territories, whatever their role in the long struggle against Polonization between the wars, were denied any significant part in the administration of the Reichsgau. The Danzig party organization simply expanded to include the Polish territory and remained under the control of the Gauleiter.

A shortage of administrative officials to serve the Kreisleiter did lead to the transfer of personnel from the Old Reich, as the prewar German territory was called. The new men never played an important political role in the Reichsgau. In any case, working conditions in the former corridor were not designed to attract the best talents. The Polish population was hostile, and few administrators wished to work in these rural areas, isolated from German "civilization." The established local administrations of the Old Reich had no desire to give up good men, when military conscription had already left them shorthanded. The eastern areas of the Greater German Reich tended to be staffed by the overaged and the incompetent. Danzig-West Prussia was no exception. It was sometimes even necessary to employ the services of former Polish officials.[5]

The highest local authority in Danzig-West Prussia was Forster, in a dual capacity as Gauleiter and Reichsstatthalter (governor). In general, the old distinction between party and state no longer made any sense. In the rural areas, with their shortage of personnel, the party and the state hierarchies were absolutely identical. Forster's authority as Gauleiter was exercised through the old Gauleitung, now run by a new deputy Gauleiter, Otto Andres, who was replaced in 1942 by Gerhard Seeger. The senate of the free city was transformed into the Office of the Governor (Reichsstatthalterei), which was directed by former Vice-President Wilhelm Huth, as Forster's deputy for governmental affairs. Most of the government departments were headed by senators from the free city period who had worked closely with Forster, including Julius Hoppenrath and Willibald Wiercinski-Keiser.[6] The equivalent departments in Gauleitung and government were usually headed by the same individuals, old Danzig party members almost to a man.

The outbreak of war eliminated the last of Forster's local Nazi rivals. Arthur Greiser was appointed Gauleiter of the Warthegau. When he went to his new post, Greiser took with him most of those Danzig officials who had stood by him against Forster. He was accompanied by Böttcher and Blume of the dissolved Senate Foreign Department, and by Police Chief Froböss.[7] As soon as he was liberated from the constraints imposed by the presidency of the free city, Greiser dropped the mask and appeared as what he had always wanted to be, a brutal, uncontrolled Nazi despot, who treated his Polish subjects with severity and his Jewish victims with the callousness appropriate to the final solution. Greiser continued to interest himself in Danzig affairs, although he could not intervene directly, and he did his best to help whatever enemies Forster happened to make for himself. When Deputy Gauleiter Otto Andres fell out with Forster and was forced to leave Danzig-West Prussia in 1942, he found a place of refuge in Poznan with Greiser.[8] But Greiser's hatred could not reach effectively across Gau borders, and within Danzig-West Prussia Forster strengthened his position to the point where it seemed absolute.

This did not occur without opposition. It was originally intended by Forster that there would be only one center of authority in the Reichsgau, the Gauleitung-Reichsstatthalterei in Danzig, headed by himself. However, the Reich Ministry of the Interior decreed that there would be three governmental presidents (Regierungspräsidenten) in Danzig-West Prussia, who would have their seats in Danzig, Bydgoszcz, and Marienwerder. Officials of the ministry freely admitted that their intention was to "ward off the danger of too strong a ducal power." [9] It was hoped that the individual Regierungspräsidenten would be at least informally responsible to the Ministry of the Interior and thus bypass Forster. The attempt failed. Huth, who also had the rank of Regierungspräsident, was able to keep the administration unified and under Forster's control. Given the unity of party and state in the Reichsgau, the Ministry of the Interior never had a real opportunity to weaken Forster's authority. With his last rivals in government and party gone, Forster did indeed resemble a "duke of West Prussia." [10]

Forster's political cronies were not all dedicated administrators. In fact, some of them seem to have been drunken, corrupt hedonists, interested primarily in dodging conscription and lording it over their subordinates. The "higher SS and police leader" in Danzig-West Prussia, Richard Hildebrandt, was repelled by what he found when he was assigned to the Reichsgau. He wrote to Himmler, "in my long party experience I have never yet met with a Gau in which things are done so arbitrarily and with so little reason and sense."[11] The SS had its own notions of how things ought to be run in the new German East. The only serious challenge to Forster's position during the war came from Heinrich Himmler's expanding SS empire. In particular, the Reichsführer SS claimed superior jurisdiction in matters of population policy. Forster's sense of independence would not allow him to yield on this crucial question. He developed an interest in officially declaring most of the Polish residents of his Gau to be "ethnic Germans," in direct opposition to Himmler's exclusive racist ideology. The dispute lasted through 1944 and wound its way through technical debates on the nature of the "German race," spiced with the sniping of Gauleiter Greiser from Poznan. Greiser united with Himmler in attempting to discredit Forster and in trying to force his surrender to SS authority. The most extraordinary thing about the dispute is that Forster won it. He was able to "germanize" almost all of the inhabitants of the Reichsgau, at least on paper, and he successfully defied the head of the SS with the remark, "If I looked like Himmler, I wouldn't talk about race."[12]

The victory over Himmler was an empty one. Forster had become a National Socialist in 1923, at the age of twenty-one. He may have sometimes forgotten that there was a reality outside the party. In this he was not alone in the NSDAP. The refusal of national socialism to be judged by external standards, even by the practical standards of success and failure, played an essential part in the long and horrible end of the Third Reich. In 1944, as the military position of the Reich grew worse, reality came crashing in on the Reichsgau Danzig-West Prussia. The creeping senility of the system first became obvious in the rural areas around the town of Tuchola (Tuchel). The Poles of the area, many of them card-carrying ethnic Germans, left their homes and farms to form partisan bands. Pillage and death were visited on genuine Germans and Polish collaborators throughout the southern part of the Reichsgau. Himmler had been, in a way, a better judge of the situation in Danzig–West Prussia than was Forster. It was indeed impossible to turn Poles into Germans overnight. Quarrels over germanization became irrelevant.

Ethnic Germans or "racial aliens," the Poles rebelled against their masters. Legal authorities were helpless south of the Gdynia-Danzig area, and the army was busy fighting the Russians.

As the grim winter of 1944–45 approached, the old men and boys of the Reichsgau took to the fields to dig hasty fortifications and to man them as members of the last-ditch reserve army, the *Volkssturm.* Forster's administration met the crisis surprisingly well. Sensible, step-by-step evacuation plans were drawn up and distributed. The Gau authorities proceeded calmly, aware of the coming storm, and behaved as if they were confident of final victory.

But in January 1945, all plans were swept away by the rapidity of events and the scarcity of resources. The German population of the Reichsgau had already been swollen by women and children evacuated from Germany's bombed-out western cities. Now a horde of refugees—men, women, children, and livestock—poured into Danzig from East Prussia. The Gau authorities there, held back by a political refusal to admit the possibility of Russian invasion, had delayed evacuation until too late. As the Russians invested Königsberg, the panicked, half-starved East Prussians made chaos of all Reichsgau preparations, warning arrangements, and transportation schedules. By late January and early February, the Russians were in the Reichsgau itself, and the German inhabitants were faced with a choice between wild flight and the doubtful mercy of the conqueror. As they scrambled for whatever transportation was available, the Poles took over. The Red Army was able to take many West Prussian towns without a fight. The swastika had already been hauled down, and the red-and-white Polish ensign was flying.[13]

At the end of February, Danzig itself was closely besieged, a Baltic pocket held desperately by a retreating German army. The last civilian transport ships to leave were torpedoed and bombed, with frightful loss of life. In March Forster appeared in Hitler's bunker in Berlin, determined to enlighten the Führer on the dire situation in Danzig. But Hitler kept his old hold on Forster, and the Gauleiter returned to the fighting convinced that new German divisions would somehow rescue the surrounded city.[14]

At the last moment, Forster left his capital by submarine. In a final broadcast, he exhorted Danzig's defenders to hold on until the end: "Danzig remains German." [15] On 30 March, the city was taken by the Russians, and the Polish flag was hoisted. According to the Red Army high command, ten thousand German soldiers were taken prisoner. Thirty-nine thousand of the defenders were dead.[16] Prolonged air and artillery bombardment had reduced the Hanseatic queen of the Baltic to a pile of rubble, brooded over by the gaunt skeleton of the Marienkirche. The remaining civilian population shared the usual lot of Germans who fell into Russian hands—pillage, rape, and murder.[17]

Forster escaped to western Germany. He was interned and then extradited to Poland. He stood trial in 1948 and was executed. His old rival, Arthur Greiser, was captured in his Gau capital of Poznan when it fell in 1945. He was tried in July 1946 and executed.[18] A recent study notes that Greiser was convicted of "waging aggressive war," among other things, "and to him goes the dubious honor of being the first person ever convicted on such a charge." [19]

German Danzig was destroyed. Most of its citizens who survive now live in West Germany, since the Poles adopted their own solution to the population question and expelled most of the Germans east of the Oder and the Neisse.[20] The free city may continue a shadowy existence in international law, although recent agreements between West Germany and Poland make that possibility more doubtful than ever. Some refugees from the free city did constitute themselves a kind of government-in-exile,[21] but one without any real hope of restoration. The stones of Danzig may remain. The Poles have done much to restore the core of the town, and the excellence of the restoration has even won the grudging admiration of former inhabitants.[22] But the German community has disappeared forever. Danzig is gone, and Polish Gdansk has taken its place.

The major responsibility for the destruction of Danzig, and of much else besides, must of course lie with the Nazi movement and with its chief local representative, Albert Forster. Forster believed he had constructed for himself an impregnable position, and he was correct, within the only context that he knew. But to the external reality represented by the invading Red Army, his fortress was a sand castle, and his power a mirage built on the delusion of the Thousand-Year Reich. Forster's political outlook reflected in an extreme form the tragedy, and the crime, of millions of Hitler's followers. Their faith in the Führer armed them against adversity, moved them to accomplish the impossible, and led them headlong into the abyss. Blind until the end, they turned Europe into a charnel house, in which the bones of the guilty and the innocent lay jumbled in indiscriminate confusion.

Note on Sources

A. Unpublished Documentary Materials

This study is based on research undertaken in several European archives and in two American microfilm collections. All documentary citations in the notes include abbreviations indicating the current depository of the material.

National Archives, Washington, D.C., microfilm collection (NA)

Politisches Archiv des Auswärtigen Amts, Bonn (PA)

The documentary collection most important to this study was that produced by the German Foreign Office (Auswärtiges Amt; AA). The AA was the channel for all official relations between Germany and the free city. The original files are now deposited in the Politisches Archiv des Auswärtigen Amts. An extensive microfilming project, the Whaddon Hall project, has produced a rather badly organized mass of film, now available in and from the British Foreign Office and the National Archives (microcopy number T-120). All AA documents that have been filmed are designated NA/T-120 in the footnotes. This is followed by the microfilm roll number, the serial number, frame numbers, and a file reference that may be used to locate the original document in the Politisches Archiv. Documents that have not been filmed and are available only in Bonn are designated PA, followed by the file reference.

The files of the Deutsches Generalkonsulat Danzig, both NA and PA, carry the abbreviation DGKD. Files in the following categories were also used:

Before the AA Reorganization of 1936

Geh. (Geheimakten 1920–36)
Pol. IV (Politische Abteilung IV)

Abt. IV-Wirtschaft-Danzig
Abt. IV-Kultur
Abt. Presse
Handakten-Direktoren: (Richard) Meyer
Handakten: Lieres
Büro RAM (Reichsaussenminister)
Büro St.S. (Staatssekretär)

After the Reorganization of 1936

Pol. I
Pol. II
Pol. V
Büro Chef AO (Auslandsorganisation)
Neue Reichskanzlei: Auswärtiges Amt
Inland II (geheim)

For further information consult George O. Kent, *A Catalog of Files and Microfilms of the German Foreign Ministry Archives, 1920–1945* (Stanford, 1962 et seq.).

The National Archives also hold a very large collection of films of miscellaneous German records, the "Alexandria project." These are being catalogued in a continuing series, *Guides to German Records Filmed at Alexandria, Va.*, a publication of the National Archives and Records Service. Since the bulk of the collection as it pertains to Danzig deals with the war years, it was of use primarily in the preparation of the epilogue of the present study. Microcopy series containing valuable information on Danzig-West Prussia include: T-71, T-74, T-77, T-81, and T-175. The reference form follows that used for T-120.

Also used was the NA collection of films made by the American Historical Association at the Berlin Document Center, microcopy T-580. The originals are now in the Bundesarchiv. A finding aid to the entire collection is available on T-580/roll 999. T-580/roll 20/Ordner 200 (Schumacher material) contains uniquely useful documents on the early history of the Gau Danzig and was vital to the preparation of chapter 2. Most other material on Danzig in T-580 deals with the war years, including the following: T-580/320/32; T-580/320–21/35; T-580/548/672–73.

Note on Sources

Bundesarchiv, Koblenz (BA)

The major collection of party and government files from the Third Reich, outside East Germany, is today in the Bundesarchiv. This collection was primarily, though not exclusively, valuable for its wartime holdings. Since a complete published catalog of the files in the BA does not exist, a precise list of the materials consulted is necessary here.

Ost 12/Gotenhafen, Stadt (1939–45)

Schumacher/200 (Danzig-Westpreussen)

Schumacher/396 (Generalstaatsanwalt Danzig, Lageberichte, 1940–44)

Ost-Dok. 8 DW, Nr. 105, 135, 143, 188

NS 1/2080, 2167 (Vermögensübersichten der Kreise und Ortsgruppen, Danzig, 1937–38)

NS 10/69–71 (Schriftwechsel mit Gau- und Kreisleitungen der NSDAP, vornehmlich Ergebenheitsadressen und Einladungen betreffend, 1933–38)

NS 25/198–202, 746, 1087, 1293 (Hauptamt für Kommunalpolitik, 1934–42)

R 22/3360 (Reichsjustizministerium, Lageberichte des Oberlandesgerichtspräsidenten und des Generalstaatsanwaltes in Danzig, 1940–45)

R 36/10, 1406, 2292, 24604 (Deutscher Gemeindetag, 1939–45)

Berlin Document Center of the United States State Department, West Berlin (BDC)

Extremely important for this study were the Nazi personnel files deposited in the Berlin Document Center of the United States State Department. The BDC has no public catalog. Files are produced when information on specific individuals is requested. The materials are organized in broad categories, roughly according to provenance, but items of varied origin may be combined in a single folder. The following BDC files were consulted:

Oberstes Parteigericht (OPG) : Hans Albert Hohnfeldt, Ernst Kendzia, Wilhelm von Wnuck

Partei-Kanzlei (PK) : Otto Andres, Paul Batzer, Edmund Beyl, Albert Forster, Hans Albert Hohnfeldt, Dr. Julius Hoppenrath, Wilhelm Huth, Werner Kampe, Ernst Kendzia, Gustav Lippkau, Georg Lippke, Wilhelm Löbsack, Leonhard Michael Rampf, Hermann Rauschning, Gerhard Seeger, Paul Wittenberg

Rasse- und Siedlungshauptamt RF-SS (RUSHA): Karl Grötzner, Erich Temp

SA: Adalbert Boeck, Otto Ivers, Max Linsmayer

SS Officers (SSO): Erich von dem Bach, Wolfgang Diewerge, Erich Dubke, Albert Forster, Arthur Greiser, Dr. Erich Grossmann, Richard Hildebrandt, Wilhelm Huth, Ernst Kendzia, Dr. Helmut Kluck, Werner Lorenz, Dr. Alexander Reiner, Lothar Rethel, Felix Strautmann, Edmund Freiherr von Thermann

Hauptarchiv der NSDAP (HA)

Of relatively minor importance for this study was the collection of microfilms known as the Hauptarchiv der NSDAP, available from the Hoover Institution, Stanford University. The HA collection is completely catalogued in G. Heinz, *NSDAP Hauptarchiv: Guide to the Hoover Microfilm Collection* (Stanford, 1964). The following HA files were found useful:

roll 11/folder 240/III Danzig (1–6)

13/260/N.S.V. Einsatz—Front—Luftangriffe etc.—besetzte Gebiete, 1942–45

19/370/H.J. Grenzlandamt

30/587/Volkstagswahl am 7. April 1935

42/839/Deutsch-Soziale Partei

47/994/Zeitungen und Zeitschriften der N. S. Presse . . . (*Danziger Vorposten*)

Archives de la Société des Nations, United Nations Library, Geneva (ASDN)

The collection of the Archives de la Société des Nations was of great interest, though valuable chiefly as a supplement to the other documentary collections. The most important political material, the correspondence of the League of Nations high commissioners, was partly destroyed during the war. The correspondence of Sean Lester suffered severely. Special collections of the high commissioners' correspondence are found in the "Section" files. But S 322 (Gravina, Rosting) is partially closed to researchers, and the relevant portions of S 332–33 (Lester, Burckhardt) are entirely closed.

The "Registry" files are more open. Files are organized in blocks of years: 19–27 (1919–27), 28–32, and 33–46. All relevant unrestricted files produced by the Section des Commissions administratives et des questions de Minorités (designated 2B) were consulted. In the footnotes, these files are referred to by their series and dossier numbers, with their carton numbers given in parentheses. For further information, see "Archives de la S.D.N.; Répertoire général," bound in three volumes and available at the U.N. Library, Geneva. An earlier version is available at the U.N., New York. See also *Guide des Archives de la Société des Nations* (Geneva, 1969), which is now available in English as well, and Herbert S. Levine, "Note: The League of Nations Archives at Geneva," *Central European History* 3 (1970): 392–96.

Three important files were restricted, and could not be seen:

33–46: 2B/18255/18255 (R 3719) Confidential Interviews with Polish Representatives, 1935

33–46: 2B/20647/20647 (R 3720) Mission of M. Krabbe to Danzig, November 1935

33–46: 2B/24871/3 dossiers (R 3720) Situation of Jews and Refugees, 1936–39.

Public Record Office, London (PRO)

The relevant files of the British Foreign Office, deposited in the Public Record Office in London, appear in the notes as PRO/FO 371. The British consuls in Danzig were keen observers of the domestic political situation, and their reports on the progressive *Gleichschaltung* of the free city proved most helpful. The collection also contains copies of most important League documents dealing with the free city, including the correspondence of the high commissioners with Geneva. These were transmitted to the FO by Geneva because the British provided the rapporteur on Danzig questions to the League council, a position occupied successively by Simon, Eden, and Halifax. Documents that cannot be seen in the original in Geneva because of wartime destruction or archival restrictions are thus available in London. In addition, the high commissioners often corresponded directly with the FO or communicated through the British consul in Danzig.

A complete guide to FO 371 is available in the PRO. The documents are bound in volumes by year. The notes follow the scheme: PRO/FO 371/volume number/document number/file numbers. Files are untitled. Documents dealing with Danzig were normally bound with those on Poland and designated "55." For 1938 and 1939 important information on Danzig is also found in files dealing with Germany (18), and with Jews, refugees, and the League. Through 1933, the files originated with the Northern Department of the FO (N documents), and from 1934 with the Central Department (C documents). In 1938 and 1939 contributions on Danzig were also made by the Western Department (W documents).

Wojewódzkie Archiwum Państwowe w Gdańsku, Danzig (Gdansk) (WAP)

There are two collections of significance for the study of the free city in the possession of the Wojewódzkie Archiwum Państwowe w Gdańsku, formerly the Danziger Staatsarchiv. The records of the senate of the free city have apparently been preserved more or less intact, but I was not permitted access to them by the Polish central archival authorities on the grounds that the files were not yet properly catalogued and classified. Had access been permitted, some uncertain points in this study would perhaps have been clarified. The records of the Polish Commissariat-General are easier of access. I consulted the most relevant section of these files, designated Komisarz Generalny Rzeczypospolitej Polskiej w Gdańsku (KGRP), I, 259. Because of an extreme limitation of time, I was able only to skim the political dispatches of the commissioners-general to the Polish Foreign Ministry, files 916 through 932. The specialized files in KGRP, I, 259 were consulted with greater thoroughness. The following files were found particularly useful: 157, 166, 604, 606, 608–9, 611–18, 713, 717, 719–

20, 771. For further information consult Czesław Stodolny, *Inwentarz akt Komisarza Generalnego Rzeczypospolitej w Gdańsku 1919–1939* (Warsaw, 1967).

Except for isolated pieces, the archives of the Gau Danzig, later Gau Danzig-Westpreussen, no longer exist. According to the administration of the WAP, these party records were evacuated late in the war and seem to have been destroyed en route to the west. The WAP therefore contains no document of interest for the war period, unless these are attached to the closed senate documents. Fortunately, the missing Gau files could be replaced by other materials, particularly the BDC, BA, and NA collections, although there remain gaps in the historical record.

Wiener Library, London

Document file 509, containing copies of correspondence between Danzig Jewish authorities and the senate, from 1933 through 1935, was consulted.

B. Private Sources

Most of the major actors on the Danzig scene are now dead. Others were unfortunately either unable or unwilling to correspond with me. Professor Carl J. Burckhardt was a cooperative correspondent. Information on Danzig was obtained in conversations with two former Danzigers, Dr. Hans Viktor Böttcher (son of Dr. Viktor Böttcher, head of the Senate Foreign Dept.) and Dr. Karl-Heinz Mattern, both now of Bonn. I was allowed to see a letter from Burckhardt to the younger Dr. Böttcher, dated 29 January 1951. Erich Brost, former editor of the *Danziger Volksstimme* (SPD) now residing in Essen, was kind enough to provide information in several letters.

Material on the Danzig opposition was made available by a source that may not be cited. This information has generally been used only to confirm judgments formed on the basis of other materials. Where it was found necessary to include information not available elsewhere, this material has been cited as "private information."

C. *The Moderow Manuscript*

The U.N. Library in Geneva, Historical Collections Section, which administers the ASDN, is in possession of a manuscript opened to researchers in 1970: W. Moderow, "Die Freie Stadt Danzig." The late Mr. Moderow was a high official in the U.N. Secretariat before his retirement. From 1921 to 1939 he was a member of the staff of the Polish commissioner-general in Danzig, a member of the Danzig Harbor Board from 1926, and a frequent participant in Danzig-Polish negotiations. Although Moderow brought a unique personal knowledge to bear on Danzig questions, his MS is a remarkably objective account of the situation in the free city. It is designed to prove that the solution to the Danzig problem adopted between the wars did not work at all badly. I benefited greatly from the new, propaganda-free insights contained in the MS, even where I could not agree with them. The MS is notable chiefly for its discussion of Danzig-Polish economic relations and its dissection of the views of Carl J. Burckhardt.

D. *Newspapers*

The National Socialist weekly (1931–33) and daily (1933–44) newspaper, the *Danziger Vorposten,* is available in the municipal library of Gdansk (Danzig) and in the New York Public Library. Both collections have gaps, but together they provide an almost complete run of the *Vorposten.* The Gdansk library also possesses partial collections of the other newspapers of the free city. The *Danziger Volksstimme* (SPD), the most important opposition paper, is available on microfilm from the Mikrofilm-Archiv der deutschsprachigen Presse e.V., Dortmund (Best.-Nr. F 103). Citations of the *Vorposten* are usually from the newspaper files themselves. The other Danzig newspapers, including the *Volksstimme,* were consulted in the Danzig library, but most citations from these newspapers refer to clippings seen in various documentary collections. For these, the file in which the clipping was seen is also noted. The following Danzig newspapers are cited in the notes (party affiliation in parentheses):

Danziger Allgemeine Zeitung (DNVP)
Danziger Landeszeitung (Center, later coordinated)
Danziger Neueste Nachrichten (independent liberal, later coordinated)
Danziger Volksstimme (SPD)
Danziger Volkszeitung (Center)
Danziger Vorposten (NSDAP)
Gazeta Gdańska (Polish)

The press library of the Royal Institute of International Affairs, Chatham House, London, provided a sampling of the international press. The library's holdings are in the form of clippings. The following newspapers appear in the footnotes:

Basler Nachrichten
Berliner Tageblatt
The Daily Herald (London)
The Daily Telegraph (London)
Diplomatische Korrespondenz (Berlin)
Frankfurter Zeitung
Journal des Nations (Geneva)
Manchester Guardian
The New York Times
The Observer (London)
The Sunday Times (London)
Le Temps (Paris)
The Times (London)
Völkischer Beobachter (Berlin)

E. The Works of Hermann Rauschning

Before becoming president of the Danzig Senate, Hermann Rauschning published:

Die Entdeutschung Westpreussens und Posens. Berlin, 1930.
Geschichte der Musik und Musikpflege in Danzig. Danzig, 1931.

Two of Rauschning's speeches as president were published in pamphlet form:

Deutsche und Polen. Danzig, 1934.

Zehn Monate nationalsozialistische Regierung in Danzig. Danzig, 1934.

Since Rauschning's speeches were altered extensively before publication, they are cited as reported in the dispatches of the German consul-general.

After breaking with the Nazis, Rauschning began a career as an emigré publicist by writing for a journal published by an anti-Hitler member of the Catholic German minority in Poland. Two particularly interesting articles, which relate directly to the Danzig question, are:

"Ein Prüfstein für den Völkerbund: Worum geht es in Danzig?" *Der Deutsche in Polen* 4, no. 2 (10 Jan. 1937).

"Der Völkerbund hat das Wort! Danzig als Unruhenherd—Danzig als Friedensfaktor in Osteuropa." *Der Deutsche in Polen* 4, no. 3 (17 Jan. 1937).

Rauschning's major theoretical work is *Die Revolution des Nihilismus,* first published in Zurich in 1938 and issued in a revised edition in 1939. For reference purposes, this study has used the somewhat abridged version edited by Golo Mann (Zurich, 1964). Of Rauschning's later works, the following memoirlike volumes are particularly relevant to Danzig:

The Conservative Revolution. New York, 1941.

Gespräche mit Hitler. New York, 1940.

Makers of Destruction. London, 1942. (American title: *Men of Chaos*.)

Other works:

Deutschland zwischen Ost und West. Berlin, Hamburg, and Stuttgart, 1950.

The Redemption of Democracy. New York, 1941.

Time of Delirium. New York, 1946.

F. Published Documentary Material and Official Publications

Amtsblatt des Reichsstatthalters in Danzig-Westpreussen. Danzig, 1939–45.

Danziger statistisches Taschenbuch/1933, 1934, 1936. Danzig, 1932, 1934, 1936.

Die deutschen Vertreibungsverluste: Bevölkerungsbilanzen für die deutschen Vertreibungsgebiete 1939/50. Wiesbaden and Stuttgart, 1958.

Documents on British Foreign Policy: 1919–1939. 3d ser. 3 vols. London, 1946–50.

Documents on German Foreign Policy. Ser. C, D. Washington, 1949 et seq.

Entscheidungen des Hohen Kommissars des Völkerbundes in der Freien Stadt Danzig: Decisions of the High Commissioner, League of Nations, Free City of Danzig. 6 vols. Danzig, 1922–33.

Ergebnisse der Volks- und Berufszählung vom 1. November 1923 in der Freien Stadt Danzig mit einem Anhang: Die Ergebnisse der Volkszählung vom 31. August 1924. Danzig, 1926.

Forster, Albert, and Wilhelm Löbsack, eds. *Das nationalsozialistische Gewissen in Danzig.* Danzig, 1936.

Gesetzblatt für die Freie Stadt Danzig. Danzig, 1920–39.

Hitler, Adolf. *The Speeches of Adolf Hitler, April 1922–August 1939.* Edited by Norman H. Baynes. 2 vols. London, 1942.

Krannhals, Detlef, ed. *Das politische Danzig, Dokumente.* Danzig, 1937.

League of Nations Official Journal. Geneva, 1920–40.

Mantoux, Paul. *Les délibérations du Conseil des Quatre (24 mars–28 juin 1919)* . 2 vols. Paris, 1955.

Reichsband. 3d ed., 1941–42. Berlin, 1943.

Reichsgesetzblatt. Berlin, 1939, 1940.

"Report of M. Carl Burckhardt." *Series of League of Nations Publications, Political.* Vol. 7. 1940.

Sammlung der Dokumente zum Rechtsstreit Danzig-Gdingen. Danzig, 1931.

Schramm, Percy Ernst, ed. *Hitlers Tischgespräche im Führerhauptquartier.* Rev. ed. Stuttgart, 1963.

Verfassung der Freien Stadt Danzig in der Fassung des Gesetzes vom 4. Juli 1930. Danzig, n.d.

Verordnungsblatt des Reichsstatthalters in Danzig-Westpreussen. Danzig, 1939–45.

G. *Memoirs and Diaries*

Beck, Józef. *Dernier rapport: Politique polonaise 1926–1939.* Paris, 1951.

Burckhardt, Carl J. *Meine Danziger Mission.* Munich, 1960.

Goebbels, Joseph. *Vom Kaiserhof zur Reichskanzlei.* Munich, 1934.

Gülzow, Gerhard. *Kirchenkampf in Danzig 1934–1945: Persönliche Erinnerungen.* Leer, 1968.

Hitler, Adolf. *Mein Kampf.* "Editorial sponsors," J. Chamberlain et al. New York, 1939.

Lehndorf, Hans Graf von. *Ein Bericht aus Ost- und Westpreussen 1945–1947.* Bonn, 1960.

Lipski, Józef. *Diplomat in Berlin 1933–1939.* Edited by W. Jedrzejewicz. New York, 1968.

Rauschning, Anna. *No Retreat.* New York and Indianapolis, 1942.

Sahm, Heinrich. *Erinnerungen aus meinen Danziger Jahren 1919–1930.* Marburg/Lahn, 1958.

Schmidt, Paul. *Statist auf diplomatischer Bühne.* Bonn, 1949.

Szembek, Jan. *Journal 1933–1939.* Paris, 1952.

Weizsäcker, Ernst von. *Erinnerungen.* Munich and Freiburg/Br., 1950.

Ziehm, Ernst. *Aus meiner politischen Arbeit in Danzig 1914–1939.* Marburg/Lahn, 1960.

Zoller, Albert, ed. *Hitler Privat.* Düsseldorf, 1949.

H. *Secondary Sources*

In the period before 1945, and especially before 1939, the Danzig question was a living issue. An enormous amount of material, much of it polemical, was published. The best guide to contemporary published sources is Fritz Prinzhorn, *Danzig—Polen—Korridor und Grenzgebiete: Eine Bibliographie mit besonderer Berücksichtigung von Politik und Wirtschaft,* 9 vols., Berichtsjahre 1931–41 (Danzig, 1932–40; Leipzig, 1940–42) ; title changes in 1940 to *Deutsche Reichsgaue im Osten und Generalgouvernement Polen.* Excellent shorter bibliographies are to be found in the works of Morrow, Leonhardt, Mason, and Kimmich, listed below.

The unified alphabetical list below contains secondary works and articles cited, with a few postwar titles that were not cited but were found useful.

Akzin, Benjamin. "Zionism." *The Universal Jewish Encyclopedia*. New York, 1969. 10: 645–67.

Allen, William S. *The Nazi Seizure of Power: The Experience of a Single German Town 1930–1935*. Chicago, 1965.

Arendt, Hannah. *Eichmann in Jerusalem*. Rev. ed. New York, 1965.

Aschkewitz, Max. *Zur Geschichte der Juden in Westpreussen 1772–1932*. Marburg/Lahn, 1968.

Askenazy, Simon (Szymon). *Dantzig and Poland*. London, 1921.

Bachem, Karl. *Vorgeschichte, Geschichte und Politik der Zentrumspartei*. Vol. 8. Cologne, 1932.

Baedeker, Kurt. "Wartendes Land an der Weichsel: Deutsche Arbeitsdienstpflicht ausserhalb der Reichsgrenzen." *Der Deutsche im Osten* 2, no. 1 (Mar. 1939): 3–9.

Bennecke, Heinrich. *Hitler und die SA*. Munich and Vienna, 1962.

Beutel, Michael, and Hans-Karl Gspann. *Das heutige Danzig*. Munich, 1956.

Bierowski, Thadée (Tadeusz). *La Ville Libre de Dantzig et la guerre polono-bolchévique de 1920*. Danzig, 1932.

Biskup, Marian. *Stosunek Gdańska do Kazimierza Jagiellończyka w okresie wojny trzynastoletniej 1454–1466*. Torun, 1953.

Bloch, Charles. *Hitler und die europäischen Mächte 1933/1934: Kontinuität oder Bruch*. Frankfurt/Main, 1966.

Boeck, Adalbert. "Danzig ist eine deutsche Stadt." *Der Türmer* 41, no. 9 (June 1939): 177–88.

Bracher, Karl Dietrich. *The German Dictatorship*. New York, 1970.

Bracher, Karl Dietrich. Wolfgang Sauer, and Gerhard Schulz. *Die nationalsozialistische Machtergreifung*. Cologne and Opladen, 1960.

Breyer, Richard. *Das Deutsche Reich und Polen 1932–1937*. Würzburg, 1955.

Broszat, Martin. *Nationalsozialistische Polenpolitik 1939–1945*. Stuttgart, 1961.

———. *Der Staat Hitlers*. Munich, 1969.

———. *200 Jahre deutsche Polenpolitik*. Munich, 1963.

Bullock, Alan. *Hitler, a Study in Tyranny*. Rev. ed. New York, 1964.

Ciećkowski, Zbigniew. "Organizacje rewizjonistyczne i paramilitarne W.M. Gdańska w przygotowaniu agresji hitlerowskiej na Polske." *Przegląd Morski*, no. 9 (1967) : 52–66.

———. "Powstanie i rozwój ruchu narodowosocjalistycznego w W.M. Gdańsku do 1933 r." *Zapiski Historyczne* 30, no. 2 (1965) : 35–72.

Cienciala, Anna. *Poland and the Western Powers, 1938–1939*. Toronto, 1968.

———. "The Significance of the Declaration of Non-Aggression of Jan. 26, 1934." *East European Quarterly* 1 (1967) : 1–30.

Déat, Marcel. *Perspectives françaises*. Paris, 1940.

Denne, Ludwig. *Das Danzig Problem in der deutschen Aussenpolitik, 1934–1939*. Bonn, 1959.

Deutsch, Harold C. *The Conspiracy against Hitler in the Twilight War*. Minneapolis, 1968.

Das Deutsche Führerlexikon 1934/1935. Berlin, 1934.

Diewerge, Wolfgang. *Der neue Reichsgau Danzig-Westpreussen*. Berlin, 1940. (In microcopy: NA/T-580/20/200.)

Dopierała, Bohdan (Bogdan) . "Beck and the Gdańsk Question (1930–1935) ." *Acta Poloniae Historica* 17 (1968) : 71–104.

———. *Gdańska polityka Józefa Becka*. Poznan, 1967.

Dormeyer, D. F. *Marktregulierung zur Rettung der Danziger Landwirtschaft*. Danzig, 1934.

Drage, Charles. *The Amiable Prussian*. London, 1958.

Echt, Samuel. "Die Geschichte der Juden in Danzig." *Deutsche Studien* 8, no. 30 (June 1970) : 145–53.

Gärtner, Margerete, ed. *Danzig and the Corridor*. Berlin, 1939.

Gasiorowski, Zygmunt J. "Did Piłsudski Attempt to Initiate a Preventive War in 1933?" *The Journal of Modern History* 27 (1955) : 135–51.

Gerechtigkeit für Danzig. (Cover title: *Die Freie Stadt Danzig*.) N.p., 1965.

Giannini, Amadeo. *The Problem of Danzig*. Rome, 1932.

Graham, Charles. "La Ville Libre dangereuse." *L'Europe nouvelle* 19 (2 May 1936) : 465–66.

Halperin, S. William. *Germany Tried Democracy*. New York, 1965.

Harder, Hans Adolf. *Danzig, Polen und der Völkerbund*. Berlin, 1928.

Heiber, Helmut. *Joseph Goebbels*. Berlin, 1962.

Herzog, Elizabeth, and Mark Zborowski. *Life Is with People: The Culture of the Shtetl*. New York, 1962.

Hilberg, Raul. *The Destruction of the European Jews*. Chicago, 1961.

Hofmannsthal, Hugo von. *Das Schriftum als geistiger Raum der Nation*. Munich, 1927.

Höhne, Heinz. *Der Orden unter dem Totenkopf: Die Geschichte der SS*. Gütersloh, 1967.

Hüttenberger, Peter. *Die Gauleiter: Studie zum Wandel des Machtgefüges in der NSDAP*. Stuttgart, 1969.

Ingrim, Robert. *Hitlers glücklichster Tag: London, am 18. Juni 1935*. Stuttgart, 1962.

Jäckel, Eberhard. *Hitler's Weltanschauung*. Middletown, Conn., 1972.

Jacobsen, Hans-Adolf. *Nationalsozialistische Aussenpolitik 1933–1938*. Frankfurt/Main and Berlin, 1968.

Janowicz, Zbigniew. *Ustrój administracyjny ziem polskich wcielonych do Rzeszy Niemieckiej 1939–1945*. Poznan, 1951.

Jung, Edgar J. *Die Herrschaft der Minderwertigen*. 2d ed. Berlin, 1930.

Kasprowicz, Bolesław. "Straty gospodarcze Gdańska jako wynik jego izolowania się od Polski w latach miedzywojennych." *Przegląd Zachodni* 12 (1956) : 311–23.

Keyser, Erich. *Danzigs Geschichte*. Danzig, 1928.

———. *Geschichte der Stadt Danzig*. Kitzingen/Main, 1951.

Kimmich, Christoph M. *The Free City: Danzig and German Foreign Policy, 1919–1934*. New Haven, 1968.

Klemperer, Klemens von. *Germany's New Conservatism*. Princeton, 1968.

Koehl, Robert. "Feudal Aspects of National Socialism." *American Political Science Review* 54 (1960) : 921–33.

———. *RKFDV: German Resettlement and Population Policy 1939–1945*. Cambridge, Mass., 1957.

Lafore, Laurence. *The End of Glory*. Philadelphia and New York, 1970.

Lebovics, Herman. *Social Conservatism and the Middle Classes in Germany, 1914–1933*. Princeton, 1969.

Leonhardt, Hans L. *Nazi Conquest of Danzig*. Chicago, 1942.

Levine, Herbert S. "Local Authority and the SS State: The Conflict over Population Policy in Danzig-West Prussia, 1939–1945." *Central European History* 2 (1969) : 331–55.

———. "The Mediator: The Efforts of Carl J. Burckhardt to Avert a Second World War," *Journal of Modern History* 45 (1973) .

Lewy, Guenter. *The Catholic Church and Nazi Germany*. New York, 1965.

Löbsack, Wilhelm. *Albert Forster*. Hamburg, 1934.

Loening, Otto. *Die Rechtsstellung der Freien Stadt Danzig*. Berlin, 1928.

Luckau, Alma. *The German Delegation at the Paris Peace Conference*. New York, 1941.

Łyczkowski, Eugeniusz. "W sprawie genezy Wolnego Miasta Gdańska." *Przegląd Zachodni* 22 (1966) : 298–309.

Makowski, Julian. *Le caractère étatique de la Ville Libre de Dantzig*. Warsaw, 1933.

Maltzahn, Irmgard von. *Deutsche Mädel auf Vorposten*. Leipzig, 1934.

Markull, Wilhelm. "Danzig: Das Schicksal einer deutschen Stadt." *Zeitschrift für Politik* 19, no. 9 (Jan. 1930) : 616–27.

Mason, John Brown. *The Danzig Dilemma*. Stanford, 1946.

Mattern, Karl-Heinz. *Die Exilregierung*. Tübingen, 1953.

Meyer, Hans Bernard. *Danzig in 144 Bildern*. Leer, 1956.

Meyer, Milton. *They Thought They Were Free*. Chicago, 1966.

Montfort, Henri de. *Dantzig, port de Pologne*. Paris, 1939.

Morrow, Ian F. D. *The Peace Settlement in the German-Polish Borderlands*. London, 1936.

Morsey, Rudolf. "Hitlers Verhandlungen mit der Zentrumsführung am 31. Januar 1933." *Vierteljahrshefte für Zeitgeschichte* 9 (1961) : 182–94.

Mosse, George L. *The Crisis of German Ideology.* New York, 1964.

Neumann, Franz. *Behemoth: The Structure and Practice of National Socialism 1933–1944.* New York, 1966.

Noakes, Jeremy. "Conflict and Development in the NSDAP 1924–1927." *Journal of Contemporary History* 1 (1966) : 3–36.

Nyomarkay, Joseph. *Charisma and Factionalism in the Nazi Party.* Minneapolis, 1967.

Orlow, Dietrich. *The History of the Nazi Party: 1919–1933.* Pittsburgh, 1969.

Peiser, Kurt. *Danzig, das Schicksal eines deutschen Hafens.* Danzig, 1940.

Pelczar, Marian. *Polski Gdańsk.* Gdansk, 1947.

Peterson, Edward N. *The Limits of Hitler's Power.* Princeton, 1969.

Polak, Henryk. "Położenie szkolnictwa polskiego w W. M. Gdańsku." *Przegląd Zachodni* 20 (1964) : 387–410.

Prill, Felician. "Sean Lester: High Commissioner in Danzig, 1933–1937." *Studies* (Dublin) 49, no. 195 (Autumn 1960) : 259–65.

Pulzer, Peter G. J. *The Rise of Political Anti-Semitism in Germany and Austria.* New York, 1964.

Redlin, Fritz. "Danzig löst die Judenfrage." *Mitteilungen über die Judenfrage* (Berlin) 3, no. 4 (26 Jan. 1939) : 5.

———. "Eine tatkräftige Lösung: Die Wahrheit über die Danziger Judenauswanderung." *Mitteilungen über die Judenfrage* 3, no. 13 (30 Mar. 1939) : 3.

Reichmann, Eva G. *Hostages of Civilization: The Social Sources of German Anti-Semitism.* Boston: 1951.

Reitlinger, Gerald. *The Final Solution: The Attempt to Exterminate the Jews of Europe.* New York, 1961.

Rieper, Gerhard. "Die militärischen Rechte Polens in der Freien Stadt und die Frage der Neutralität Danzigs." diss. Ph.D. Würzburg, 1933.

Robertson, E. M. *Hitler's Pre-War Policy and Military Plans 1933–1939.* London, 1963.

Roos, Hans. *A History of Modern Poland.* New York, 1966.

———. *Polen und Europa.* Tübingen, 1957.

Sauer, Wolfgang. "National Socialism: Totalitarianism or Fascism?" *American Historical Review* 73 (Dec. 1967) : 404–24.

Sawatzki, Günther. *Danzig ist deutsch.* Berlin, 1939.

Schäfer, Wolfgang, *NSDAP: Entwicklung und Struktur der Staatspartei des dritten Reiches.* Hannover and Frankfurt/Main, 1957.

Schimitzek, Stanisław. *Truth or Conjecture? German Civilian War Losses in the East.* Poznan, 1966.

Schleunes, Karl A. *The Twisted Road to Auschwitz: Nazi Policy toward German Jews 1933–1939.* Urbana and Chicago, 1970.

Schmitt, Carl. *Staat, Bewegung, Volk: Die Dreigliederung der politischen Einheit.* Hamburg, 1933.

Schoenbaum, David. *Hitler's Social Revolution.* Garden City, N.Y., 1966.

Schüddekopf, Ernst Otto. *Linke Leute von Rechts.* Stuttgart, 1960.

Schweitzer, Arthur. *Big Business in the Third Reich.* Bloomington, Ind., 1964.

Sellenthin, H. G. *Geschichte der Juden in Berlin und des Gebäudes Fasanenstrasse 79/80.* Berlin, 1959.

Siebeneichen, A., and H. Strasburger. *Spór o Gdynię.* Torun, 1930.

Simson, Paul. *Geschichte der Stadt Danzig.* 3 vols. Danzig, 1913–18.

Sodeikat, Ernst. "Der Nationalsozialismus und die Danziger Opposition." *Vierteljahrshefte für Zeitgeschichte* 14 (1966) : 139–74.

———. "Die Verfolgung und der Widerstand der Juden in der Freien Stadt Danzig von 1933 bis 1945." *Bulletin des Leo Baeck Instituts* 8, no. 30 (1965) : 107–49.

Steen, Hans. *Blaue Jungen schlagen Polen.* Stuttgart, 1941.

Stephen, Walther. *Danzig: Gründung und Strassennamen.* Marburg/Lahn, 1954.

Stern, Fritz. *The Politics of Cultural Despair: A Study in the Rise of Germanic Ideology.* 2d ed. Berkeley, 1965.

Stockhorst, Erich. *Fünftausend Köpfe: Wer war was im Dritten Reich*. Velbert, 1967.

Strohmenger, Hanns. *Danzigs Heimkehr ins Reich*. Danzig, 1939.

Stucken, Rudolf. *Deutsche Geld- und Kreditpolitik*. Hamburg, 1937.

Taylor, A. J. P. *The Origins of the Second World War*. New York, 1962.

Taylor, Telford. *Nuremberg and Vietnam: An American Tragedy*. Chicago, 1970.

Toland, John. *The Last Hundred Days*. New York, 1966.

Trevor-Roper, H. R. "A. J. P. Taylor, Hitler, and the War." *Encounter* 17, no. 7 (July 1961) : 88–96.

———. "Hitlers Kriegsziele." *Vierteljahrshefte für Zeitgeschichte* 8 (1960) : 121–33.

Trzebiatowski, Klemens. "Szkolnictwo i oswiata polska w Wolnym Mieście Gdańsku 1918–1939." *Przegląd Zachodni* 12 (1956) : 324–38.

Vogelsang, Thilo. *Reichswehr, Staat und NSDAP*. Stuttgart, 1962.

Waite, Robert G. L. *Vanguard of Nazism: The Free Corps Movement in Post-War Germany, 1918–1923*. Cambridge, Mass., 1952.

Weinberg, Gerhard L. "The Defeat of Germany in 1918 and the European Balance of Power." *Central European History* 2 (1969) : 248–60.

———. *The Foreign Policy of Hitler's Germany: Diplomatic Revolution in Europe, 1933–36*. Chicago, 1970.

———. "A Proposed Compromise over Danzig in 1939?" *Journal of Central European Affairs* 14 (1954) : 334–38.

Wer ist's. Vol. 10. Berlin, 1935.

Wertheimer, Mildred S. "Nazi Pressure in Danzig." *Geneva Special Studies* 7, no. 3 (May 1936) : 1–16.

Wilder, Jan Antoni. "The Danzig Problem from Within." *The Slavonic (and East European) Review* 15 (1936–37) : 357–67.

Wynot, Edward D., Jr. " 'A Necessary Cruelty': The Emergence of Official Anti-Semitism in Poland, 1936–39." *American Historical Review* 76 (1971) : 1035–58.

Notes

Introduction

1. Marcel Déat, *Perspectives françaises* (Paris, 1940), p. 31. "Mourir pour Dantzig?" appeared originally in *l'Œuvre,* 4 May 1939. On Déat see Emily H. Goodman, "The Socialism of Marcel Déat," dissertation, Stanford University, 1973.

2. Some would disagree, most notably A. J. P. Taylor, *The Origins of the Second World War* (New York, 1962).

3. The only work that deals specifically with the Nazis in the free city is Hans L. Leonhardt, *Nazi Conquest of Danzig* (Chicago, 1942). Leonhardt was himself involved with the Danzig opposition to the Nazis, but he had little knowledge of the internal affairs of the NSDAP, and his account contains a number of errors.

4. The broader aspects of the debate on the nature of national socialism are examined in Wolfgang Sauer, "National Socialism: Totalitarianism or Fascism?" *American Historical Review* 73 (December 1967): 404–24. Several new studies have attempted to break away from the older tendency to view the Third Reich and the Nazi movement as monolithic, totalitarian entities, in order more precisely to describe their political anatomies. See, e.g., Joseph Nyomarkay, *Charisma and Factionalism in the Nazi Party* (Minneapolis, 1967); David Schoenbaum, *Hitler's Social Revolution* (Garden City, N.Y., 1966); Edward N. Peterson, *The Limits of Hitler's Power* (Princeton, 1969); and Peter Hüttenberger, *Die Gauleiter* (Stuttgart, 1969). General studies of particular importance include Dietrich Orlow, *The History of the Nazi Party: 1919–1933* (Pittsburgh, 1969); Martin Broszat, *Der Staat Hitlers* (Munich, 1969); and Karl Dietrich Bracher, *The German Dictatorship* (New York, 1970).

5. On local history, see esp. Peterson, *Limits of Hitler's Power,* and William S. Allen, *The Nazi Seizure of Power: The Experience of a Single German Town 1930–1935* (Chicago, 1965).

Chapter 1

1. Walther Stephen, *Danzig: Gründung und Strassennamen* (Marburg/Lahn, 1954), and Marian Biskup, *Stosunek Gdańska do Kazimierza Jagiellończyka w okresie wojny trzynastoletniej 1454–1466* (Torun, 1953).

2. John Brown Mason, *The Danzig Dilemma* (Stanford, 1946), pp. 14–34, summarizes Danzig history before 1920. The standard older work is Paul Simson, *Geschichte der Stadt Danzig,* 3 vols. (Danzig, 1913–18). For the German interpretation, see Erich Keyser, *Danzigs Geschichte* (Danzig, 1928), and Keyser, *Geschichte der Stadt Danzig* (Kitzingen/Main, 1951). This attitude remains the official position of the Danzig refugee organization, the Vertretung der Danziger. See *Gerechtigkeit für Danzig* (cover title: *Die Freie Stadt Danzig*) (n.p., 1965), pp. 10–11. The classical Polish statement is in Simon Askenazy, *Dantzig and Poland* (London, 1921), esp. pp. 14–23.

3. Mason, *Danzig Dilemma,* p. 30, and Ian F. D. Morrow, *The Peace Settlement in the German-Polish Borderlands* (London, 1936), p. 31.

4. Morrow, *Peace Settlement,* pp. 30–33, and Christoph M. Kimmich, *The Free City: Danzig and German Foreign Policy, 1919–34* (New Haven, 1968), p. 2.

5. For photographs of Danzig see Hans Bernard Meyer, *Danzig in 144 Bildern* (Leer, 1956); the text is marred by propaganda. A typical German-oriented guidebook is Günther Sawatzki, *Danzig ist deutsch* (Berlin, 1939). For a Polish orientation cf. Henri de Montfort, *Dantzig, port de Pologne* (Paris, 1939), and Marian Pelczar, *Polski Gdańsk* (Gdansk, 1947).

6. Mason, *Danzig Dilemma,* p. 33.

7. Ibid., pp. 35–60, and Kimmich, *Free City,* pp. 1–22, summarize the literature on the Peace Conference as it relates to Danzig.

8. Henrich Sahm, *Erinnerungen aus meinen Danziger Jahren 1919–1930* (Marburg/Lahn, 1958), p. 1; Wilhelm Markull, "Danzig: Das Schicksal einer deutschen Stadt," *Zeitschrift für Politik* 19, no. 9 (January 1930): 619; and Askenazy, "Prefatory Note," *Dantzig and Poland,* all recognize Lloyd George's role. Cf. Kimmich, *Free City,* pp. 6–11, and Eugeniusz Lyczkowski, "W sprawie genezy Wolnego Miasta Gdanska," *Przegląd Zachodni* (1966): 298–309.

9. Kimmich, *Free City,* pp. 8–10.

10. Alma Luckau, *The German Delegation at the Paris Peace Conference* (New York, 1941), pp. 318–19, 336–37.

11. Paul Mantoux, *Les délibérations du Conseil des Quatre (24 mars–28 juin 1919)* (Paris, 1955), 1:200.

12. Gerhard L. Weinberg, "The Defeat of Germany in 1918 and the European Balance of Power," *Central European History* 2 (1969): 248–60.

13. Kimmich, *Free City,* p. 19.

14. W. Moderow, "Die Freie Stadt Danzig," Historical Collections Section, United Nations Library, Geneva (cited below as Moderow MS), p. 9.

15. The Danzig-Polish convention and the proclamation of the free city are reprinted in Mason, *Danzig Dilemma,* pp. 323–32. Cf. Sahm,

Erinnerungen, pp. 18–30. For the constitution see Special Supplement no. 7 (July 1922), *LNOJ.*

16. Mason, *Danzig Dilemma,* pp. 77–88.

17. Cited in ibid., p. 78.

18. *Entscheidungen des Hohen Kommissars des Völkerbundes in der Freien Stadt Danzig: Decisions of the High Commissioner, League of Nations, Free City of Danzig* (Danzig, 1922–33), 1924, p. 70.

19. Moderow MS, pp. 6–7.

20. Mason, *Danzig Dilemma,* esp. pp. 228–47. Cf. Hans Adolf Harder, *Danzig, Polen und der Völkerbund* (Berlin, 1928); Otto Loening, *Die Rechtsstellung der Freien Stadt Danzig* (Berlin, 1928); Julian Makowski, *Le caractère étatique de la Ville Libre de Dantzig* (Warsaw, 1933); and Morrow, *Peace Settlement,* pp. 17–180.

21. Moderow MS, esp. pp. 32, 40.

22. Mason, *Danzig Dilemma,* p. 103n.

23. See the section of the WAP entitled Komisarz Generalny Rzeczypospolitej Polskiej w Gdańsku (Commissariat-General of the Republic of Poland in Danzig) (cited below as WAP/KGRP), I, 259/717 and 719.

24. Mason, *Danzig Dilemma,* pp. 5–7. Cf. Moderow MS, pp. 99–101.

25. See, e.g., Arthur Greiser, Vermerk (extract), 12 November 1937, in files of the Deutsches Generalkonsulat (German Consulate-General) Danzig, PA (cited below as PA/DGKD), II 17, 2.

26. On Danzig's Jews see Max Aschkewitz, *Zur Geschichte der Juden in Westpreussen 1772–1932* (Marburg/Lahn, 1968), and "Die Geschichte der Juden in Danzig: Zu einem Manuskript von Samuel Echt," *Deutsche Studien* 8, no. 30 (June 1970): 145–48.

27. *Verfassung der Freien Stadt Danzig in der Fassung des Gesetzes vom 4. Juli 1930* (Danzig, n.d.).

28. Mason, *Danzig Dilemma,* pp. 70–71. Kimmich, *Free City,* pp. 42, 52. Cf. Jan Antoni Wilder, "The Danzig Problem from Within," *The Slavonic (and East European) Review* 15 (1936–37): 357–67.

29. Amadeo Giannini, *The Problem of Danzig* (Rome, 1932), p. 23. Absolute proof is provided by Kimmich, *Free City.*

30. A dissertation dealing with domestic politics before the Nazi takeover is being prepared by Witold Sypniewski (Krakow). The best published sources are Sahm, *Erinnerungen,* and Ernst Ziehm, *Aus meiner politischen Arbeit in Danzig 1914–1939* (Marburg/Lahn, 1960).

31. Mason, *Danzig Dilemma,* pp. 178–79.

32. Ibid., pp. 116–17; Sahm, *Erinnerungen,* pp. 13–18; Thadée Bierowski, *La Ville Libre de Dantzig et la guerre polono-bolchévique de 1920* (Danzig, 1932). Cf. Gerhard Rieper, "Die militärischen Rechte Polens in der Freien Stadt und die Frage der Neutralität Danzigs" (Ph.D. diss., Würzburg, 1933).

33. Mason, *Danzig Dilemma,* pp. 130–38; Morrow, *Peace Settlement,*

pp. 124–58; Moderow MS, chap. 5; and *Sammlung der Dokumente zum Rechtsstreit Danzig-Gdingen* (Danzig, 1931).

34. Edmund von Thermann (German consul-general, Danzig) to AA, 31 May 1933, Pa/Pol. IV: Wi (Geh.) 1 Nr.1, Bd. 2.

35. Mason, *Danzig Dilemma,* p. 92.

Chapter 2

1. Wolfgang Diewerge, *Der neue Reichsgau Danzig-Westpreussen: Ein Arbeitsbericht vom Aufbauwerk im deutschen Osten* (Berlin, 1940), p. 26, available on microfilm, NA/microcopy no. T-580/roll 20/Ordner 200.

2. There are two collections of documents from 1925 to 1930: NA/T-580/20/200, which is a microfilm made from a BA file, Schumacher/200, but includes some additional material, and OPG-Hohnfeldt, a file in the BDC.

3. Personalbogen, n.d., BDC/OPG-Hohnfeldt, and Hohnfeldt to Hauptgeschäftsstelle der NSDAP, 6 October 1925, NA/T-580/20/200.

4. On the free corps see Robert G. L. Waite, *Vanguard of Nazism: The Free Corps Movement in Post-War Germany, 1918–1923* (Cambridge, Mass., 1952).

5. On *völkisch* ideology and politics see Peter G. J. Pulzer, *The Rise of Political Anti-Semitism in Germany and Austria* (New York, 1964); Fritz Stern, *The Politics of Cultural Despair* (Berkeley, 1965); George L. Mosse, *The Crisis of German Ideology* (New York, 1964); and Klemens von Klemperer, *Germany's New Conservatism* (Princeton, 1968).

6. On the DSP, see Dietrich Orlow, *The History of the Nazi Party: 1919–1933* (Pittsburgh, 1969), pp. 26–30, 42, and Jeremy Noakes, "Conflict and Development in the NSDAP 1924–1927," *Journal of Contemporary History* 1 (1966):3–36. Cf. the material on the DSP in HA/roll 42/folder 839.

7. Walter Maass (stellv. Gauleiter Danzig) to Reichsleitung der NSDAP, 1 June 1928, BDC/OPG-Hohnfeldt.

8. Hohnfeldt correspondence, October 1925–March 1926, NA/T-580/20/200. The formation of a new Gau frequently depended more on the "availability of a willing man" than on other factors. See Orlow, *Nazi Party,* p. 58.

9. Documents for March 1926, NA/T-580/20/200.

10. Hohnfeldt to Hauptgeschäftsstelle, 17 and 29 March 1926, NA/T-580/20/200.

11. Orlow, *Nazi Party,* chap. 4.

12. Hohnfeldt correspondence, May–August 1926, NA/T-580/20/200.

13. Ibid., August–December 1926. Cf. Noakes, "Conflict and Development," pp. 15ff., and Orlow, *Nazi Party,* pp. 59ff.

14. RL-Propaganda-Abteilung to Gauleitung Danzig, 21 March 1927, NA/T-580/20/200.

15. Orlow, *Nazi Party,* pp. 119–20.

16. Hohnfeldt correspondence, April 1927–June 1928, NA/T-580/20/200. Maass correspondence, June–November 1928, BDC/OPG-Hohnfeldt.

17. Resolutions passed in June 1929 by various Danzig associations, forwarded to League of Nations, 17 August 1929, in ASDN/years 28–32: section 2B/series 12952/dossier 12952 (carton R 1909).

18. Maass to Organisationsabteilung der Reichsleitung, 28 January 1930, NA/T-580/20/200. On Reich party membership see Alan Bullock, *Hitler, a Study in Tyranny,* rev. ed. (New York, 1964), p. 150; Orlow, *Nazi Party,* pp. 179ff.; and Wolfgang Schäfer, *NSDAP* (Hannover and Frankfurt/Main, 1957), pp. 11, 17.

19. Orlow, *Nazi Party,* p. 82.

20. Documents, January–March 1930, NA/T-580/20/200.

21. Koch to Buch, 30 July 1930; Kurt Schubert to Göring, n.d., BDC/OPG-Hohnfeldt.

22. For membership in June 1930 see Wilhelm Löbsack and Albert Forster, *Das nationalsozialistische Gewissen in Danzig* (Danzig, 1936), p. 279. Membership of 400 in 1929 may be inferred from NA/T-580/20/200.

23. On the depression see Christoph M. Kimmich, *The Free City* (New Haven, 1968), p. 106.

24. Commissioner-General Strasburger to High Commissioner Gravina, 18 June, 19 September 1930, ASDN/28–32: 2B/12952/12952 (R 1909). Cf. WAP/KGRP, I, 259/608.

25. On Stennes see Charles Drage, *The Amiable Prussian* (London, 1958), and Ernst Otto Schüddekopf, *Linke Leute von Rechts* (Stuttgart, 1960), pp. 322–23.

26. Koch to Buch, 30 July 1930, BDC/OPG-Hohnfeldt. Cf. Heinrich Bennecke, *Hitler und die SA* (Munich and Vienna, 1962), pp. 247–48.

27. Wnuck, Vertrag . . . (1940), BDC/OPG-Wnuck.

28. *Danziger Vorposten,* 7 April 1933. Erich Stockhorst, *Fünftausend Köpfe* (Velbert, 1967), p. 163.

29. Koch to Buch, 30 July, BDC/OPG-Hohnfeldt.

30. Documents, July–August 1930, BDC/OPG-Hohnfeldt.

31. Heinz Höhne, *Der Orden unter dem Totenkopf* (Gütersloh, 1967), pp. 64–66, and Helmut Heiber, *Joseph Goebbels* (Berlin, 1962), pp. 97–98.

32. Koch to Wnuck, 5 September 1930; Buch to Thiede, 16 September 1930, BDC/OPG-Hohnfeldt.

33. Reinhardt, SA Bericht, 5 September 1930, BDC/OPG-Hohnfeldt.

34. Anon., "Kurzer Bericht über die am 8.9.30 in Danzig einberufene Generalmitgliederversammlung . . . ," 22 September 1930; Danzig

Ortsgruppenleiter to Hitler, 8 September 1930, BDC/OPG-Hohnfeldt.

35. Orlow, *Nazi Party,* p. 86.

36. Documents for September 1930, BDC/OPG-Hohnfeldt.

37. On the nature of Hitler's leadership see Orlow, *Nazi Party,* and Joseph Nyomarkay, *Charisma and Factionalism in the Nazi Party* (Minneapolis, 1967).

38. Documents, 30 September–5 October 1930, BDC/OPG-Hohnfeldt.

39. Greiser to Göring, 4 October 1930, BDC/OPG-Hohnfeldt.

40. Documents for October 1930, BDC/OPG-Hohnfeldt, and NA/T-580/20/200.

Chapter 3

1. Wilhelm Löbsack, *Albert Forster* (Hamburg, 1934), pp. 9–26, and *Das Deutsche Führerlexikon 1934/1935* (Berlin, 1934), p. 128.

2. Löbsack, *Albert Forster,* p. 32.

3. Hitler, Vollmacht, 15 October 1930, reproduced, ibid., p. 33.

4. Albert Forster and Wilhelm Löbsack, eds., *Das nationalsozialistische Gewissen in Danzig* (Danzig, 1936), p. 16.

5. Nat. Soc. candidates to Forster, 23 October 1930, BDC/OPG-Hohnfeldt.

6. Löbsack, *Albert Forster,* p. 38, and BDC/SA-Linsmayer.

7. Forster and Löbsack, *Gewissen,* pp. 19ff., and Löbsack, *Albert Forster,* p. 37. Cf. William S. Allen, *The Nazi Seizure of Power* (Chicago, 1965), pp. 31–32, 294–95.

8. Greiser to Göring, 9, 11 October 1930, BDC/OPG-Hohnfeldt. Strasburger to Gravina, 18 October 1930, WAP/KGRP, I, 259/608, pp. 41–42.

9. Löbsack, *Albert Forster,* p. 37. *Danziger Statistisches Taschenbuch 1933* (Danzig, 1932), pp. 157, 159. Gravina to Sec'y-Gen., 18 November 1930, ASDN/28–32: 2B/1437/1437 (R 1897).

10. Werner (HJ Danzig) to Grenzlandamt der HJ, 30 January 1931, HA/roll 19/frame 370. Irmgard von Maltzahn, *Deutsche Mädel auf Vorposten* (Leipzig, 1934).

11. Documents, 15 October 1930–17 February 1937, HA/47/994.

12. Dietrich Orlow, *The History of the Nazi Party: 1919–1933* (Pittsburgh, 1969), pp. 131–33, 151ff., covers the reorientation of party strategy in the Reich.

13. Löbsack, *Albert Forster,* pp. 20, 24. On rural Bavaria cf. Edward N. Peterson, *The Limits of Hitler's Power* (Princeton, 1969), chaps. 5, 7, 8.

14. Forster, "Richtlinien zum Abhalten von Versammlungen auf dem Lande," 6 January 1931 (misdated 1930), NA/T-580/20/200.

15. Forster and Löbsack, *Gewissen,* pp. 31, 35ff., and the *Vorposten,* 1931, esp. the column: "Aus der Bewegung."

16. *Vorposten,* 30 October 1931. The figures are unsubstantiated.

17. Greiser to Reichsleitung, 3 January 1931, NA/T-580/20/200.

18. Forster and Löbsack, *Gewissen,* p. 279.

19. For 1936 office holders see HA/11/240/III Danzig. Cf. lists in BDC/OPG-Hohnfeldt and NA/T-580/20/200.

20. Orlow, *Nazi Party,* pp. 14–30.

21. See, e.g., Alan Bullock, *Hitler, a Study in Tyranny,* rev. ed. (New York, 1964), p. 151; S. William Halperin, *Germany Tried Democracy* (New York, 1965), p. 406; and Allen, *Nazi Seizure,* pp. 65–83.

22. Bolesław Kasprowicz, "Straty gospodarcze Gdańska jako wynik jego izolowania się od Polski w latach międzywojennych," *Przegląd Zachodni* 12 (1956): 311–23.

23. Based on statistics in Ian F. D. Morrow, *The Peace Settlement in the German-Polish Borderlands* (London, 1936), pp. 499, 507–8.

24. Christoph M. Kimmich, *The Free City* (New Haven, 1968), pp. 106–7. Koester (German consulate-general) to AA, 20 February 1933, PA/Abt. IV-Wirtschaft-Danzig: Wi (Geh.) 1 Nr. 1.

25. John Brown Mason, *The Danzig Dilemma* (Stanford, 1946), pp. 130–38, 178–84; Morrow, *Peace Settlement,* pp. 124–58; A. Siebeneichen and H. Strasburger, *Spór o Gdynię* (Torun, 1930), and *Sammlung der Dokumente zum Rechtsstreit Danzig-Gdingen* (Danzig, 1931).

26. PA/DGKD: Wo 4, Bd. 3.

27. Cited in Heinrich Sahm, *Erinnerungen aus meinen Danziger Jahren 1919–1930* (Marburg/Lahn, 1958), p. 172.

28. Greiser, circular, 18 April 1931, WAP/KGRP, I, 259/608, p. 52.

29. "Zurück zum Reich. Gegen vertragliche Willkür."

30. WAP/KGRP, I, 259/606, 608.

31. *Vorposten,* 1931–32, esp. 27 November 1931, and Löbsack, *Albert Forster,* pp. 39, 45–47.

32. Löbsack, *Albert Forster,* p. 45, and *Vorposten,* 22 May 1931.

33. Budding (Regierungspräsident Marienwerder) to Severing (Prus. min. of the interior), 3 March 1931, PA/DGKD: II 1, Bd. 5. *Vorposten,* 22 May 1931.

34. *Vorposten,* 15 April 1932, and Löbsack, *Albert Forster,* p. 51 and photograph facing p. 48.

35. Ernst Ziehm, *Aus meiner politischen Arbeit in Danzig 1914–1939* (Marburg/Lahn, 1960), p. 148.

36. Ibid., pp. 142–43.

37. E.g., Milbradt to Hitler, 24 October 1930, BDC/OPG-Hohnfeldt.

38. Orlow, *Nazi Party,* p. 188.

39. Löbsack, *Albert Forster,* p. 38, and *Danziger Beobachter,* 19 December 1930, cited in Forster and Löbsack, *Gewissen,* p. 27.

40. Thermann to AA, 11 December 1930, PA/Pol. IV: Po 5 Dz, Bd. 5.

41. Ziehm, *Politischen Arbeit,* pp. 143–46.

42. Unsigned memorandum, 13 December 1930, NA/T-580/20/200. Forster and Löbsack, *Gewissen,* pp. 26–28.

43. Orlow, *Nazi Party,* p. 191.

44. Thermann to AA, 19, 31 March 1931, PA/Pol IV: Po 5 Dz, Bd. 5.

45. *Vorposten,* 27 February and 23 October 1931.

46. E.g., *Vorposten,* 10 July and 4 September 1931, 15 January 1932.

47. *Vorposten,* spring 1931, and WAP/KGRP, I, 259/606, 608.

48. *Vorposten,* 3 June 1932.

49. Karl Dietrich Bracher, in Bracher, Wolfgang Sauer, and Gerhard Schulz, *Die nationalsozialistische Machtergreifung* (Cologne and Opladen, 1960), pp. 38–40.

50. Gravina to Rosting, 17 April 1932, ASDN/28–32: 2B/34205/34205 (R 1919).

51. *Vorposten,* 10 June, 1, 15 July 1932.

52. WAP/KGRP, I, 259/613, pp. 26–45, 105.

53. Hermann Rauschning, *Gespräche mit Hitler* (New York, 1940), pp. 31–32. Löbsack, *Albert Forster,* p. 53 and photograph facing p. 48. *Vorposten,* 9 September 1932. Gravina to Rosting, 17 April 1932, ASDN/28–32: 2B/34205/34205 (R 1919).

54. Heinrich Bennecke, *Hitler und die SA* (Munich and Vienna, 1962), pp. 203–8. NA/T-81/roll 91/frames 105060–62/EAP 231-c-01/3.

55. Cf. Joseph Goebbels, *Vom Kaiserhof zur Reichskanzlei* (Munich, 1934), p. 191, for cooperation with KPD during Berlin transit strike.

56. *Vorposten,* 23 and 30 September 1932.

57. Bullock, *Hitler,* pp. 230–43, and Orlow, *Nazi Party,* pp. 286ff.

58. Pol. IV, Aufzeichnung, n.d. (October 1933), NA/T-120/roll 2787/series 6023/frames H 044553–54/Pol. IV: Po 2 Dz, Bd. 3. Anna Rauschning, *No Retreat* (New York and Indianapolis, 1942), pp. 11–22, 85–95. *Führerlexikon,* p. 370. On the German minority and Rauschning's role see Richard Breyer, *Das Deutsche Reich und Polen 1932–1937* (Würzburg, 1955), pp. 38–63.

59. Rauschning's later published works: *Die Revolution des Nihilismus* (Zurich, 1938, 1939), citations from slightly abridged 1964 ed., edited by Golo Mann; *Gespräche mit Hitler; The Conservative Revolution* (New York, 1941); *The Redemption of Democracy* (New York, 1941); *Makers of Destruction* (London, 1942), American title: *Men of Chaos; Time of Delirium* (New York, 1946); *Deutschland zwischen Ost und West* (Berlin, Hamburg, and Stuttgart, 1950). The description of Rauschning's outlook is based on these works. When Rauschning's *Gespräche mit Hitler* first appeared, it was dismissed as the propaganda of an embittered ex-Nazi. After the publication of Percy Ernst Schramm, ed., *Hitlers Tischgespräche im Führerhauptquartier,* rev. ed. (Stuttgart, 1963), the accounts of the Führer's conversations given by Rauschning seemed more authentic. See H. R. Trevor-Roper, *The Last Days of Hitler,* 3d ed. (New York, 1962), p. 66n. The *Gespräche* have been

found reliable where they can be checked against documents, and they have been used as a primary source in this study. Rauschning's *Conservative Revolution* has also been found generally reliable. In *Die Revolution des Nihilismus* and *Makers of Destruction* conversations and events are reported with insufficient circumstantial background to allow for documentary substantiation. These works have been used with caution. For a rather negative interpretation of Rauschning's work and influence see Eberhard Jäckel, *Hitler's Weltanschauung* (Middletown, Conn., 1972), pp. 15ff., 124–25, n.22.

60. (Berlin, 1930).

61. Klemens von Klemperer, *Germany's New Conservatism* (Princeton, 1968). Cf. Fritz Stern, *The Politics of Cultural Despair* (Berkeley, 1965), pp. 231–325.

62. *Conservative Revolution,* p. 51. Hugo von Hofmannsthal, *Das Schriftum als geistiger Raum der Nation* (Munich, 1927), p. 16. Edgar J. Jung, *Die Herrschaft der Minderwertigen* (Berlin, 1930).

63. Rauschning, *Die Revolution des Nihilismus,* p. 140.

64. Rauschning, *Conservative Revolution,* p. 56.

65. Morrow, *Peace Settlement,* pp. 296, 502.

66. Kimmich, *Free City,* pp. 47, 122–23.

67. D. F. Dormeyer, *Marktregulierung zur Rettung der Danziger Landwirtschaft* (Danzig, 1934), p. 5. Thermann to AA, 1 September 1932, PA/Abt. IV-Wirtschaft-Danzig: Wi (Geh.) 1 Nr. 1.

68. Rauschning, *Conservative Revolution,* pp. 56–57. Ziehm, *Politischen Arbeit,* p. 193. *Vorposten,* 17 February, 7 April 1933. Hans L. Leonhardt, *Nazi Conquest of Danzig* (Chicago, 1942), p. 191.

69. Dormeyer, *Marktregulierung,* pp. 6–7, and Anna Rauschning, *No Retreat,* pp. 105–6.

70. Orlow, *Nazi Party,* pp. 194, 202, 241. *Führerlexikon,* p. 370.

71. Leonhardt, *Nazi Conquest,* p. 56. Leonhardt unwittingly strengthens this contention by stating mistakenly that Rauschning became head of the *Landbund* before he joined the NSDAP, and that he held the post of "Vice-Gauleiter." The latter error is repeated in Carl J. Burckhardt, *Meine Danziger Mission* (Munich, 1960), p. 34, and in Ludwig Denne, *Das Danzig Problem in der deutschen Aussenpolitik* (Bonn, 1959), p. 45. Rauschning's name appeared only three times in the *Vorposten* before April 1933, in the issues of 8 January 1932, and 17 February and 31 March 1933.

72. Thermann to Neurath, 3 February 1933, NA/T-120/3512/9062/E 634776–79/Pol. IV: Po 5 Dz, Bd. 6.

73. *Vorposten,* 10, 17 February 1933. Koester to AA, 23 February 1933, NA/T-120/3512/9062/E 634781–82/Pol. IV: Po 5 Dz, Bd. 6.

74. Kimmich, *Free City,* pp. 130–34. Hans Roos, *Polen und Europa* (Tübingen, 1957), pp. 61–71. Bogdan Dopierała, *Gdańska polityka*

Józefa Becka (Poznan, 1967), pp. 52ff. Józef Beck, *Dernier rapport* (Paris, 1951), pp. 25–26.

75. Ziehm, *Politischen Arbeit,* p. 186.

76. Ibid., pp. 189–91. The negotiations may be traced in detail in the following: NA/T-120/3512/9062/E 634780–802/Pol. IV: Po 5 Dz. Bd. 6; Meyer, memorandum, 3 April 1933, NA/T-20/3404/8825/E 614285/Handakten-Direktoren: Meyer, Danzig: Politisches; and Thermann to AA, 31 March 1933, NA/T-120/2916/6207/E 469135–39/Geh.: Polen/Danzig.

77. *Vorposten,* 21 April 1933.

78. Rauschning, *Conservative Revolution,* pp. 218–26.

79. Leonhardt, *Nazi Conquest,* p. 56.

80. Rauschning, *Gespräche,* p. 53.

81. Cameron to Sir John Simon (Brit. foreign minister), 29 June 1933, in PRO/FO 371/17235/N 4927/1275/55.

82. Hitler directly reassured the British on Danzig. See Horace Rumbold (Brit. ambassador, Berlin) to FO, 16 March 1933, PRO/FO 371/17235/N 1735/1275/55.

83. *Vorposten,* April–May 1933.

84. Ziehm to Rosting (2 letters), 17 May 1933, ASDN/33–46: 2B/3398/3398 (R 3709), and Rosting to Sec'y-Gen., 16 May 1933, ASDN/33–46: 2B/4140/4140 (R 3712).

85. Leonhardt, *Nazi Conquest,* pp. 58–59.

86. Cited in Löbsack, *Albert Forster,* p. 57.

87. *Taschenbuch,* p. 159.

Chapter 4

1. John Brown Mason, *The Danzig Dilemma* (Stanford, 1946), p. 88.

2. Thilo Vogelsang, *Reichswehr, Staat und NSDAP* (Stuttgart, 1962), p. 118. Cf. Dietrich Orlow, *The History of the Nazi Party: 1919–1933* (Pittsburgh, 1969), p. 216.

3. *Vorposten,* 1 June 1933, and *Frankfurter Zeitung,* 30 May 1933.

4. Hermann Rauschning, *The Conservative Revolution* (New York, 1941), p. 6. On the DNVP, see Thermann to Meyer, 8 June 1933, NA/T-120/3404/8825/E 614282–83/Handakten-Direktoren: Meyer, Danzig: Politisches. Cf. Karl Dietrich Bracher, Wolfgang Sauer, and Gerhard Schulz, *Die nationalsozialistische Machtergreifung* (Cologne and Opladen, 1960), pp. 204–14.

5. Karl Bachem, *Vorgeschichte, Geschichte und Politik der Zentrumspartei* 8 (Cologne, 1932): 257.

6. Guenter Lewy, *The Catholic Church and Nazi Germany* (New York, 1965), pp. 21, 27, and Rudolf Morsey, "Hitlers Verhandlungen mit der Zentrumsführung am 31. Januar 1933," *Vierteljahrshefte für Zeitgeschichte* 9 (1961): 182–94.

7. Lewy, *Catholic Church,* pp. 94–98.

8. Forster to Reichsleitung, Kartei-Abt., 29 August 1933, BDC/PK-Hoppenrath.

9. Thermann to AA, 29 June 1933, NA/T-120/3214/7574/E 542853–54/Pol. IV: Po 5 Dz, Bd. 7. Rosting, general report, 6 January 1934, *LNOJ* 15 (1934): 995. *Vorposten,* 21 June 1933. BDC/SSO-Huth, and Kluck.

10. *Vorposten,* 7 April 1933.

11. Documents for June 1933, NA/T-120/2954/6211/E 469613–29/Geh.: Polen/Danzig, Wi 7.

12. *Vorposten,* 19 May 1933. ASDN/33–46: 2B/4380, 5837/3398 (R 3709–10).

13. *Vorposten,* 27 June, 7 September 1933. Thermann to AA, 14 September 1933, NA/T-120/3512/9062/E 634924–25/Pol. IV: Po 5 Dz, Bd. 8.

14. *Vorposten,* 6 September 1933.

15. Ernst Ziehm, *Aus meiner politischen Arbeit in Danzig* (Marburg/Lahn, 1960), p. 59. Cf. Hans L. Leonhardt, *Nazi Conquest of Danzig* (Chicago, 1942), pp. 82–83, and Danzig dispatches for September 1933, NA/T-120/3512/9062/E 634924–28/Pol. IV: Po 5 Dz, Bd. 8.

16. Martin Broszat, *200 Jahre deutsche Polenpolitik* (Munich, 1963), pp. 182–86; Hans Roos, *A History of Modern Poland* (New York, 1966), pp. 129–30; and Roos, *Polen und Europa* (Tübingen, 1957), p. 65. For a differing view cf. Zygmunt J. Gasiorowski, "Did Piłsudski Attempt to Initiate a Preventive War in 1933?" *The Journal of Modern History* 27 (1955): 135–51. The best brief discussion of Polish-German relations in 1933 is in Gerhard L. Weinberg, *The Foreign Policy of Hitler's Germany* (Chicago, 1970), pp. 57–74.

17. Adolf Hitler, *Die Südtiroler Frage und das Deutsche Bündnisproblem* (Munich, 1926). This pamphlet became part of vol. 2 of *Mein Kampf,* J. Chamberlain, et al., "editorial sponsors" (New York, 1939), pp. 911ff.

18. Christoph M. Kimmich, *The Free City* (New Haven, 1968), p. 140.

19. *Vorposten* and *Manchester Guardian,* 19 May 1933. Albert Forster and Wilhelm Löbsack, *Das nationalsozialistische Gewissen in Danzig* (Danzig, 1936), pp. 154–56. Moltke (German minister Warsaw) to AA, 19 May 1933, *DGFP,* series C, vol. 1, no. 253. Erskine to Simon, 6 June 1933, PRO/FO 371/17226/N 4347/38/55.

20. Hermann Rauschning, *Gespräche mit Hitler* (New York, 1940), p. 84. *Vorposten,* 1 June 1933. Kimmich, *Free City,* p. 142, cites Rauschning, "Regierungserklärung," 23 June 1933, orig. in *Gesetzblatt für die Freie Stadt Danzig* (Danzig, 1920–39), 26 June 1933.

21. Schliep (German legation Warsaw) to AA, 5 July 1933, NA/T-120/3516/9081/E 637589–95/Pol. IV: Po 3 Dz, Bd. 25.

22. Kimmich, *Free City,* p. 143.

23. Simon, report to the council, 28 September 1933, *LNOJ* 14 (1933): 1330–31. Thermann to AA, 13 July 1933, NA/T-120/3516/9081/E 637598–600/Pol. IV: Po 3 Dz, Bd. 26. ASDN/33–46: 2B/6014/6014 (R 3718).

24. Rosting to Sec'y-Gen., 5 August 1933, *LNOJ* 14 (1933): 1156–57. Thermann to AA, 26 July 1933, NA/T-120/3516/9081/E 637603–15/Pol. IV: Po 3 Dz, Bd. 26. Text of agreement in *LNOJ* 14 (1933): pp. 1157–61. Cf. Klemens Trzebiatowski, "Szkolnictwo i oświata polska w Wolnym Mieście Gdańsku 1918–1939," *Przegląd Zachodni* 12 (1956): 324–38, and Henryk Polak, "Położenie szkolnictwa polskiego w W. M. Gdańsku," *Przegląd Zachodni* 20 (1964): 387–410.

25. Text in *LNOJ* 14 (1933): pp. 1542–43.

26. On "full use" and the Gdynia-Danzig conflict, see Ian F. D. Morrow, *The Peace Settlement in the German-Polish Borderlands* (London, 1936), pp. 124–58; Kimmich, *Free City,* pp. 144–45; Bogdan Dopierała, *Gdańska polityka Józefa Becka* (Poznan, 1967), chap. 1; and Dopierała, "Beck and the Gdańsk Question (1930–1935)," *Acta Poloniae Historica* 17 (1968): 71–104.

27. Rauschning, *Conservative Revolution,* pp. 120, 122, and *Die Revolution des Nihilismus,* Golo Mann, ed. (Zürich, 1964), pp. 269–99.

28. Rauschning, *Gespräche,* p. 109.

29. *Vorposten,* 6 September 1933.

30. Kimmich, *Free City,* esp. chap. 4.

31. Hermann Rauschning, *Makers of Destruction* (London, 1942), pp. 95–99. Documents, August–September 1933, NA/T-120/3516/9081/E 637603–21/Pol. IV: Po 3 Dz, Bd. 26; NA/T-120/3024/6601/E 495059–64/Geh.: Polen/Danzig, Pol 3, Bd. 5.

32. Rosting to Sec'y-Gen., 8 August 1933, ASDN/33–46: 2B/6014/6014 (R 3718).

33. Neurath, memoranda, 25, 26 September 1933, *DGFP,* C, 1 nos. 449, 451.

34. The pact is analyzed in relation to Germany's international position in Charles Bloch, *Hitler und die europäischen Mächte 1933/1934* (Frankfurt/Main, 1966), pp. 49–63. Cf. Weinberg, *Foreign Policy,* pp. 69–74, and Anna M. Cienciala, "The Significance of the Declaration of Non-Aggression of Jan. 26, 1934," *East European Quarterly* 1 (1967): 1–30.

35. Weinberg, *Foreign Policy,* p. 63.

36. Papée to Senate, 31 August 1933, NA/T-120/3516/9081/E 637649–50/Pol. IV: Po 3 Dz, Bd. 26.

37. *Vorposten,* 6, 7, 16 September 1933. Cf. Leonhardt, *Nazi Conquest,* p. 70, and Rosting, general report, 6 January 1934, *LNOJ* 15 (1934): 997.

38. Koester to AA, 23 September 1933, NA/T-120/3516/9081/E

637668–69/Pol. IV: Po 3 Dz, Bd. 26. Cf. *Vorposten,* 22, 23 September 1933, and Rosting to Sec'y-Gen., 23 September 1933, ASDN/33–46: 2B/6912/5469 (R 3718).

39. Neurath, memorandum, 17 October 1933, *DGFP,* C, 2, no. 11. Rauschning, *Die Revolution,* p. 282, and *Gespräche,* p. 107.

40. Mason, *Danzig Dilemma,* pp. 179–86.

41. Kimmich, *Free City,* pp. 150–51. Rauschning, *Gespräche,* p. 107. Rauschning to Pilsudski, December 1933 (in Radowitz to AA, 2 January 1934), Radowitz to AA, 11 January 1934, NA/T-120/3516/9081/E 637714–15, E 637719–24/Pol. IV: Po 3 Dz, Bd. 27. Moltke to Neurath, 13 December 1933, NA/T–120/2915/6024/E 468613–14/Geh.: Polen/ Danzig, Fi 4.

42. Sean Lester (high commissioner) to Sec'y-Gen., 24 August 1934, *LNOJ* 15 (1934): 1422–23. Cf. Morrow, *Peace Settlement,* pp. 478–79, and Mason, *Danzig Dilemma,* pp. 184–87.

43. Radowitz to AA, 20 March 1934, NA/T-120/3516/9081/E 637726–49/Pol. IV: Po 3 Dz, Bd. 27.

44. Józef Beck, *Dernier rapport* (Paris, 1951), p. 27. The Poles frequently referred to their failure to support the Danzig opposition when they demanded Nazi cooperation on other matters. See, e.g., Józef Lipski, *Diplomat in Berlin, 1933–1939,* W. Jędrzejewicz, ed. (New York, 1968), pp. 208ff.

45. The most complete discussion of the political *Gleichschaltung* of Danzig and the formation of an opposition is in Leonhardt, *Nazi Conquest,* on which the discussion in Ludwig Denne, *Das Danzig Problem in der deutschen Aussenpolitik* (Bonn, 1959), pp. 33–75, is based.

46. Texts in *Gesetzblatt für die Freie Stadt Danzig,* 26, 30 June, 10 October 1933.

47. Moderow MS, p. 96.

48. SPD Danzig (signed "Brill") to Rosting, 15 June 1933, ASDN/ 33–46: 2B/5199/4140 (R 3712).

49. Rosting, general report, 6 January 1934, *LNOJ* 15 (1934): 998.

50. Hermann Thomat, Denkschrift, 11 December 1933, ASDN/33–46: 2B/9046/9046 (R 3718).

51. Lewy, *Catholic Church,* pp. 74–76.

52. Koester to AA, 28 September 1933, PA/DGKD:II 8, Bd. 5.

53. *Danziger Neueste Nachrichten,* 1 November 1933; trans. and Rosting to Sec'y-Gen., 4 November 1933, *LNOJ* 15 (1934): 214–15.

54. *LNOJ* 15 (1934): 214–21. Documents, November–December 1934, NA/T-120/3516/9083/E 638037–105/Pol. IV: Po 12 Dz, Bd. 3. R. Mackenzie Buchan (Brit. consul Danzig) to Simon, 13 November 1933, PRO/FO 371/172236/N 8359/1275/55. Leonhardt, *Nazi Conquest,* pp. 75–76.

55. *Wer ist's,* p. 1170.

56. Koester to AA, 28 September 1933, PA/DGKD: II 8, Bd. 5.

57. Lester to Sec'y-Gen., 3 November 1933, 1 February 1934, ASDN/33–46: 2B/7792, 9494/7792 (R 3720), 3799 (R 3711). Radowitz to AA, 28 March 1934, NA/T-120/3512/9062/E 634937–46/Pol. IV: Po 5 Dz, Bd. 8. *Gesetzblatt,* 17 January, 4 April 1934. *LNOJ* 16 (1935): 797–99.

58. *Danziger Allgemeine Zeitung,* 24 March 1934, clipping, PA/DGKD: II 8, Bd. 5. Wiercinski-Keiser to AA, 9 July 1934, NA/T-120/5646/L 1580/L 480016–17/Geh.: Polen/Danzig, Pol. 25.

59. *Ergebnisse der Volks- und Berufszählung vom 1. November 1923 in der Freien Stadt Danzig* (Danzig, 1926), p. 15.

60. Lewy, *Catholic Church,* pp. 115ff.

61. *Vorposten,* 11 April 1934.

62. O'Rourke, Hirtenbrief, 17 June 1934, PA/Pol. IV: Po 16 Dz. *LNOJ* 16 (1935): 762–66. ASDN/33–46: 2B/15254/4140 (R 3713).

63. Documents for July 1934, PA/DGKD: II 8, Bd. 5.

64. Leonhardt, *Nazi Conquest,* pp. 95–97. Radowitz to AA, 20 November 1934, NA/T-120/3512/9062/E 634984–87/Pol. IV: Po 5 Dz, Bd. 9. *LNOJ* 16 (1935): 789–806.

65. Confirmed by Erich Brost, former editor of the *Volksstimme,* in a letter to the author, 15 January 1969.

66. Leonhardt, *Nazi Conquest,* chap. 3.

67. Rosting to Sec'y-Gen., 2 November 1933, ASDN/33–46: 2B/3398/3398 (R 3709).

68. Rauschning, *Conservative Revolution,* pp. 73–74. On the German background of corporative economic thought see Herman Lebovics, *Social Conservatism and the Middle Classes in Germany, 1914–1933* (Princeton, 1969). Cf. Gerhard Schulz, in Bracher, Sauer, and Schulz, *Machtergreifung,* pt. 2, chap. 4, esp. pp. 627–34; David Schoenbaum, *Hitler's Social Revolution* (Garden City, N.Y., 1966); and Arthur Schweitzer, *Big Business in the Third Reich* (Bloomington, Ind., 1964).

69. *Vorposten,* 14, 20 July, 5 August 1933, 20 December 1934. Rauschning, *Conservative Revolution,* p. 77, and *Gespräche,* pp. 167–69. Koester to Meyer, 5 December 1933, NA/T–120/3404/8825/E 614266–9/Handakten-Direktoren: Meyer, Danzig: Politisches.

70. Rauschning, *Gespräche,* p. 19.

71. Rauschning, *Makers of Destruction,* p. 260.

72. Koester to Meyer, 27 November 1933, NA/T-120/3404/8825/E 614272–75/Handakten-Direktoren: Meyer, Danzig: Politisches. Röhm, Befehl, 9 January 1934, BDC/SSO-Greiser. Rauschning, *Gespräche,* p. 145.

73. Rauschning, *Gespräche,* pp. 97–100.

74. Koester to Meyer, 5 December 1933, NA/T-120/3404/8825/E 614266–69/Handakten-Direktoren: Meyer, Danzig: Politisches.

75. Rauschning, memorandum, 8 December 1933, NA/T-120/3404/8825/E 614271/Handakten-Direktoren: Meyer, Danzig: Politisches.

76. Documents, April–October 1934, NA/T-120/3405/8826/E 614325–408/Handakten-Direktoren: Meyer, Danzig: Finanzen und Währung. Documents, January and September 1934, NA/T-120/2915/6203/E 468462, E 468493–94/Geh.: Polen/Danzig, Fi 3. Cf. Rauschning, *Gespräche,* pp. 191–93.

77. Rauschning, *Gespräche,* pp. 182–85, 191. Cf. Lester to Strang (FO), 22 February 1934, PRO/FO, 371/17783/C 1322/155/55.

78. Radowitz to AA (includes text of Rauschning speech), 7 April 1934, NA/T-120/3516/9081/E 637753–72/Pol. IV: Po 3 Dz, Bd. 27.

79. Forster and Löbsack, *Gewissen,* p. 190.

80. Radowitz to Meyer, 7, 9 May 1934, NA/T-120/3404/8825/E 614259–65/Handakten-Direktoren: Meyer, Danzig: Politisches.

81. Lester to Sec'y-Gen., 13 July, 28 September 1934, PRO/FO 371/17784/C 5856, C 6994/155/55. Rauschning, *Gespräche,* p. 204.

Chapter 5

1. Ernst Sodeikat, "Die Verfolgung und der Widerstand der Juden in der Freien Stadt Danzig von 1933 bis 1945," *Bulletin des Leo Baeck Instituts* 8, no. 30 (1965): 118–22. Rauschning, memorandum (in Rauschning to Neurath, 28 September 1934), pp. 10–11, NA/T-120/2916/6207/E 469173–74/Geh.: Polen/Danzig, Pol 11 Nr. 1. Koester to AA, 28 September 1934, NA/T-120/4268/M 18/M 000726–29/Pol. IV: Po 5 Dz, Bd. 9. Rauschning to Meyer, 11 October 1934, NA/T-120/3404/8825/E 614222–23/Handakten-Direktoren: Meyer, Danzig: Politisches.

2. Rauschning to Neurath, 28, 29 September 1934; Neurath to Hitler, 29 September 1934, NA/T-120/2916/6207/E 469162–63, E 469228–29/Geh.: Polen/Danzig, Pol 5. Cf. Rauschning, *Gespräche mit Hitler* (New York, 1940), p. 205, and Rauschning, *The Conservative Revolution* (New York, 1941), pp. 5–6. The Rauschning memorandum is published in *DGFP,* C, 3, no. 224.

3. Blume (senate foreign dept.), Vermerk, 1 October 1934, PA/DGKD: II 1, Bd. 6. Documents, 4 October–15 November 1934, NA/T-120/2916/6207/E 46196–216/Geh.: Polen/Danzig, Pol 5; NA/T-120/3404/8825/E 614209–18/Handakten-Direktoren: Meyer, Danzig: Politisches. Cf. Rauschning, *Gespräche,* pp. 205–6.

4. Rauschning to Hitler, 8 October 1934, NA/T-120/2916/6207/E 469212–13/Geh.: Polen/Danzig, Pol 5. Radowitz to AA, 23 October 1934, NA/T-120/3404/8825/E 614219/Handakten-Direktoren: Meyer, Danzig: Politisches.

5. Radowitz to AA, 24 November 1934, NA/T-120/2916/6207/E 469248/Geh.: Polen/Danzig, Pol 5. Rauschning's correspondence regarding his resignation, most of it with Wilhelm von Wnuck, acting as Volkstag president, found its way into Poland in the summer of 1935,

apparently through Polish agents in Danzig. See NA/T-120/715/1167/327838–68/Inland II (g) : Geh. Reichssachen, Bd. 11 1943. Rauschning himself made the correspondence available to the opposition, and it appears as a petition appendix in NA/T-120/3513/9062/E 635938–74/Pol. IV: Po 5 Dz, Bd. 14, trans. in *LNOJ* 17 (1936) : 193ff, and in Rauschning, *Conservative Revolution,* pp. 14–30. Cf. Mildred S. Wertheimer, "Nazi Pressure in Danzig," *Geneva Special Studies* 7, no. 3 (May 1936) : 5–7.

6. Koester to AA, 27 November 1934, NA/T-120/2916/6207/E 469249–52/Geh.: Polen/Danzig, Pol 5.

7. Koester to AA, 28 November 1934, NA/T-120/3512/9062/E 635008/ Pol. IV: Po 5 Dz, Bd. 9.

8. Texts in *LNOJ* 16 (1935) : 762–66, 789–806.

9. *LNOJ* 16 (1935) : 139–41. Wertheimer, "Nazi Pressure," p. 7. Lester to Avenol (Sec'y-Gen.), 5, 13 February 1935, PRO/FO 371/18893/C 1150/331/55. Cf. Ernst Sodeikat, "Der Nationalsozialismus und die Danziger Opposition," *Vierteljahrshefte für Zeitgeschichte* 14 (1966) : 144–45.

10. Radowitz to AA, 14 February 1935, NA/T-120/3512/9062/E 635068–71/Pol. IV: Po 5 Dz, Bd. 10.

11. Lester to Avenol, 13 February 1935, PRO/FO 371/18893/C 1150/331/55.

12. William S. Allen, *The Nazi Seizure of Power* (Chicago, 1965), chap. 17.

13. Albert Forster and Wilhelm Löbsack, *Das nationalsozialistische Gewissen in Danzig* (Danzig, 1936), p. 200.

14. Phipps (Brit. ambassador Berlin) to Simon, 10 April 1935, PRO/FO 371/18893/C 3107/331/55.

15. On the international situation, see E. M. Robertson, *Hitler's Pre-War Policy and Military Plans 1933–1939* (London, 1963), pp. 43–61; Gerhard L. Weinberg, *The Foreign Policy of Hitler's Germany* (Chicago, 1970), pp. 205ff.; and Robert Ingrim, *Hitlers glücklichster Tag: London, am 18. Juni 1935* (Stuttgart, 1962).

16. Paul Schmidt, *Statist auf diplomatischer Bühne* (Bonn, 1949), pp. 293–303, gives a good account.

17. Radowitz, memorandum, 20 February 1935, *DGFP,* C, 3, no. 500. Forster and Löbsack, *Gewissen,* pp. 201–3. Senate, Aufruf, WAP/KGRP, I, 259/157, p. 107. Greiser-Lester correspondence, *LNOJ* 16 (1935) : 826–29. Lester to Avenol, 4 March 1935, PRO/FO 371/18893/C 2427/331/55.

18. Radowitz to Meyer, 15 March 1935, NA/T-120/3404/8825/E 614184/Handakten-Direktoren: Meyer, Danzig: Politisches. Forster to Radowitz, 26 March 1935, PA/DGKD: II 2, Bd. 4. Forster and Löbsack, *Gewissen,* p. 205. Cf. *Vorposten,* 16 March–8 April 1935.

19. Hans L. Leonhardt, *Nazi Conquest of Danzig* (Chicago, 1942),

pp. 110ff. Sodeikat, "Opposition," pp. 143–45. *LNOJ* 16 (1935): 819–30. WAP/KGRP, I, 259/719–20. ASDN/33–46: 2B/15638/4140 (R 3713). PA/DGKD: II 4c. It has been claimed that the NSDAP spent the equivalent of 200,000 pounds sterling on the elections, most of it from the Reich. See Jan Antoni Wilder, "The Danzig Problem from Within," *The Slavonic (and East European) Review* 15 (1936–37): 362. This claim is unsubstantiated. Contemporary commentators failed to distinguish between funds spent in Danzig and funds spent in the Reich. See, e.g., Wertheimer, "Nazi Pressure," p. 8.

20. Radowitz to AA, 20 March 1935, NA/T-120/3512/9062/E 635144–45/Pol. IV: Po 5 Dz, Bd. 10.

21. NA/T-120/3512/9062/E 635149–73/Pol. IV: Po 5 Dz, Bd. 10.

22. Radowitz, memorandum, 20 February 1935, *DGFP,* C, 3, no. 500.

23. Sodeikat, "Opposition," p. 145. The report of Forster's conduct relies on Sodeikat's private sources and is unconfirmed.

24. Officially, 139,423 of 235,062 valid votes. Lester to Sec'y-Gen., 6 May 1935, *LNOJ* 16 (1935): 824–25.

25. PA/DGKD: II 19, Bd. 1. Erich Brost to author, 15 January 1969.

26. *Danziger Statistisches Taschenbuch 1934* (Danzig, 1934), p. 161.

27. Ernst Ziehm, *Aus meiner politischen Arbeit in Danzig 1914–1939* (Marburg/Lahn, 1960), p. 197.

28. Radowitz to AA, 9 April 1935, encl. Rauschning to Forster, open letter (Liste Weise, n.d.), NA/T-120/3512/9062/E 635185–88/Pol. IV: Po 5 Dz, Bd. 11. Cf. Rauschning, *Conservative Revolution,* pp. 31–32, in which the open letter is reprinted in part.

29. The significance of the vote for Weise's list has been overestimated. See Leonhardt, *Nazi Conquest,* p. 121, and Wertheimer, "Nazi Pressure," p. 7. Wertheimer's statement that the German Nationalist vote increased between 1933 and 1935 is incorrect and based on a misreading of Lester to Sec'y-Gen., 6 May 1935, *LNOJ* 16 (1935): 824–25.

30. Photographic appendix, Greiser to Lester, 15 May 1935, ASDN/33–46: 2B/15638/4140 (R 3713).

31. See, e.g., *The Times* (London), 8, 9 April 1935; *New York Times,* 7 April 1935; and Stephen Duggan, "The Significance of the Election in Danzig," address over the Columbia Broadcasting System, 12 April 1935, mimeographed copy in New York Public Library.

32. Forster and Löbsack, *Gewissen,* pp. 207–8. *Frankfurter Zeitung,* 9 April 1935. Radowitz to Meyer, 8 April 1935, NA/T-120/3512/9062/E 635177/Pol. IV: Po 5 Dz, Bd. 11. Cf. Phipps to Simon, 10 April 1935, PRO/FO 371/18893/C 3107/331/55.

33. BDC/SSO-Greiser.

34. Von dem Bach-Zelewski to Himmler, 8 April 1935, BDC/SSO-von dem Bach.

35. Franz Neumann, *Behemoth* (New York, 1966), p. 333.

36. Rudolf Stucken, *Deutsche Geld- und Kreditpolitik* (Hamburg, 1937), pp. 153ff. NA/T-120/3405/8826/E 614367–86/Handakten-Direktoren: Meyer, Danzig: Finanzen und Währung.

37. Rauschning to Neurath, 1 February 1934, NA/T-120/3405/8826/E 614412–50/Handakten-Direktoren: Meyer, Danzig: Finanzen und Währung.

38. Sodeikat, "Opposition," p. 147. Meyer, Aufzeichnung, 18 April 1934, NA/T-120/3405/8826/E 614406–408/Handakten-Direktoren: Meyer, Danzig: Finanzen und Währung. Rauschning, speech, 7 April 1934, NA/T-120/3516/9081/E 637756–72/Pol. IV: Po 3 Dz, Bd. 27.

39. Moderow MS, p. 75, and H. J. Potter (Bank of England), memorandum, November 1935, PRO/FO 371/19959/C 316/316/55, esp. p. 23.

40. Meyer, Aufzeichnung, 2 May 1935, NA/T-120/3405/8826/E 614298–302/Handakten-Direktoren: Meyer, Danzig: Finanzen und Währung.

41. Documents, 3 May–3 June 1935, NA/T-120/3512/9062/E 635201/Pol. IV: Po 5 Dz, Bd. 11; NA/T-120/3516/9082/E 637969–72, E 637984/Abt. IV-Wirtschaft-Danzig: Fi 16; NA/T-120/3808/K 220/K 060288–96/Geh.: Polen/Danzig, Wi 1; NA/T-120/3405/8826/E 614294–96/Handakten-Direktoren: Meyer, Danzig: Finanzen und Währung. Cf. Sodeikat, "Opposition," p. 148, and Leonhardt, *Nazi Conquest,* pp. 138–39.

42. Protocol, n.d. (encl. in Göring to Neurath, 21 May 1935), NA/T-120/2626/5552/E 394583/Handakten-Direktoren: Meyer, Danzig I. Cf. Wilder, "Danzig Problem," p. 363.

43. BDC/OPG-von Wnuck.

44. Wilder, "Danzig Problem," p. 361.

45. NA/T-120/3405/8826/E 614294–96, E 614472–75/Handakten-Direktoren: Meyer, Danzig I. NA/T-120/2625/5552/E 394497–529/Handakten-Direktoren: Meyer, Danzig I. Conversation with Schacht reported in Lipski to Beck, 13 June 1935, in Józef Lipski *Diplomat in Berlin, 1933–1939,* W. Jędrzejewicz, ed. (New York, 1968), pp. 209–12.

46. Radowitz to Meyer, 16 May 1935, NA/T-120/2626/5552/E 394600–602/Handakten-Direktoren: Meyer, Danzig I.

47. NA/T-120/2625–26/5552/Handakten-Direktoren: Meyer, Danzig I.

48. NA/T-120/2626/5552/Handakten-Direktoren: Meyer, Danzig II, esp. Schaefer (president, Bank of Danzig), memorandum, 26 July 1935, and Meyer, Aufzeichnung, 26 July 1935, E 395890–91, E 394898. Lipski, *Diplomat,* pp. 208–17.

49. Weinberg, *Foreign Policy,* pp. 190–92, places the dispute in the context of German-Polish relations. The contemporary literature on Danzig-Polish economic relations is voluminous. For a convenient statistical summary, see Wertheimer, "Nazi Pressure," p. 9. After 1934

the Polish viewpoint was not adequately publicized, perhaps as a result of the German treaty. The German-Danzig attitude is plain from *Ostland-Berichte: Reihe B: Wirtschaftsnachrichten* (Danzig, October 1933–36). German propaganda of 1939 may be sampled in Margerete Gärtner, ed., *Danzig and the Corridor* (Berlin, 1939). Evidence on the July crisis of 1935 is given in an unsigned memorandum, n.d. (probably originating in Danzig, encl. in Radowitz to AA, 27 July 1935), NA/T-120/2626/5552/E 394853–80/Handakten-Direktoren: Meyer, Danzig II. See also Potter, memorandum, November 1935, PRO/FO 371/19959/C 316/316/55. Two somewhat contradictory Polish views are given in Moderow MS, chaps. 5 and 6, and Bolesław Kasprowicz, "Straty gospodarcze Gdańska jako wynik jego izolowania się od Polski w latach międzywojennych," *Przegląd Zachodni* 12 (1956): 311–23.

50. Meyer, memorandum, 22 July 1935, and Greiser to Papée, 23 July 1935, NA/T-120/2626/5552/E 394940, E 394928/Handakten-Direktoren: Meyer, Danzig II.

51. Documents, 22–26 July 1935, NA/T-120/2625/5552/E 394702–9, E 394907–8, E 395007, E 395018–20/Handakten-Direktoren: Meyer, Danzig II. Meyer, Aufzeichnung, 26 July 1935, NA/T-120/3405/8828/E 614496–97/Handakten-Direktoren: Meyer, Danzig II.

52. Adelmann, protocol, 30 July 1935, NA/T-120/2626/5552/E 394838–43/Handakten-Direktoren: Meyer, Danzig II. Cf. *Vorposten,* 20 August 1935, and Radowitz to AA, 22 August 1935, NA/T-120/2787/6033/H 044502/Pol. IV: Po 2 Dz, Bd. 3, for disavowal by Gauleitung of rumors.

53. Documents, 22–31 July 1935, NA/T-120/2626/5552/E 394821, E 394978, E 394895–96, E 395007/Handakten-Direktoren: Meyer, Danzig II.

54. NA/T-120/2626/5552/E 394725–832/Handakten-Direktoren: Meyer, Danzig II. NA/T-120/3405/8828/E 614487–92/Handakten-Direktoren: Meyer, Danzig II.

55. Meyer, memorandum 4 August 1935, NA/T-120/2626/5552/E 394757–58/Handakten-Direktoren: Meyer, Danzig II. Cf. Józef Beck, *Dernier rapport* (Paris, 1951), p. 102.

56. Telephonat aus Danzig, 9 August 1933, NA/T-120/2626/5552/E 394658–61/Handakten-Direktoren: Meyer, Danzig II. Leonhardt, *Nazi Conquest,* p. 144.

57. BDC/OPG-Hohnfeldt.

58. Radowitz to Meyer, 19 October 1934, NA/T-120/3405/8826/E 614325–26/Handakten-Direktoren: Meyer, Danzig: Finanzen und Währung.

59. According to Dr. Karl-Heinz Mattern, formerly of Danzig, who knew Linsmayer. Information given in a conversation with the author, Bonn, 23 August 1968.

60. *Vorposten,* 2 July 1934. *Le Temps,* 26 July 1934. On the SA's

dislike of Greiser, see Hermann Rauschning, *Makers of Destruction* (London, 1942), p. 265.

61. BDC/SSO-Reiner.

62. [Reinhard Heydrich], Aktennotiz, 26 November 1934, BDC/SSO-Greiser. Radowitz to Meyer, 19 October 1934, NA/T-120/3405/8826/E 614325–26/Handakten-Direktoren: Meyer, Danzig: Finanzen und Währung.

63. Lester to Avenol, 27 February 1935, PRO/FO 371/18893/C 2427/331/55.

64. Ibid., and Wnuck to Forster, 28 November 1934, BDC/OPG-Wnuck.

65. BDC/OPG-Wnuck. DGKD to AA, 29 June 1935, PA/DGKD: II 1, Bd. 6.

66. Helferich to Neurath, 31 July 1935, NA/T-120/2916/6206/E 469061–68/Geh.: Polen/Danzig, Pol 2. The good relationship between Hoppenrath and Forster is confirmed by Hoppenrath, "Stellungnahme zu der Schrift des damaligen Senators Prof. Dr. Kluck . . . ," 25 October 1955, in BA, Ost-Dok. 8 DW, Nr. 105.

67. Helferich to Neurath, and Helferich to Bülow, 10 August 1935, NA/T-120/2626/5552/E 394648–52/Handakten-Direktoren: Meyer, Danzig II.

68. Bülow to Göring, 5 September 1935, NA/T-120/2626/5552/E 394624/Handakten-Direktoren: Meyer, Danzig II. Neurath, minute, 17 October 1935, NA/T-120/2916/6206/E 469069–70/Geh.: Polen/Danzig, Pol 2.

69. Documents, 25, 28 November 1935, NA/T-120/3513/9062/E 635795–802/Pol. IV: Po 5 Dz, Bd. 11.

70. Walther von Hagens (Danzig Supreme Court president), Eidesstattliche Versicherung, 20 May 1949, BA/Ost-Dok. 8 DW, Nr. 188, pp. 2–3. Lester to Avenol, 18, 19 November 1935, PRO/FO 371/18894/C 8019/331/55.

71. Kluck, Denkschrift, 30 July 1936, BDC/SSO-Kluck (also in BA/Ost-Dok. 8 DW, Nr. 105). Cf. Kluck, Bericht, 21 October 1955, BA/Ost-Dok. 8 DW, Nr. 105.

72. Bach-Zelewski to Reiner, 14 May 1934, BDC/SSO-Reiner, and BDC/SSO-Grossmann, and Kluck.

73. This is a major theme of Joseph Nyomarkay, *Charisma and Factionalism in the Nazi Party* (Minneapolis, 1967).

Chapter 6

1. *Manchester Guardian,* 27 May 1933.

2. Mildred S. Wertheimer, "Nazi Pressure in Danzig," *Geneva Special Studies* 7, no. 3 (May 1936): 2.

3. For the Reich, see William S. Allen, *The Nazi Seizure of Power*

(Chicago, 1965), esp. chaps. 14, 17. Cf. Karl Dietrich Bracher, *The German Dictatorship* (New York, 1970), and Bracher, Sauer, and Schulz, *Die nationalsozialistische Machtergreifung* (Cologne and Opladen, 1960).

4. Hermann Rauschning, *Makers of Destruction* (London, 1942), pp. 95–96. Hans-Adolf Jacobsen, *Nationalsozialistische Aussenpolitik 1933–1938* (Frankfurt/Main and Berlin, 1968), pp. 36–37. BDC/SSO-Thermann.

5. See the Radowitz-Richard Meyer correspondence, esp. in NA/T-120/3404/8825/Handakten-Direktoren: Meyer, Danzig: Politisches.

6. PA/Pol. V: Po 28, Bände 1–2. PA/DGKD: II 4 a, b, c. PA/DGKD: II 5, Bd. 1.

7. On Protestant oppositional activities, see Gerhard Gülzow, *Kirchenkampf in Danzig 1934–1945* (Leer, 1968), and PA/DGKD: II 9, Bände 1–2.

8. Allen, *Nazi Seizure,* chap. 14.

9. WAP/KGRP, I, 259, esp. files 713, 717, 719.

10. For the Reich see Franz Neumann, *Behemoth* (New York, 1966), and Arthur Schweitzer, *Big Business in the Third Reich* (Bloomington, Ind., 1964).

11. The details of the initial structure were announced in the *Vorposten,* July–August 1933. Reports continued to appear through 1934 but were scarce thereafter. For details of Danzig's economy see *Ostland-Berichte, Reihe B: Wirtschaftsnachrichten* (Danzig, October 1933–1936; ceased publication thereafter).

12. Ernst Sodeikat, "Der Nationalsozialismus und die Danziger Opposition," *Vierteljahrshefte für Zeitgeschichte* 14 (1966): 150–51. Koester to AA, 24 February 1934, PA/DGKD: II 27. ASDN/33–46: 2B/21404/21404 (R 3720).

13. On the labor service see Kurt Baedeker, "Wartendes Land an der Weichsel: Deutsche Arbeitsdienstpflicht ausserhalb der Reichsgrenzen," *Der Deutsche im Osten* 2, no. 1 (March 1939): 3–9. On the transfer of Danzigers to the Reich, see *LNOJ* 17 (1936), p. 179; Greiser, Vorwort, in Fritz Markmann and Johann Thies, *Danzig* (Leipzig, 1939), p. 3; and *Berliner Tageblatt,* 2 June 1937.

14. Albert Forster and Wilhelm Löbsack, *Das nationalsozialistische Gewissen in Danzig* (Danzig, 1936), p. 279. Wolfgang Schäfer, *NSDAP* (Hannover and Frankfurt/Main, 1957), pp. 35–36.

15. Sodeikat, "Opposition," p. 153.

16. Ibid., pp. 154–55. Radowitz to AA, 26 August 1935, NA/T-120/3513/9062/E 635645–48/Pol. IV: Po 5 Dz, Bd. 12.

17. Radowitz to AA, 11, 16 May 1935, NA/T-120/3512/9062/E 635220–31, E 635236/Pol. IV: Po 5 Dz, Bd. 11.

18. Adelmann to Roediger, 14 November 1935, NA/T-120/3512/9062/E 635787/Pol. IV: Po 5 Dz, Bd. 12. Cf. Hans L. Leonhardt, *Nazi*

Conquest of Danzig (Chicago, 1942), pp. 164ff., and Sodeikat, "Opposition," pp. 158–60.

19. Hagens to Forster, 23 November 1935, BA/Ost-Dok. 8 DW, Nr. 143, pp. 10–11. Carl Schmitt, *Staat, Bewegung, Volk: Die Dreigliederung der politischen Einheit* (Hamburg, 1933), p. 43.

20. NA/T-120/3513/9063/E 635591–681/Pol. IV: Po 5 Dz, Bd. 12. Hagens, Eidesstattliche Versicherung, 20 May 1949, BA/Ost-Dok. 8 DW, Nr. 188, pp. 2–3. Lester to Avenol, 16 July 1935, PRO/FO 371/18894/C 6071/331/55. ASDN/33–46: 2B/19795/3398 (R 3710). Cf. Leonhardt, *Nazi Conquest,* p. 170.

21. Radowitz to AA, 30 August 1935, NA/T-120/3512/9062/E 635653–55/Pol. IV: Po 5 Dz, Bd. 12. Hagens, Vermerk, 28 October 1935, BA/Ost-Dok. 8 DW, Nr. 143, pp. 5–9, 12–13. Hagens, Eidesstattliche Versicherung, 20 May 1949, BA/Ost-Dok. 8 DW, Nr. 188, pp. 2–3. Cf. Sodeikat, "Opposition," pp. 153, 161–62n; Carl J. Burckhardt, *Meine Danziger Mission* (Munich, 1960), p. 89; and Leonhardt, *Nazi Conquest,* pp. 170–71.

22. Luckwald to AA, 31 December 1936, PA/DGKD: II 1, Bd. 7. Hagens, Eidesstattliche Versicherung, 20 May 1949, BA/Ost-Dok. 8 DW, Nr. 188, pp. 2–3.

23. Text in *LNOJ* 17 (1936): 184–88. See also Radowitz to AA, 21 November 1935, NA/T-120/3513/9062/E 635790–93/Pol. IV: Po 5 Dz, Bd. 12. Cf. ASDN/33–46: 2B/21333/3398 (R 3710).

24. For the texts, see *LNOJ* 16–17 (1935–36). For the documentary background see the appropriate files in the ASDN. These files also contain letters of complaint and formal petitions that, for various reasons, were not placed before the council. The best discussions of the petitions are in Leonhardt, *Nazi Conquest.*

25. Greiser, Regierungserklärung, 27 November 1935 (in Radowitz to AA, 28 November 1935), NA/T-120/3513/9062/E 635825–43/Pol. IV: Po 5 Dz, Bd. 12; trans. in *LNOJ* 17 (1936): 180–82. Robinson (Brit. consul Danzig) to Hoare, 11 December 1935, PRO/FO 371/18895/C 8280/331/55. Lester to Krabbe, 5 December 1935, and P. J. Makay (International Control Office) to League treasurer, 7 December 1935 (deals with cost of League to Danzig) ASDN/33–46: 2B/21913/3398 (R 3710).

26. Lester to Avenol, extract from private diary for 30 November 1935, PRO/FO 371/18895/C 8243/331/55. Böttcher, Vermerk, 30 November 1935, NA/T-120/3717/8087/E 638867–68/DGKD: Besprechungen mit dem Hohen Kommissar, Bd. 2. Radowitz, Aufzeichnung, 3 December 1935, NA/T-120/2916/6207/E 469305–307/Geh.: Polen/Danzig, Pol 5. Radowitz to AA, 4 December 1935, NA/T-120/3513/9062/E 635848/Pol. IV: Po 5 Dz, Bd. 2.

27. *LNOJ* 17 (1936): 188–89.

28. ASDN/S 322/5.

29. Meyer (German delegation Geneva) to AA, two telegrams, 11 October 1933, NA/T-120/3510/9052/E 634093–95/Geh.: Polen/Danzig, Pol 11 no. 1, Bd. 7. Documents for October 1933, PRO/FO 371/17228/82/55. On Lester see Felician Prill, "Sean Lester: High Commissioner in Danzig, 1933–1937," *Studies* (Dublin) 49, no. 195 (Autumn 1960): 259–65. A dissertation on Lester is being prepared by Stephen Barcroft, of Trinity University, Dublin.

30. Bülow-Schwante (AA) to German Legation Dublin, 30 October 1933; Schlemann (Dublin) to AA, 1 November 1933, NA/T-120/3510/9052/E 634111–12/Geh.: Polen/Danzig, Pol 11, no. 1, Bd. 7.

31. Lester to Avenol, 3 November, 4 December 1934, PRO/FO 371/17784/C 8006, C 8905/155/55.

32. ASDN/33–46: 2B/17939/3398 (R 3710).

33. Lester to Avenol, 5, 22 February 1935; Strang, FO minute, 18 July 1935, PRO/FO 371/18893–94/C 1550, C 1947, C 5552/331/55.

34. Lester to Avenol, extract from private diary for 28 November 1935, PRO/FO 371/18895/C 8243/331/55.

35. Rumbold, minute, 28 December 1935, PRO/FO 371/18895/C 8425/331/55. On Rumbold see Franklin L. Ford, "Three Observers in Berlin: Rumbold, Dodd, and François-Poncet," in *The Diplomats,* Gordon A. Craig and Felix Gilbert, eds. (Princeton, 1953), pp. 437–47.

36. Radowitz to AA, 4 September 1935, NA/T-120/2787/6033/H 044667–70/Pol. IV: Po 2 Dz, Bd. 3. Blume (senate foreign dept.), Vermerk, 5 September 1935, NA/T-120/3517/8087/E 638838–43/DGKD: Besprechungen mit dem Hohen Kommissar, Bd. 2. Cf. Leonhardt, *Nazi Conquest,* pp. 231–32.

37. Lester to Avenol, extract from private diary for 28 November 1935, PRO/FO 371/18895/C 8243/331/55. The effect of the Ethiopian crisis on Nazi foreign policy is summarized in Jacobsen, *Aussenpolitik,* pp. 416ff.

38. PRO/FO 371/18895/C 8120, C 8180, C 8268/331/55. PRO/FO 371/19950/C 33/33/55. NA/T-120/3513/9062/E 635904–6076/Pol. IV: Po 5 Dz, Bände 12, 14–15.

39. Stevenson, FO memorandum, 7 January 1936 (with attached minutes by Rumbold, 10 January, and by Baxter, 12 January); Weise to Eden, 23 December 1935, PRO/FO 371/19950/C 118, C 133/33/55. Hans Lazarus appears to have been identical with Hans Leonhardt. See his own account of the trip in Leonhardt, *Nazi Conquest,* pp. 191–96. These sources have been supplemented by confidential material in the author's possession.

40. Leonhardt, *Nazi Conquest,* p. 214.

41. Roediger, Aufzeichnungen, 23, 24 January 1936; Roediger to Moltke, 29 January 1936, NA/T-120/3513/9062/E 636078–83, E 636113–15, E 636138/Pol. IV: Po 5 Dz, Bd. 15. *The Times,* 25 January 1936. *Frankfurter Zeitung,* 26 January 1936. For the mistaken belief that

Greiser was carrying out Hitler's orders see Charles Graham, "La Ville Libre dangereuse," *L'Europe nouvelle* 19 (1936) : 465–66, and *Manchester Guardian,* 27 January 1936. The error is repeated in Leonhardt, *Nazi Conquest,* p. 208, and Burckhardt, *Danziger Mission,* p. 43.

42. Greiser, speech, 31 January 1936 (in Radowitz to AA, 1 February 1936), NA/T-120/3513/9062/E 636157–70/Pol. IV: Po 5 Dz, Bd. 15.

43. Roediger to Radowitz, 10 February 1936, NA/T-120/3513/9062/E 636194/Pol. IV: Po 5 Dz, Bd. 15.

44. Lester to Avenol, 4, 24 February 1936, PRO/FO 371/19951/C 1162, C 1383/33/55. Eckner (DGKD) to AA, 20 April 1936, NA/T-120/3513/9062/E 636220–22/Pol. IV: Po 5 Dz, Bd. 15.

45. Gamm (DNVP) to Senate, 4 March 1936 (in Radowitz to AA, 26 March 1936), NA/T-120/3513/9062/E 636200–217/Pol. IV: Po 5 Dz, Bd. 15. Leonhardt, *Nazi Conquest,* pp. 214–16.

46. Lester to Avenol, 5 May 1936, *LNOJ* 17 (1936) : 511 (see also pp. 543–44).

47. Leonhardt, *Nazi Conquest,* pp. 226–27.

48. Ibid., pp. 227–30. Kluck, Denkschrift, 30 July 1936, BDC/SSO-Kluck. Forster and Löbsack, *Gewissen,* pp. 240–45. Robinson to Eden, 15 June 1936; Lester to Avenol, 15, 16 June 1936, PRO/FO 371/19951/C 4371, C 4517/33/55. *Völkischer Beobachter,* 14 June 1936. *The Times,* 15 June 1936. *New York Times,* 17 June 1936.

49. Blume, Vermerk, 26 June 1936, PA/Pol. I: Völkerbundbeziehungen, Deutschland-Polen/Danzig. Leonhardt, *Nazi Conquest,* pp. 233–34. Burckhardt, *Danziger Mission,* p. 89. Trans. of *Vorposten* article, *LNOJ* 17 (1936) : pp. 901–2. Forster to Brückner (Adjutant des Führers), 25 June 1936, BA/NS 10/70, p. 10. *The Times* and *Le Temps,* 28, 29, 30 June 1936.

50. *LNOJ* 17 (1936) : 895–99.

51. Krauel (German consul Geneva) to AA, 5 July 1936 (reports conversation with Greiser), PA/Pol. I: Völkerbundbeziehungen, Deutschland-Polen/Danzig.

52. Text of speech in *LNOJ* 17 (1936), pp. 763–66. Leonhardt, *Nazi Conquest,* pp. 238–39. *The Times, Le Temps,* and *Manchester Guardian,* 6 July 1936. *Basler Nachrichten,* 5 July 1936. *Frankfurter Zeitung,* 6 July 1936, gives a favorable report of Greiser's behavior.

53. Unsigned minute, n.d. (July 1937), NA/T-120/120/116/66324–26/Büro RAM: Danzig.

54. *The Daily Telegraph,* 6 July 1936. Leonhardt, *Nazi Conquest,* p. 249. Lester to Avenol, 12 September 1936, appendix 2, *LNOJ* 17 (1936) : 1363–64. Lester to Avenol, 1 August 1936, PRO/FO 371/19954/C 5831/33/55.

55. *LNOJ* 17 (1936) : 762–63. Józef Lipski, *Diplomat in Berlin,*

1933–1939, W. Jędrzejewicz, ed. (New York, 1968) pp. 257–66. Cf. ASDN/33–46: 2B/25756/25756 (R 3720).

56. *LNOJ* 17 (1936): 1190–91. Cf. PRO/FO 371/19950–56/33/55; Prill, "Sean Lester," p. 264; and Bohdan (Bogdan) Dopierała, "Beck and the Gdansk Question (1930–1935)," *Acta Poloniae Historica* 17 (1968): 103–4.

57. ASDN/33–46: 2B/25619/25619 (R 3720), esp. McKinnon Wood (Legal Section), memorandum, 16 September 1936.

58. Lester, minute (on Krabbe, memorandum, 26 November 1937), 2 December 1937, ASDN/33–46: 2B/31586/4140 (R 3715).

59. *Gesetzblatt der Freien Stadt Danzig,* 18 July 1936, trans. in *LNOJ* 17 (1936): 1365–73. Cf. Leonhardt, *Nazi Conquest,* pp. 247–48.

60. For a schedule of newspaper bans, see *LNOJ* 17 (1936): 1365. Acts of repression may be followed in the reports of the Brit. consul in Danzig, in PRO/FO 371/19950–56/33/55. Cf. Leonhardt, *Nazi Conquest,* pp. 250–59, and Sodeikat, "Opposition," pp. 170ff.

61. Leonhardt, *Nazi Conquest,* pp. 267–68. Leonhardt's sneer at Weise (p. 311) seems hardly justified.

62. Robinson to Eden, March–May 1937, PRO/FO 371/20757/5/55.

63. Documents, April–May 1937, PA/DGKD: II 8, Bd. 5.

64. Grolmann (DGKD) to AA, dispatch, 15 June 1938; O'Rourke, Hirtenbrief, 12 June 1938 (read 26 June), PA/DGKD: II 8, Bd. 6.

65. Bassler (senate), Vermerk, 27 August 1938, PA/DGKD: II 8, Bd. 6.

66. Unless otherwise noted, the information in the following section is taken from a 20-page booklet issued by the Gauorganisationsamt Danzig, "Statistik des Gaues Danzig der NSDAP: Nur für den Dienstgebrauch," December 1937, HA/30/587.

67. Forster and Löbsack, *Gewissen,* p. 279.

68. David Schoenbaum, *Hitler's Social Revolution* (Garden City, N.Y., 1966), p. 73.

69. For example, the *Ergebnisse der Volks- und Berufszählung vom 1. November 1923 in der Freien Stadt Danzig* (Danzig, 1926), p. 77, lists 31,459 laborers engaged in industry and artisan trades, but it is impossible to tell how many of these were *Handwerker* and how many *Arbeiter,* in the sense of the party survey.

70. The numbers of the Danzig police are given in Greiser to Lester, 6 August 1935, PA/Pol. IV: VW 6 Dz.

71. Schäfer, *NSDAP,* pp. 38–39.

Chapter 7

1. A. J. P. Taylor, *The Origins of the Second World War* (New York, 1962). Cf. H. R. Trevor-Roper, "A. J. P. Taylor, Hitler, and the

War," *Encounter* 17, no. 7 (July 1961): 88–96, and Trevor-Roper, "Hitlers Kriegsziele," *Vierteljahrshefte für Zeitgeschichte* 8 (1960): 121–33. For more recent opinion see, e.g., Hans-Adolf Jacobsen, *Nationalsozialistische Aussenpolitik 1933–1938* (Frankfurt/Main and Berlin, 1968), chap. 5 (esp. p. 598n), and Laurence Lafore, *The End of Glory* (Philadelphia and New York, 1970), esp. pp. 13–15, 179–87. See further Eberhard Jäckel, *Hitler's Weltanschauung* (Middletown, Conn., 1972). The Taylor thesis is dead, insofar as it pertains to Nazi and Hitlerian motivation and planning.

2. E.g.: Anna Cienciala, *Poland and the Western Powers, 1938–1939* (Toronto, 1968), pp. 177–237; Carl J. Burckhardt, *Meine Danziger Mission* (Munich, 1960); Ludwig Denne, *Das Danzig Problem in der deutschen Aussenpolitik, 1934–1939* (Bonn, 1959); Bogdan Dopierała, *Gdańska polityka Józefa Becka* (Poznan, 1967), pp. 224–369; and the Moderow MS.

3. Ernst Sodeikat, "Die Verfolgung und der Widerstand der Juden in der Freien Stadt Danzig von 1933 bis 1945," *Bulletin des Leo Baeck Instituts* 8, no. 30 (1965): 109–10. Max Aschkewitz, *Zur Geschichte der Juden in Westpreussen 1772–1932* (Marburg/Lahn, 1968). Samuel Echt, "Die Geschichte der Juden in Danzig," *Deutsche Studien* 8, no. 30 (June 1970): 145–53, esp. pp. 145–46. This last is a summary of a book-length MS by Echt on the Jews in the free city, to be published by the Ost-Akademie, Lüneburg. For statistical purposes, the term *Jew* is limited here to members of the Jewish religious community. The population of Berlin, in comparison, was 4 percent Jewish in 1910, 3.8 percent in 1933, and 1.7 percent in 1939. See H.G. Sellenthin, *Geschichte der Juden in Berlin und des Gebäudes Fasanenstrasse 79/80* (Berlin, 1959), p. 101.

4. *Manchester Guardian,* 27 May 1933.

5. Elizabeth Herzog and Mark Zborowski, *Life Is with People: The Culture of the Shtetl* (New York, 1962), pp. 152ff.

6. As attested by many German Jews, e.g., in Eva G. Reichmann, *Hostages of Civilization* (Boston, 1951), p. 238.

7. For the development of the "final solution," see Hannah Arendt, *Eichmann in Jerusalem,* rev. ed. (New York, 1965); Gerald Reitlinger, *The Final Solution* (New York, 1961); Raul Hilberg, *The Destruction of the European Jews* (Chicago, 1961); and Karl A. Schleunes, *The Twisted Road to Auschwitz* (Urbana and Chicago, 1970). For a comparison of the pogrom with Hitler's goals, see Jäckel, *Weltanschauung,* pp. 48ff.

8. *LNOJ* 14 (1933): 1543.

9. *LNOJ* 16 (1935): 830–49. Walther Wohler (Senate Dept. of the Interior), Niederschrift, 8 November 1934, PA/DGKD: II 17, Bd. 1. Radowitz to AA, 14 February 1934, PA/Pol. IV: Po 17 Dz, Bd. 1. Sodeikat, "Juden," pp. 113–17. Correspondence between Danzig Jewish

authorities and Senate, 1933–35, document file 509, Wiener Library, London.

10. Radowitz to AA, draft telegram, 15 July 1935, PA/DGKD: II 17, Bd. 1. Received version, NA/T-120/4947/L 1396/L 363779/Pol. IV: Po Juden/Dz.

11. Barth (Senate Dept. of Propaganda), Vermerk, 15 July 1935, PA/DGKD: II 17, Bd. 1. Sodeikat, "Juden," pp. 122–28. *LNOJ* 16 (1935): 1321–25.

12. Radowitz to AA, 15 July 1935; Batzer to Greiser, 30 July 1935, NA/T-120/4947/L 1396/L 363779–83/Pol. IV: Po Juden/Dz. Cf. Luckwald (consul-general) to AA, 23 October 1937, PA/DGKD: II 17, Bd. 1.

13. Burckhardt, *Danziger Mission,* pp. 205–6. Fritz Redlin, "Danzig löst die Judenfrage" and "Eine tatkräftige Lösung: Die Wahrheit über die Danziger Judenauswanderung," *Mitteilungen über die Judenfrage* (Berlin) 3, no. 4 (26 January 1939): 5, and no. 13 (30 March 1939): 3.

14. Burckhardt, *Danziger Mission,* pp. 95–97. *Manchester Guardian* and *Journal des Nations,* 9 April 1937. *Frankfurter Zeitung,* 10 April 1937. Böttcher, Vermerk, 10 April 1937, PA/DGKD: Verschiedene Geheimsachen, Bd. 3. Böttcher, Vermerk, 21 April 1937, NA/T-120/3194/7249/E 532055–58/DGKD: Besprechungen mit dem Hohen Kommissar, Bd. 4.

15. *Völkischer Beobachter,* 7 May 1937.

16. Burckhardt, *Danziger Mission,* p. 103.

17. Sodeikat, "Juden," pp. 128–31. *Berliner Tageblatt,* 12 October 1937. *Manchester Guardian, Daily Telegraph, The Times,* 25 October 1937. *Frankfurter Zeitung,* 26 October 1937.

18. Robinson to Eden, 25 October 1937; Burckhardt to Avenol, 12 November 1937, PRO/FO 371/30759/C 7610, C 8088/5/55. Sitzung des Schnellgerichts am 27.10.1937 (in Grolmann to AA, 16 November 1937), PA/DGKD: II 17, Bd. 2.

19. E.g., Greiser to Lester, 24 August 1935, *LNOJ* 16 (1935): 1325. On the Polish political background see Edward D. Wynot, Jr., " 'A Necessary Cruelty': The Emergence of Official Anti-Semitism in Poland, 1936–39," *American Historical Review* 76 (1971): 1035–58.

20. Greiser, Vermerk (extract), 12 November 1937; Luckwald to AA, 16 December 1937, PA/DGKD: II 17, Bd. 2.

21. Burckhardt, *Danziger Mission,* pp. 194ff. Böttcher, Vermerk, 3 December 1937, PA/DGKD: II 17, Bd. 2. Böttcher, Vermerk, 15 December 1937, NA/T-120/3194/7249/E 533064–67/DGKD: Besprechungen mit dem Hohen Kommissar, Bd. 4. Krabbe to Stevenson, 10 November 1937, PRO/FO 371/20759/C 7871/5/55.

22. *Frankfurter Zeitung,* 30 May 1938. *Daily Herald,* 4 June, 9 August 1938.

23. Redlin, "Danzig löst die Judenfrage." Janson (consul-general) to AA, 3 January 1939, PA/DGKD: Pol. 4, no. 5.

24. Walters to Randall, 19 October 1938, PRO/FO 371/21803/C 12793/197/55. Shepherd to Halifax, 24 October 1938, PRO/FO 371/21636/C 13205/1667/62. *Vorposten,* 10 October 1938. *Manchester Guardian,* 13 October 1938.

25. Schleunes, *Twisted Road,* pp. 236ff. Milton Meyer, *They Thought They Were Free* (Chicago, 1966), focuses on *Kristallnacht* in Marburg.

26. Sodeikat, "Juden," p. 133. Greiser-Chodacki correspondence, December 1938–January 1939, PA/DGKD: Pol. 4, no. 5. Janson to AA, 19 November 1938, PA/DGKD: II 2, Bd. 8. *Frankfurter Zeitung,* 15 November 1938. Wilhelm Zarske, "Auch Danzig macht reinen Tisch mit Juda," *Völkischer Beobachter,* 15 November 1938. There is no explanation available for the lag between the outbreak of violence in the Reich and that in Danzig.

27. *Gesetzblatt,* 23 November 1938. *Frankfurter Zeitung,* 24 November 1938. Burckhardt, *Danziger Mission,* p. 219.

28. Böttcher, Vermerk, 1 October 1938, NA/T-120/3194/7249/E 532084–85/DGKD: Besprechungen mit dem Hohen Kommissar, Bd. 4. Weizsäcker, minute, 19 December 1938, NA/T-120/120/116/66389/Büro RAM: Danzig. Burckhardt, *Danziger Mission,* pp. 219ff.

29. Documents, April–December 1938, PRO/FO 371/21635/C 3309/1667/62; PRO/FO 371/21638/C 15461/1667/62; PRO/FO 371/22539/W 16012/104/98.

30. Synagogen-Gemeinde Danzig to League council, 28 November 1938 (in Shepherd to Halifax, 2 December 1938), PRO/FO 371/22539/W 16012/104/98. A relevant League file, ASDN/33–46:2B/25619 (R 3720) is restricted, but some information may be gained from ASDN/33–46: 2B/36189/3799 (R 3712), which deals with questions of Danzig citizenship.

31. Echt, "Die Geschichte," pp. 148–49. Burckhardt, *Danziger Mission,* p. 222. *The Times,* 21 December 1938. Sodeikat, "Juden," p. 135.

32. Benjamin Akzin, "Zionism," *The Universal Jewish Encyclopedia* (New York, 1969), 10: 662–64.

33. Shepherd to Halifax, 13 February 1939, PRO/FO 371/24085/W 3092/551/48.

34. Randall, Conversation with Mr. Cooper (Home Office), 12 January 1939, PRO/FO 371/24085/W 708/551/48. See further the remainder of this file, for January.

35. Echt, "Die Geschichte." Burckhardt, *Danziger Mission,* pp. 206–7. Redlin, "Danzig löst die Judenfrage." PRO/FO 371/24085/551/48. PRO/FO 371/24089/1369/48. PA/Pol V: Po 6. PA/DGKD: Pol 4, no. 5. On Shepherd and Burckhardt see Shepherd to Halifax, 24 December 1938; Hankey (Warsaw) to Randall, 18 Dec. 1938, PRO/FO 371/

21804/C 15881/197/55; Burckhardt to Walters, 10 February 1939, PRO/FO 371/23133/C 1905/92/55.

36. *Manchester Guardian,* 8 December 1938. *Gesetzblatt,* 2, 15 February, 4, 12 March, 10 May, 22, 28 July 1939. Redlin, "Eine tatkräftige Lösung." Führer des S.D. Unterabschnitts Danzig to Kloetzel (DGKD), 4 April 1939, PA/DGKD: Pol 4, no. 5.

37. Böttcher to Janson, 23 December 1938, PA/DGKD: Pol 4, no. 5. *Gesetzblatt,* 11 January 1939.

38. Sodeikat, "Juden," pp. 143–47. Echt, "Die Geschichte," p. 147.

39. *The Sunday Times,* 19 June 1938. *Le Temps,* 20 June 1938. PRO/FO 371/21801/197/55, May–June 1938. PA/DGKD: II 2, Bd. 8, May–June 1938. Erich Kordt to Weizsäcker, 30 May 1938, NA/T-120/120/116/66363/Büro RAM: Danzig. Schliep (AA-Pol. V.), memorandum, 24 May 1938, PA/Pol. I: Völkerbundbeziehungen, Deutschland-Polen/Danzig.

40. Grolmann to AA, 20 June 1938, PA/DGKD: II 2, Bd. 8. *Völkischer Beobachter,* 21 June 1938. Cf. Shepherd to Halifax, 10 May, 21 July 1938, PRO/FO 371/21801–802/C 4357, C 7509/197/55.

41. Shepherd to Halifax, 21 July 1938, PRO/FO 371/21802/C 7508/197/55.

42. The principal authority for these matters is Burckhardt, whose reports appear throughout PRO/FO 371/21801–802/197/55.

43. Cienciala, *Poland,* and Denne, *Danzig Problem,* pp. 128–39.

44. Leonhardt, *Nazi Conquest,* pp. 308–9.

45. Strang, FO minute, 5 February 1937, PRO/FO 371/20756/C 1047/5/55.

46. Burckhardt's general political views are expressed in *Meine Danziger Mission* as well as in a letter to Dr. Hans Viktor Böttcher, the son of the director of the senate foreign dept., 29 January 1951 (in possession of Böttcher). His views are criticized in Moderow MS, chap. 10. The most important documentary sources for Burckhardt's activities are the British files, PRO/FO 371/5/55 (1937), 197/55 (1938), and 92/55 and 54/18 (1939). German sources include PA/DGKD: Besprechungen mit dem Hoken Kommissar, Bd. 4, 1937–39, and Völkerbund und Hoher Kommissar, Bd. 1, 1939 (partially filmed as NA/T-120/3194–95/7249, 7261). Burckhardt's diplomatic activities during his tenure as high commissioner are discussed in Herbert S. Levine, "The Mediator: The Efforts of Carl J. Burckhardt to Avert a Second World War," *Journal of Modern History,* 45 (1973).

47. Burckhardt's lengthy citations are accurate, insofar as they can be confirmed through PRO/FO 371. The League files he used are largely closed to researchers.

48. Eden to Kennard, 25 February 1937, PRO/FO 371/20756/C 1756/5/55. Burckhardt, *Danziger Mission,* pp. 69ff. Cf. Leonhardt, *Nazi*

Conquest, pp. 331–38, and "Report of M. Carl Burckhardt," *Series of League of Nations Publications, Political,* vol. 7 (1940).

49. Burckhardt, *Danziger Mission,* pp. 51ff.

50. Ibid., p. 75. Some examples: Krauel to AA, 31 December 1937; Böttcher, Vermerk, 7 February 1938, PA/Pol. I: Völkerbundbeziehungen, Deutschland-Polen/Danzig. Böttcher, Vermerke, 2 March 1937, 10 January 1938; Greiser, Vermerk, 12 August 1937, NA/T-120/3194/7249/E 532048–49, E 532059–61/DGKD: Besprechungen mit dem Hohen Kommissar, Bd. 4.

51. Burckhardt, *Danziger Mission,* pp. 176–81.

52. On Weizsäcker see his *Erinnerungen* (Munich and Freiburg, 1950). On Weizsäcker, Burckhardt, and the "German resistance" see Harold C. Deutsch, *The Conspiracy against Hitler in the Twilight War* (Minneapolis, 1968), pp. 16–22. Deutsch agrees that the German documents dealing with Burckhardt should not be taken at face value.

53. Record of a meeting of Committee of Three, Geneva, 20 September 1938, PRO/FO 371/21803/C 10487/197/55.

54. Kennard to Eden, 11 March 1937, PRO/FO 371/20757/C 2107/5/55. Shepherd to Halifax, 21 July 1938; Walters to Stevenson, 8 August 1938 (encloses Burckhardt to Walters, 2 August 1938), PRO/FO 371/21802/C 7509, C 8119/197/55.

55. For a contrary view see Leonhardt, *Nazi Conquest,* pp. 331–38.

56. *Daily Herald* and *Manchester Guardian,* 10 August 1938. *Daily Herald* and *New York Times,* 21 April 1939. Although these and similar reports cannot properly be verified, the *New York Times* seems to have been best informed.

57. Erich Brost, cited by Burckhardt, Record of a meeting of Committee of Three, 28 January 1938, PRO/FO 371/21800/C 627/197/55.

58. Record of a meeting of Committee of Three, 20 September 1938, PRO/FO 371/21803/C 10487/197/55.

59. Deutsch, *Conspiracy,* pp. 37, 82–83, 103. Burckhardt, *Danziger Mission,* pp. 181–87. Warner (Brit. minister Berne) to Halifax, 5 September 1938; Stevenson to Strang, 8 September 1938, *Documents on British Foreign Policy: 1919–1939,* 3d ser. (London, 1946–50), 2:242, 689–92.

60. *The Speeches of Adolf Hitler, April 1922–August 1939,* Norman H. Baynes, ed. (London, 1942), 2: 1536.

61. Weizsäcker, minute, 17 October 1938, PA/Büro Chef AO: Danzig. Böttcher, Vermerk, 18 November 1938, PA/DGKD: II 2, Bd. 8. Cf. PRO/FO 371/21803/C 13192, C 13862, C 14439/197/55.

62. Documents, December 1938–February 1939, PRO/FO 371/21804/C 15236, C 15377/197/55; PRO/FO 371/23132–33/C 99, C 2418/92/55. Cienciala, *Poland,* pp. 162–63, 181–82.

63. Shepherd to Halifax, 6 March 1939, PRO/FO 371/23133/C 2808/92/55.

64. For German-Polish relations in this period see Cienciala, *Poland,* pp. 180–98. Cf. E. M. Robertson, *Hitler's Pre-War Policy and Military Plans 1933–1939* (London, 1963), pp. 150–57.

65. Cienciala, *Poland,* p. 186. *Vorposten,* 29 November 1938. Hewel, Aktennotiz, 13 January 1939, NA/T-120/120/116/66401/Büro RAM: Danzig.

66. Gerhard L. Weinberg, "A Proposed Compromise over Danzig in 1939?" *Journal of Central European Affairs* 14 (1954): 334–38, suggests this possibility, but Cienciala, *Poland,* pp. 190–92, insists that the Poles made a final no-compromise decision in January.

67. Cienciala, *Poland,* pp. 207–45.

68. *Speeches of Adolf Hitler,* 2: 1629–32.

69. Samples of Reich and Danzig propaganda may be found in Adalbert Boeck, "Danzig ist eine deutsche Stadt," *Der Türmer* 41, no. 9 (June 1939): 177–88, Margarete Gärtner, ed., *Danzig and the Corridor* (Berlin, 1939), and *Vorposten,* April–August 1939.

70. Documents, February–March 1939, PRO/FO 371/23133/C 1905, C 3670, C 3818/92/55. Krabbe, minute, 21 February 1939; McKinnon Wood, minute, 23 February 1939, ASDN/33–46: 2B/4393/3398 (R 3709).

71. Meyer, protocol, 31 May 1935, NA/T-120/2625/3552/E 394515–16/Handakten-Direktoren: Meyer, Danzig I. Neurath, minute, 17 October 1935, NA/T-120/2916/6206/E 469069–70/Geh.: Polen/Danzig, Pol 2.

72. Documents, 2 May 1935–29 April 1936, NA/T-120/3525/9163/E 644514–41/DGKD: Reichswehr, Bd. 2.

73. Greiser, confidential circular, 18 August 1937, PA/DGKD: Verschiedene Geheimsachen, Bd. 3.

74. NA/T-120/1421/2897/Pol. V: Po 14.

75. According to Burckhardt. See Makins, memorandum, 12 September 1938, PRO/FO 371/21803/C 9858/197/55.

76. Kennard to Halifax, 12 May 1939; Shepherd to Halifax, 16 May 1939, PRO/FO 371/23019/C 7095, C 7150/54/18.

77. Some of these preparations are mentioned in Günther Sawatzki, *Danzig ist deutsch* (Berlin, 1939); Hanns Strohmenger, *Danzigs Heimkehr ins Reich* (Danzig, 1939); and Hans Steen, *Blaue Jungen schlagen Polen* (Stuttgart, 1941). The number of international press reports defies enumeration. Extremely precise are the dispatches of Gerald Shepherd to the British Foreign Office, May–July 1939, PRO/FO 371/23019–21/54/18. The British consul left Danzig on leave and was replaced on 10 July by acting Consul Francis Shepherd. The latter was rather less perceptive than his predecessor and under Burckhardt's influence. See his reports, July–September 1939, PRO/FO 371/23024–28/54/18. File 54/18 also contains reports of the views of Burckhardt, which varied widely. For open German admission of some military

activity in Danzig, see *Völkischer Beobachter,* 25 July, 25 August 1939, and *Frankfurter Zeitung,* 28 August 1939.

78. Denne, *Danzig Problem,* pp. 231–54. WAP/KGRP, I, 259/771. NA/T-120/3293/8049/Pol. V: Po 52–1. NA/T-120/3200/7693/Pol. V: Po 61. NA/T-120/1016/1724/Pol. V: Po 3, Bände 15–16. Cf. Moderow MS, p. 27.

79. *New York Times,* 25 August 1939.

80. Woermann (AA-Pol. I) to DGKD, 19 August 1939, PA/DGKD: Pers Si 2.

81. Robertson, *Pre-War Policy,* p. 180.

82. Greiser, Vermerk, 24 August 1939, NA/T-120/3194/7249/E 532092–93/DGKD: Besprechungen mit dem Hohen Kommissar, Bd. 4. *Vorposten* and *Frankfurter Zeitung,* 25 August 1939.

83. Woermann to DGKD, 13 May, 24 August 1939, NA/T-120/3307/8287/E 588336/DGKD: Paket 151/7.

84. Weizsäcker to DGKD, two telegrams, 25 August 1939, PA/DGKD: Pers Si 2.

85. Robertson, *Pre-War Policy,* pp. 182–84.

86. Weizsäcker to DGKD, sealed instructions and activating telegram, 19 and 31 August 1939, PA/DGKD: Pers Si 2. *New York Times,* 25, 28 August 1939. Preston (Kovno) to Halifax, 2 September 1939 (report from Burckhardt); Francis Shepherd to Halifax, 4 September 1939 (from Riga), PRO/FO 371/23028/C 12801, C 13880/54/18. Cf. "Final Report of M. Carl Burckhardt."

Chapter 8

1. The literature on the Polish campaign is considerable. For a propagandistic but essentially accurate contemporary view from Danzig see Hans Steen, *Blaue Jungen schlagen Polen* (Stuttgart, 1941), and Hanns Strohmenger, *Danzigs Heimkehr ins Reich* (Danzig, 1939).

2. "Erlässe des Führers und Reichskanzlers über Gliederung und Verwaltung der Ostgebiete," 8 October, 2 November 1939, 29 January 1940, *Reichsgesetzblatt* (Berlin), 1939, pp. 2042, 2135, and 1940, p. 251. Martin Bormann, Anordnung, 19 March 1940, NA/T-580/20/200. Reichswirtschaftsminister, confidential circular, 1 November 1939, NA/T-71/88/88/591813–14/RWM 18/47. Unless otherwise noted, organizational details given in the text are from Wolfgang Diewerge, *Der neue Reichsgau Danzig-Westpreussen* (Berlin, 1940), NA/T-580/20/200, and Zbigniew Janowicz, *Ustrój administracyjny ziem polskich wcielonych do Rzeszy Niemieckiej 1939–1945* (Poznan, 1951).

3. Kurt Peiser, *Danzig, das Schicksal eines deutschen Hafens* (Danzig, 1940), p. 37. Erich Keyser, memorandum, n.d. (September 1939), with notation by Forster, 5 April 1943, BA/Ost 12/Gotenhafen, Stadt/4 (see further, 2, 68, 72).

4. For a list of names see *Reichsband,* 3d ed., 1941–42 (Berlin, 1943), pp. 26–42.

5. The best single source of political information on Danzig-West Prussia, and esp. on conditions in the former Polish territories, is BA/Reichsjustizministerium/R 22/3360 (Lageberichte des Oberlandesgerichtspräsidenten und des Generalstaatsanwaltes in Danzig 1940–45).

6. Diewerge, *Danzig-Westpreussen,* pp. 99ff., NA/T-580/20/200.

7. According to information given the author by Dr. Hans Viktor Böttcher in a conversation, Bonn, 12 August 1968.

8. BDC/PK-Andres.

9. Storr, Vermerkung, 9 February 1940, BA/Hauptamt für Kommunalpolitik/NS 25/202.

10. The analogy of national socialism with feudalism has been attempted in Robert Koehl, "Feudal Aspects of National Socialism," *American Political Science Review* 54 (December 1960): 921–33. Cf. Joseph Nyomarkay, *Charisma and Factionalism in the Nazi Party* (Minneapolis, 1967), pp. 33–34.

11. Hildebrandt to Himmler, 19 February 1941, BDC/PK-Kampe, Werner. See also the remainder of the file, and BDC/PK-Seeger, Gerhard.

12. Documents, January–May 1943, BDC/SSO-Forster. The two major works on Nazi population policy in the Polish territories are Robert Koehl, *RKFDV: German Resettlement and Population Policy 1939–1945* (Cambridge, Mass., 1957), and Martin Broszat, *Nationalsozialistische Polenpolitik 1939–1945* (Stuttgart, 1961). On the Himmler-Forster dispute see Herbert S. Levine, "Local Authority and the SS State: The Conflict over Population Policy in Danzig-West Prussia, 1939–1945," *Central European History* 2 (1969): 331–55.

13. Lageberichte, 1944–45, BA/Reichsjustizministerium/R 22/3360. *Vorposten,* August–November 1944. Cf. Hans Graf von Lehndorf, *Ein Bericht aus Ost- und Westpreussen 1945–1947* (Bonn, 1960).

14. Albert Zoller, ed., *Hitler Privat* (Düsseldorf, 1949), pp. 230–31.

15. According to Dr. Karl-Heinz Mattern, formerly of Danzig, in a conversation with the author, Bonn, 23 August 1968.

16. *The Times,* 31 March 1945.

17. For a summary of survivors' reports see John Toland, *The Last Hundred Days* (New York, 1966), pp. 300–303. Cf. n. 20, below.

18. The facts of condemnation and execution are confirmed in a letter to the author from the Main Commission of Inquiry into Nazi Crimes in Poland (Polish Ministry of Justice), 24 May 1971.

19. Telford Taylor, *Nuremberg and Vietnam: An American Tragedy* (Chicago, 1970), p. 87n.

20. The grim conditions in the German east have been thoroughly described in the series published by the West German government: "Dokumentation der Vertreibung der Deutschen aus Ost-Mitteleuropa."

The standard West German statistical study is *Die deutschen Vertreibungsverluste* (Wiesbaden and Stuttgart, 1958). For a detailed Polish refutation see Stanisław Schimitzek, *Truth or Conjecture? German Civilian War Losses in the East* (Poznan, 1966).

21. Karl-Heinz Mattern, *Die Exilregierung* (Tübingen, 1953), pp. 55–58.

22. Willi Michael Beutel and Hans-Karl Gspann, *Das heutige Danzig* (Munich, 1956). The restoration is still proceeding slowly, and much of the center of town remained rubble in May 1968 during my visit. The excellence of what has been done is remarkable.

Index